GROWING UP GRANT

A Gay Life in the Shadow of Ulysses S. Grant

Ulysses Grant Dietz

Published by IngramSpark
Ulysses Grant Dietz
11 Woodhill Drive
Maplewood, New Jersey 07040

Book Layout © 2017 BookDesignTemplates.com

Growing Up Grant/ Ulysses Grant Dietz -- 1st ed.
ISBN: 978-0-578-98018-80

I dedicate this book to Gary, to Grace and Alex,

and to all the people, living and dead,

who have made me who I am.

Whence I came

Ulysses S. Grant and Julia Boggs Dent

Robert Edwin Dietz and Anna Hadwick

(Great-great-grandparents)

Frederick Dent Grant and Ida Marie Honoré

John Edwin Dietz and Olga Sanderson

(Great-grandparents)

Ulysses S. Grant (III) and Edith Root

Robert Edwin Dietz (II) and Barbara Bancroft Johnson

(Grandparents)

Julia Grant and John Sanderson Dietz

(Parents)

Ulysses Grant Dietz

CONTENTS

A WALK IN THE PARK WITH RUDY 1

Speculation #1 THE NAME 7

UPSTATE 11

LEAVE IT TO BEAVER 27

THE WONDER YEARS 37

Speculation #2 THE PROPHECY..47

MY ROOTS 51

Speculation #3 LEAVING THE NEST 57

THREE WEDDINGS AND A FUNERAL 61

I ONLY MET THE PRINCESS ONCE 71

Speculation #4 THE PROPOSAL 77

DANCING ON THE EDGE OF THE GILDED AGE................................81

Speculation#5 FRED AND IDA 99

THE END OF THE WORLD 105

RECONSTRUCTION 121

A SEPARATE PEACE...133

BOYS IN THE BAND 141

SEQUINS AT YALE..159

A Short Story BORN AGAIN..167

FOR KEEPS 187

Speculation #6 THE BARGAIN 207

FINIAL LAND...213

THE ANTI-AMERICAN WING 225

LEAVE IT TO BEAVER REPRISE 235

Speculation #7 GERTIE GOES AWAY...249

COME TO JESUS..255

MOUTHS OF BABES 267

HETERONORMATIVITY 293

FAREWELL TO UPSTATE 309

OTHER PEOPLE'S MONEY 315

Speculation #8 SPIRIT OF CHRISTMAS YET TO COME...................... 335

BREAKFAST EVERY FIFTEEN MINUTES 341

I am lying in my bed at school, staring at the ceiling. I am sixteen, in my second year at prep school. It is late 1971.

As I lie there, my mind reeling with anxiety, I say to myself: "How can I be like this? Edie is dead. Ned is dead. Jed might go to prison. How can I do this to my parents? How can God do this to my family?

Then I hear a voice. For the first time in my young life a voice speaks to me out of nowhere. In the moment, at sixteen, I figure it must be God.

Here's what it says: *Be happy. Live a good life.*

Huh.

CHAPTER ONE

A WALK IN THE PARK
WITH RUDY

I t's April 27, 1997, and I'm walking up Riverside Drive with Rudy Giuliani, mayor of New York. To be honest, Rudy is ignoring me. Wearing a cheap-looking black suit, he is in fact working the crowd as I walk uptown toward Grant's Tomb to the mayor's right, surrounded loosely by security men and well-wishers. It is President Ulysses S. Grant's birthday, and we are leading a sort of parade to launch the celebration of the centennial re-dedication of the General Grant National Memorial, better known as Grant's Tomb. Rudy is running for reelection, and once we shake hands in front of the cameras in Riverside Park, he pays me no further heed. I am not alone this day, but I am at the front of the procession, solely because of my name, with the mayor of New York somewhere off to my left.

On that cool, sunny April morning, I looked fabulous. I was wearing my favorite suit and a yellow silk necktie with a repeat pattern of the White House. This slightly surreal moment was the culmination of a long adventure in which I had been a willing puppet, a name for the press, a face for the public. My brother Jed was behind me somewhere, with my two adolescent nephews, Robert and Elihu. There were probably more cousins back there, as well as my niece Edith. We were, all of us, descendants of the eighteenth U.S. President, Ulysses S. Grant and First Lady Julia Dent Grant; but I was the only Ulysses.

I was the face and the name that the press, when it bothered to pay attention, had come to know.

My own family was there, too. Gary, my partner of nearly twenty-two years, was also close at hand, with our two children: Alexander, who was two and a half, and Grace, one and a half. They, weirdly, had been assigned an old-fashioned closed horse-drawn carriage, which was part of the parade, though it shielded them from public view. Now and then, I noticed press people approach the carriage, as if wondering what celebrity was hidden inside, but no real notice was made of this man and the little non-white children. Nobody asked what their relationship was to the Grants or, specifically, to me. I suspect that was the Park Service's intention all along: to keep my unconventional family discreetly off-camera.

When the meandering group finished their "march" to the broad sycamore-lined plaza in front of Grant's Tomb, there was still more family, cousins from near and far; all likewise descendants of the general and his devoted wife whose remains lay, side by side, in the great, fifteen-story silvery granite mausoleum that looms over the northern end of Riverside Park.

On the same date, a decade earlier, I had been invited by the National Park Service to come and give a brief speech for U.S. Grant's annual birthday commemoration at the Tomb. At that point I had not been there since I was a small child in the early 1960s, when my parents, John and Julia Dietz, brought my little brother Ned and me to see the Tomb. We had really come to New York to see the Bronx Zoo, but I remember the Tomb in a vague, dreamlike sort of way. Though my parents called me Grant, I recall being introduced to the park ranger on duty as Ulysses. The ranger seemed very pleased to meet me. I did not then understand that I was the only Ulysses in my generation, of all the descendants of the general and his lady. At that point it was enough of a challenge to make a capital G, much less attempt to spell my real first name. The fact that I was Ulysses was an abstract idea, not yet part of my identity.

The April 1987 commemoration was seven years into my life in New Jersey, where I had moved from Delaware in 1980 to be a curator at the Newark Museum. At thirty-one, I was used to public speaking, indeed had begun to relish the attention and the applause of the curatorial lecture circuit. Who knew that people would pay you to talk to them about silver or furniture or glass or ceramics?

I don't recall what I said that day in 1987, up on the granite steps in front of the great Doric portico, which was swathed in bunting and American flags that fluttered in the spring breeze. At that point I knew virtually nothing about my namesake and ancestor, and very little about the Civil War. I had read Julia Dent Grant's memoirs, published in 1975, but never the general's own. The general's widow had purposely set aside her own manuscript in deference to her husband's best-selling (and profitable) memoirs. My mother and her sisters, daughters of Ulysses S Grant III, finally submitted the manuscript for publication after their father's death in 1968. I had read my great-great-grandmother's memoirs with the curiosity of a nascent curator, interested not in stories of politics and war, but in the more personal narrative of the life of this woman from whom I was descended. I felt pride in my ancestry but had never given much consideration to what that meant to me, other than the occasional embarrassment I felt at the negative mythology that went with the name. I knew the Big Three myths about Ulysses S. Grant: he was a bad student at West Point (therefore, somehow, stupid); he was the worst president ever; and he was a drunk. Any one of these, in my experience thus far, would inevitably be brought up by anyone I met, as soon as they learned the reason I was called Ulysses.

I doubt I addressed any of that in my three-minute speech in 1987, but whatever I said was quickly eclipsed by what followed. After the ceremony, I was introduced by eager Park Service staffers to an elegant, middle-aged African American woman named Alma. There, on live television (Channel 4 with Connie Collins), I was told that Alma's late husband, who had been named Ulysses as well, was thought by his family to be a descendant of the general. I shook hands with Alma and smiled – I hope warmly – at this kind-faced woman. Inside, however, my brain was in a tailspin.

The implication was that President Grant had somehow fathered an illegitimate child from a Black woman during his years in Washington. This was not something I had ever heard before; nor, I discovered, was it something that this nice woman's in-laws had any wisp of documentation to support. It was simply the fact that her late husband's name had been Ulysses, and what with all the conversation about Thomas Jefferson and Sally Hemmings in the air at the time, there had been speculation. That this might be awkward for both me and Alma on live news coverage had not, apparently, been considered by the National Park Service. That this might not be history, but sensationalism, had not been fully thought through either. For me, this was not about race; this was about the assumption that Ulysses S. Grant would cheat on his wife. This was unacceptable. Ulysses S. Grant was not Thomas Jefferson.

In retrospect, that morning in 1987 altered my worldview, although I didn't know it at the time. I wrote a strongly worded letter to the Park Service, suggesting that they not pull a stunt like this on me again, if they ever expected me to show up at the Tomb. I don't remember what, if any, response they sent me. As it happened, other events unfolded that would affect my long-term relationship with the National Park Service.

It was also at this moment more than thirty years ago that the Park Service's decreasing budget, and the increasingly evident lack of care at the Tomb (and throughout New York City's federal parks), came to public notice. Over the coming years I would get drawn into the battle over the future of Grant's Tomb, a campaign led by a fervent young Columbia University law student named Frank Scaturro. Frank would lead the charge, appealing to local Congressmen, cajoling city bureaucrats; and, finally, using me to deliver veiled threats to remove the presidential couple's remains. In the end, helped by his political allies and years of faithful effort, Frank would force the U.S. Department of the Interior, which oversees the National Park Service, to fund renovations to what is, after all, a presidential gravesite and a uniquely important historic shrine.

All I did was smile and wave. All I did was be Ulysses.

In the decade following this quiet debacle, I got involved with the re-established Grant Monument Association, and also with the Ulysses S. Grant Association (USGA). My grandfather Grant had been an officer of the former, and a founding trustee of the latter. The USGA's charismatic and erudite executive director, John Y. Simon, would be my real introduction to the life of my famous namesake. Inspired by him and by the members of the USGA, I would begin to chip away at my own shameful ignorance about the much-maligned general and president and his life.

By the time of the centennial of the Tomb in 1997, which was a brilliant, windy April day, the place was splendid. Its silvery-white walls shimmered in the sun. The flags and patriotic bunting were bright and plentiful. The graffiti was gone, the grandiose beaux-arts interior had been restored, the leaks filled. Julia and her beloved Ulys lay side by side in their massive red granite sarcophagi below the towering colonnaded dome, and thousands of people had come to pay their respects. I stood before this huge crowd and gave a twenty-minute speech on Ulysses S. Grant, his wife Julia, and what they meant to me.

I compared them to England's Victoria and Albert as one of the great love stories of the nineteenth century. I talked about their lives, and the incredible sweep of history they had witnessed together during their nearly thirty-seven years of marriage. Unlike my talk in 1987, this time I knew what I was talking about.

I have no idea if Rudy Giuliani was paying attention to my speech, or even if he was still there. CSPAN recorded every minute of that morning's two-hour ceremony, right to the very end when, in the rough cut of the video, as the camera begins to fade to black, you can just hear my son Alex exclaiming to my partner Gary, "Daddy, I think Grace has a poopy diaper.

CHAPTER TWO

Speculation #1
THE NAME

Julia lay as still as she could, enjoying the breeze of the oscillating fan as it passed back and forth across her bed. She could feel a sheen of perspiration on her face, her dark hair clinging to her forehead. The open windows, even this high in the building, did little to mitigate the sweltering heat. According to her nurse, the morning paper reported that this was the hottest July twenty-second on record, and Julia had no reason to doubt it.

Next to her, in a white-painted metal bassinet, slept her newborn child. Julia turned her head to look at him, his face scrunched up, fists tight, twitching slightly in his first sleep outside her womb. She smiled, embracing the exhaustion she felt as the sign of a job well done. It had been a long labor, nearly twelve hours. But her little boy was here, all his bits and pieces accounted for. Healthy. Alive. That's all that mattered. She flinched from the memories of two others, not so lucky. She instead turned her thoughts to his big brother and sister, waiting excitedly at home. Julia smiled again. Three. She had done it. There were times when it had all seemed so impossible.

The door squeaked, and Julia turned her head toward the sound to see the nurse's white-capped head pop around it.

"Mr. Dietz is here, ma'am. I just wanted to check that you were awake," she said with a smile.

"Oh, good. Thank you," Julia said, returning the smile.

The nurse disappeared, and Julia's husband John replaced her, entering the room with a sheepish smile, clutching his hat to his chest.

"How are you, Petey?" he asked.

"I'm fine, Pete," Julia answered, smiling at the use of the pet names they'd given each other when they were first married a decade earlier. "Tired, but well. Come see your new little boy."

John Dietz entered and crossed the room to the near side of the bed. He was tall and slim, slightly pigeon-toed, but not without grace. He wore a light summer suit, his dark wavy hair cropped close to his scalp. Large dark eyes looked out from behind eyeglasses with colorless plastic frames. He leaned over and, brushing the damp bangs off her forehead, gave her a gentle kiss. Then he peered over at the bassinet on the far side of the bed, where the baby lay.

"I was hoping he'd be awake," he said quietly.

"Why don't you go pick him up? He's slept a lot."

John moved around the bed and hesitated by the bassinet. Julia reassured him with another smile and, setting his hat on the bed, he leaned down. With great care and practiced skill, he lifted the swaddled bundle up, putting one long-fingered hand under the newborn's head, cooing softly with delight as he held his third child for the first time.

"Look at all that hair!" he said, noting the thatch of dark fuzz that covered his new son's tiny pate.

"It may fall out," his wife responded, "and the dark color doesn't mean it will stay that way."

John beamed at her. "My hair was like this as a baby, but then I turned blond. Then dark again as I got older. I guess we'll just have to wait and see with this one."

He came back around to the other side of the bed and perched carefully on the edge of the mattress. Julia smiled at seeing the pure rapture on his face. Her husband loved babies. He was so good with them and had always helped with Jed and Edie when they were little, with none of the trepidation that some of his male peers showed in dealing with infants. The baby stirred, stretched his tiny arms, and opened bleary dark-blue eyes to a world that must have seemed alien to him. He didn't cry. He just stared.

Looking up from his son's face to his wife, John's eyes crinkled in a broad smile. "Have you thought about the name some more?"

Returning his smile, and feeling her energy return in the glow of her husband's happiness, Julia replied: "Yes. I talked to Father earlier."

Smirking, Sandy asked, "And was he delighted?"

"Yes. And appalled as well."

At her husband's expression of surprise, she continued, "Well, flattered and pleased, certainly. But he was a little shocked that we'd choose such an old-fashioned and difficult name in this day and age. After all, Father was born in 1881, and even then he was teased about his name in school."

Sandy rolled his eyes. "That's because of his notorious grandfather, who was still alive, as I recall from my history lessons. That was a tough name to live up to." He cocked his head, as he often did when asking a question. "Was he really worried about our calling him Ulysses?"

Julia's expression grew thoughtful. "He was. He told me that, here and now in 1955, it would be better to give him a regular name, like yours or your father's.

Sandy snorted, startling the baby, who squeaked, and then subsided back into his peaceful staring as his father rocked him. "Well, Jed's John like me; and there are already two Roberts in the family. I like the idea of a little Ulysses to liven things up."

"I think it's more than just that. Father is painfully aware of how U.S. Grant's star has fallen in the course of his lifetime. It's as if he's a little bit ashamed."

"I don't believe that for a minute."

"I'm not sure I do either. But his hesitation is real. I don't quite know what to make of it." Sandy settled himself more comfortably onto the bed, jiggling the baby slightly to lull him back to sleep.

"Look, Petey, you're the youngest child, and your sisters have all given their children other names. Even if he has qualms, I know the general would be hurt if we changed our minds now, no matter what he says."

He fixed his eyes on his wife's. "I know you want to give your father this gift, Julia. I do too. We'll figure out a nickname."

At that suggestion, Julia's blue eyes widened.

"That's it!" A smile broadened her mouth and animated her face, casting away any remaining look of fatigue. "We'll name him Ulysses Grant Dietz." She paused.

"Yes?" John prompted, raising his brows.

"But we'll call him Grant."

CHAPTER THREE

UPSTATE

Syracuse, New York in the 1950s was the embodiment of American post-war prosperity and optimism. It is hard for anyone born after 1980 to look at all those small and mid-sized cities today, scattered across the national landscape like so many casualties of war, and understand the level of prosperity and national optimism they represented when I was born, smack in the middle of the Baby Boom. Before the United States moved so much of our industrial production offshore, every city and town in the country made something important. New York State had a string of these cities sweeping like a sparkly capitalist necklace west across the Mohawk Valley (eventually, the New York State Thruway) from the state capital at Albany, to the great industrial center at Buffalo, with Niagara Falls just above it. Syracuse, one of the original Erie Canal towns, was at the hub of Central New York, the county seat of Onondaga County. The New York State Fair was held in Syracuse each summer. For me, growing up there, it was the center of the world.

At 200,000 people or so, Syracuse was a small pond in which my family became big fish without much effort. They were also something like carpet-baggers since there had been no Dietz family living in Syracuse before 1940. There had long been a Dietz presence, however, manifest in the large white brick letters running down the side of a towering Victorian smokestack near downtown. The R.E. Dietz Company had purchased the manufacturing operation of a kerosene lantern company in the late nineteenth century. Until we moved upstate, the Syracuse factory was run by others in our name. Founded by my great-great-grandfather, Robert Edwin Dietz, the company started out in Brooklyn in 1840 as a small operation producing whale oil lamps. By 1845, Robert and his brothers had moved into lower Manhattan, where the family firm would remain in one form or another for a century. Oil lamps sound quaint, but in the 1840s and 50s, in the era when oil was discovered and from it kerosene was first produced, oil lamps became cutting edge technology. The Dietz family fortune was founded on the shift from whale oil to kerosene, when Robert Dietz's brother Michael patented the first flat-wick kerosene burner in America. In the age of gaslight, portable table-top lighting for the home was big business. By the end of the nineteenth century, there were sales offices in New York, London, and Chicago, along with the manufacturing plants in what is now Tribeca in Manhattan, and in Syracuse. By the time domestic electricity finally defeated gaslight, the Dietz Company had shifted its focus to construction and automotive lighting.

In 1940 my Uncle Gerry (that's a hard G) married a local girl, Cynthia Goodhart, and settled in Syracuse. He was the family's advance guard. My father, John Sanderson (known as Sandy) attended the wedding, and took as his plus-one a smart young editor at Harper Brothers in New York named Julia Grant. Presumably, Sandy had discovered why his date bore the name she did, since her father, recently-promoted Brigadier General Ulysses S. Grant III, was then stationed in Cleveland with the Army Corps of Engineers. When Sandy and Julia married in 1945, just days after the end of World War II, they moved to Syracuse. My grandparents, Barbara and Robert E. Dietz II, followed suit in 1950, building a house in the neighborhood where their two sons already lived. My grandfather's sister, Ethelinda Dietz Nichols, the widow of New York bon vivant Morton Colton Nichols, left her house in Greenwich for Syracuse soon after that.

Aunt Ethel and grandfather were the sole owners of the R.E. Dietz Company, as their father, John Edwin Dietz, was the only Dietz of his generation to produce heirs. By the time I was born in 1955, the East Coast Dietz clan was deeply entrenched in the heart of Central New York. As far as my life was concerned, it was as if the family's two centuries in Manhattan had never happened.

Just my luck.

My favorite bit of family arcana is a slim volume bound in dark green cloth, produced in 1914 by my great-great uncle Fred Dietz. Called *A Leaf From the Past*, it is a deliciously turgid amalgam of New York City history, family genealogy, and product placement. It is in this little book that the Dietz coat of arms was first published, reflecting the moment when men in my family began to wear signet rings with the Dietz arms engraved on them: two gold lions *passant* on a field *gules* (i.e., red). There is indeed a town in Germany called Dietz (spelled Diez until the eighteenth century), complete with a medieval castle. My ancestors, however, emigrated from somewhere completely different—a Franco-German town in Alsace called Barr—centuries after leaving Die[t]z. In Barr they were all leather tanners, a skill they brought with them to the New World. Which is to say, they ran out of employment in Alscace and sent the youngest away to seek their fortunes in New York City in America.

The timing of this family history is highly suggestive, and I suspect that part of Fred Dietz's motivation in publishing the book was to disassociate the family from the enormous German-speaking immigrant community present in New York by 1900, as well as the anti-German sentiment stirred up by the outbreak World War I in 1914.

The truth is that the Dietz clan, by 1900, was long divorced from any sense of German identity. Distancing themselves from more recent German immigrants and linking the family name to both old aristocracy and Knickerbocker New York would have served both social and commercial purposes. A great deal of the early part of *A Leaf From the Past* is devoted to affirming the Dietz family's colonial roots in Manhattan, making much of extensive landholdings in Harlem in the early nineteenth century. Meandering and typically snooze-worthy passages quote from Robert Edwin Dietz's journals to detail the family's German, Anglo-German, and Dutch heritage. Robert Edwin himself married an Anglo-Irish woman named Anna Hadwick in 1846. The family lore that Anna was Robert's housekeeper is mysteriously absent from *A Leaf From the Past*. They were a handsome couple, and Anna brought two crucial elements into my family: red hair and the Episcopal Church.

A Leaf From the Past also reeks of calculated social climbing. I suspect that agenda can be laid at the expensively-shod feet of my great-grandmother, Olga Sanderson Dietz, who married my great-grandfather John Edwin Dietz (known as Teddy) in the 1880s. Olga was, by family tradition, half Scottish and half Russian, and met Teddy when he was working in the Chicago office of the R.E. Dietz Company. She may have married him for his money, but surely had a personal social agenda, as did many wives of upwardly-mobile men in the Gilded Age. I suspect it was she who made sure that the family signet rings came from Cartier's New York store, engraved with an aristocratic German coat of arms that was authentic, if not authentically ours by right. It was she who dragged her daughter, my great-aunt Ethel, all over Europe, trying to snag a moneyed somebody for her. It was Olga who had Marion Sims Wyeth design a house for her on El Bravo Way in Palm Beach in 1924, naming it *Casa del Greco*. As far as I can tell, my great-grandfather Teddy never set foot in Palm Beach, nor did he travel with his wife. Once her children were born, Olga seems to have spent as much time as possible away from her husband, who finally (according to my father) drank himself to death in the late 1930s. By all accounts, Olga was not warm, but, when it came to building the Dietz social brand, she got the job done.

None of that, however, figured into my formative years in Syracuse. My parents brought memories of Manhattan life with them as a young married couple, and never picked up my aunt Cynthia's distinctive upstate accent, although they would live in or near Syracuse for the rest of their lives. I grew up in Sedgwick Farm, a restricted neighborhood developed in the 1920s on the city's east side. Sedgwick Drive, its centerpiece, was a long, winding double street with a wide grass median. Lined with elm trees before the blight killed them all in the late 1960s, Sedgwick was a veritable tunnel of green, the tall wine-glass profile of the trees arching across the generous expanse of the street.

The Dietz family that came to populate Syracuse during Harry Truman's presidency represented the narrowing of a complicated Gilded Age narrative into the gentle mundanity of post-war suburbia. My grandfather Robert and his older sister Ethel were almost archetypal products of a striving Victorian in-dustrialist and his status-conscious wife. In a pattern that would be repeated, interestingly, in other branches of my family, Teddy and Olga had only two children. Ethelinda, born in 1888, was named for an aunt of her father's, who was a successful theatrical ingénue known by her stage name Linda Dietz. Her brother, named for his grandfather (but, more importantly, the founder of the family company), came a year later. Teddy and Olga had a house on the west side of Manhattan, not too far off Fifth Avenue in the West Fifties, but also maintained a large stone house in Greenwich, Connecticut.

Family lore from their childhood was minimal, but my grandfather Robert and Aunt Ethel, even with their bickering, were always close, in a fondly antagonistic way. Their lives evolved along such weirdly different paths that their closeness seems in retrospect to have been somewhat miraculous. I have a melancholy mental image of Ethel and Robert as little children, both with big dark eyes they inherited from their mother, huddled together in their nursery as the sounds of a dinner party drift up from below. With a gentle but distant father, and a domineering mother who had a clear plan for each of them, I see them as almost Trollopian caricatures of what we imagine Victorian children to have been.

Ethel described two things from her own youth that stuck in my young mind. The first was being forced to wear one of the earliest orthodontic devices, intended to cure a distinct overbite. She regaled us as children with tales of being dragged around by her mother, showing off the torturous (but also fashionable and expensive) braces, much to her mortification. She also reported being left in European hotel rooms as a girl (presumably with her mother's lady's maid nearby keeping an eye on her) while her mother partied in places like Biarritz and Divonne-les-Bains. It gave her a lifelong horror of staying in hotels alone.

Grandfather never seems to have been part of these voyages, and must have remained in New York with his father, learning the business and getting whatever private education he needed to prepare him for Princeton. Grandfather understood early on that he was the heir to the Dietz corporate legacy, and it was solemnly noted in *A Leaf From the Past* that the future of the family bloodline depended upon his procreation. But here's the twist: in 1910 he was diagnosed with tuberculosis, and discreetly exiled to a sanatorium in Santa Fe to live or die under his own recognizance. In *A Leaf From the Past*, he was written off with the slightly bizarre assertion that he had not been able to take the strain of office confinement and had sought "outdoor life." Tuberculosis, memorialized as "consumption" in nineteenth-century literature, was the scourge of urban industrial America before the advent of sulfa drugs (antibiotics). It was also a contagious disease associated with poverty and filth, and thus bore connotations both shameful and dangerous—very much as AIDS would to my generation.

Grandfather didn't die, and his sister survived her mother's machinations.

While in Santa Fe, Robert met Barbara Bancroft Johnson, daughter of Edward Jewett Johnson, a Boston insurance executive who lived in a house called Dun-Cairn in Winchester, Massachusetts. Her mother was Mary Louise Dun Johnson, known as Mamie. Barbara had been on the verge of attending Smith College, when she was assigned to go west with her brother, Gerry Johnson, who had been stricken with TB. Gerry, with a hard G, was named for the signer of the Declaration of Independence, Elbridge Gerry (again, with the hard G, the source of the term gerrymandering). I have no idea if this was a family connection or not. Barbara, my grandmother Dietz, always claimed to be descended from two signers of the Declaration of Independence, but if she mentioned them by name, I wasn't paying attention.

Poor great-uncle Gerry died, but Barbara fell in love, and in 1914 she married Robert in Winchester. They returned to New Mexico, purchased forty acres on the Rio Grande north of downtown Albuquerque, and settled down as farmers in a single-story house already built on the land. They named their place Nassau Farm, purportedly a reference to the German province of Hesse-Nassau, where the town of Dietz is located. That story smacks of Olga's social ambition, because it's also true that Robert's father was born on the family's farm in Hempstead, New York, in the heart of Nassau County. The family had owned this land since the 1840s and expanded the extant farmhouse into a large colonial revival country house in around 1890. Both Robert and his sister spent summers there with their elderly grandparents in the 1890s. Remember also that Grandfather was supposed to have gone to Princeton, where one finds

Nassau Street and Nassau Hall. I guess it's safe to say that the name "Nassau" resonated with my grandfather one way or another.

Barbara and Robert weren't typical farmers. They were part of a substantial community of East Coast and Midwestern exiles who sought out the dry desert climate of New Mexico. They had cattle and pigs, and an orchard of fruit trees. According to my father, Grandfather also grew experimental strains of tobacco for the U.S. Government. All of this was irrigated by the Rio Grande, and the address of what grew to 150 acres was on Rio Grande Road, later changed to its current Rio Grande Boulevard. The products of Nassau Farm were only intended to support the family. Grandfather was, in my father's words, a remittance man. He received a monthly allowance from his family in New York. It seems harsh to think that he was paid to stay away, presumably for his health, but he and Barbara remained in Albuquerque until his father's death in 1936.

Robert was a gentleman farmer, though he took his work seriously. He and Barbara raised four children at Nassau Farm. Robert E. Dietz III, born in 1915, was the first child, followed by Gerry Johnson Dietz and then, in 1919, by my father. A fourth child, Olga Sanderson Dietz, the baby, enjoyed the double benefit of being the youngest child and the only girl with three older brothers. Robert and Barbara expanded the house in the late 1920s into a large two-story stucco building that looked vaguely Prairie School, with a curved tiled staircase, a large beamed living room, and manicured lawns separated by hedges from the animal pens and fields of crops.

Ethel, for her part, found her own way, undoubtedly prodded by her energetic mother. A souvenir of her years on the marriage trail in Europe with her mother is a pair of little brooches in the form of a 1906 Napier touring car. Beautifully detailed, one is enameled in lavender on gold, for daytime wear; while the other is pavé with diamonds set in platinum, for evening. The actual automobile belonged, as I remember the story, to the son of an English sausage manufacturer. There is a photograph, presumably taken by the driver, showing Olga seated in the car. The sidelights of the Napier—and of many European cars of the early twentieth century—were kerosene powered and made by Dietz in the New York factory. At this same period Olga owned a Renault limousine with Dietz driving lights, which they used in New York. Great-grandmother no doubt presented her daughter as an heiress, hoping to up the ante. Despite the jewelry, the sausage scion was an also-ran. In the end someone else got the prize.

In 1911 Ethelinda Dietz married Morton Colton Nichols, known to her and her brother's children as Tim. Born in 1870, Tim Nichols was forty-one to Ethel's twenty-two, and, if my research is correct, had two failed marriages under his belt by the time he snagged Ethel, the most recent of which had only ended in 1906. Harvard class of 1892, Tim was the son of William Gilman Nichols, who from 1890 to 1907 had been the president of Herter Brothers, a celebrated decorating firm involved in the renovation of the White House by McKim, Mead, and White under Teddy and Edith Roosevelt. Tim's parents had a sprawling English-manor-style country house called *Petronia* on Long Island Sound in Rye, New York.

By the time they married, Tim must have appeared a little shopworn, but pictures of him from the 1890s show a tall, slim young man with large blue eyes and aristocratic good looks. A dandy for sure, Tim was also a rake and a skirt chaser. Family legend has it that before his marriage to Ethel he broke the bank at Monte Carlo, and there's no question he was cosmopolitan and charming. I'm inclined not to believe family rumors that he married Ethel for her money, although given the fast life he lived, having a wife with access to cash wouldn't have been unwelcome. Ethel was not a great beauty, but images of her prove she was elegant and attractive. She was also polished and witty, something of which her mother would have made sure. Marrying a twice-divorced man nearly twice her age suggests that my great aunt might have been a wee bit desperate to liberate herself from the controlling presence of the indomitable Olga. Tim was charming, he was glamorous, and he was *there.*

Less appealing stories about Uncle Tim include his persistent infidelity, as well as darkly whispered rumors that he forced Ethel to have an abortion early in their marriage because he didn't want children. They never did have children, and the man my father called "Uncle Tim" committed suicide in 1932 at the Pierre Hotel in New York, by a combination of poison and hanging. Ethel never remarried.

In the year before he died, Tim wrote Ethel a great many letters from the Westward Ho hotel in Phoenix.[1] The truth is that Tim was suffering from serious health problems, described at the time of his death as sinus troubles, but this was probably another code word for TB or possibly emphysema. I read through those letters avidly before my father destroyed them as too personal to be kept after Ethel's death in 1986 at the age of 98. I was struck by the tone of intimate friendship in them, not to mention the fact that Ethel had saved them.

In my New Jersey dining room hangs an oval portrait of Morton Nichols at the age of five, cut down (according to Aunt Ethel) from a larger rectangular portrait. The childish Tim is decked out in a dark velvet Lord Fauntleroy suit, with a big red silk bow, his golden locks falling to his shoulders. His big blue eyes stare languidly out at the viewer, serene and confident to the point of arrogance. Ethel treasured this portrait and kept it over the mantelpiece in her bedroom in Syracuse. She never spoke of Tim with anything other than fondness.

In the early 1930s, having lost millions in the Crash of 1929 and rocked by her husband's shocking death, Ethel had moved to an elegant little clapboard house on Steamboat Road in Greenwich, Connecticut, right on the water. She added two servant's rooms in the attic (thus demonstrating that, in spite of her losses, she was not impoverished) and brought in antique mantelpieces and furniture from the house she and Tim had built in Nyack in the early 1910s.

A vivid memory of my Syracuse childhood is Ethel talking about the architect who renovated the Greenwich house bringing his boyfriend (she used that word) over to Steamboat Road for dinner. I was a teenager at this point and was only getting the first glimmers of my own sexuality, and this little social nugget from the 1930s became embedded deeply in my mind.

After a quarter century of exile, Robert and Barbara moved back to New York City in 1937, leaving their eldest son, my Uncle Bob, in charge of Nassau Farm. Teddy Dietz had died, and my grandfather, as the only male heir, had to

---

[1] The *Westward Ho!* Stationery was distinctive, but I failed to note the location of the hotel before the letters were destroyed. Thus I've decided it must have been the hotel in Phoenix, which appears to have been the only one with this name in the period.

take the reins. They rented in the Manhattan neighborhood of Murray Hill, ending up in a narrow five-story brownstone at 113 East 35th Street. This is puzzling, as my grandmother had suffered terribly from joint pain since her late thirties. My only guess is that there was an elevator since the stairs would have been impossible for her to manage.

By the late 1930s my aunt Olga was boarding at Shipley in Bryn Mawr, Pennsylvania. Uncle Gerry was at Yale. Sandy, having graduated from Deerfield Academy in 1937, failed to get into Williams College and decided to work in the theater rather than go to college. For a while he commuted from his job as Ethel Merman's stage manager on Broadway to Petronia, the Nichols estate in Rye. Then he moved into the top floor of the Dietz house on East 35th Street.

Julia Grant, who would become my mother, had graduated from Bryn Mawr College in 1938, and gotten a job at Harper Brothers after spending a year working at Hamilton College. She loved the world of publishing but had no illusions as to her future. She was candidly told she was passed over for promotions because, as a woman, she would probably get married and leave. Of course, that's exactly what she did, and never felt more than mild irritation over this systemic sexism. I remember Mom confessing to me that the manuscript for Betty Smith's *A Tree Grows in Brooklyn* came across her desk and she dismissed it. It later became an enormous success, spawning both a musical and a film.

Julia had happy memories of working with Frank MacGregor, the Vice President of Harper's who would later take author James Baldwin under his wing. She had gotten to know MacGregor through an older couple, Gertrude and Bob Hawley, who were colleagues at Harpers. They became good friends, and she recalled spending weekends during World War II with Mac and his boyfriend in the country. This was another bit of information that I stored away like a treasure during my adolescence.

Julia had met the Dietz family in Albuquerque through a Bryn Mawr classmate, Mary Widmer. In 1937, three young women had driven in my mother's car from Pennsylvania to New Mexico. There, Julia attended a party where she met my father when he was still a teenager. The social world in Albuquerque was small, and the Dietzes were right in the middle of it. At the time, young

Sandy Dietz made little impression on the worldly twenty-two-year-old Miss Grant. When, in 1940, she learned that Barbara and Robert had moved to her Manhattan neighborhood, she invited them over for drinks in her studio apartment. Hearing that their son lived with them, she called Sandy and asked him to bring the ice. Talking to me in her late eighties, Mom's only comment to me about this was: "I took a good look at him and decided he was pretty cute."

When the United States entered the war in 1941 after the bombing of Pearl Harbor, Sandy was called up. He and Julia wanted to marry before he shipped out, but both sets of parents scuttled that plan. Julia's parents, Ulysses and Edith Grant, were by that time living in a sublet on Park Avenue, and my grandfather had been made the head of national civil defense by President Franklin Roosevelt. My father remembers going to have dinner with the Grants, in his new private's uniform, and finding his would-be father-in-law, Brigadier General Ulysses S. Grant III, dressed in civilian evening clothes. He always felt that this refusal to pull rank on his daughter's fiancé was both considerate and a sign of approval. The Grants liked Sandy, and they liked the Dietzes, but nobody thought that rushing into marriage just as a war was starting was a good idea.

After his long stint in the theater, my father had gotten a job at a Manhattan bank, mostly likely with some parental pressure to learn practical skills. This meant that, once he was overseas, Sandy was put in the financial offices, working with the paymaster to keep the soldiers' cash flowing. Although he received a Bronze Star in 1944 for his service in the army, he never saw combat at the front. His company came through Omaha Beach twelve days after D-Day, my father and his fellow soldiers bringing in the pay for those who had survived. He moved with the army on its final push into France, entering Paris soon after the liberation. Photographs show that he wore the little ribbon noting his bronze star at his wedding in August 1945, above his campaign ribbons. He never mentioned the Bronze Star to me or my brother. I only found it after our parents' deaths, as we were clearing out our mother's house.

Julia and Sandy spent their honeymoon at the Adirondack League Club, and then moved to Syracuse, into temporary quarters in a duplex on Durston Avenue. My father started work at the R.E. Dietz Company, alongside his brother Gerry, whose wife Cynthia would become my mother's first and fastest Upstate friend.

My parents built a seven-room house at the far end of Sedgwick Farm, on Mertens Avenue, where Sedgwick Drive's stately progress of Tudor/Colonial/Spanish houses petered out into an uninspired assortment of small postwar ranches and Cape Cod shoeboxes. Sandy and Julia painted their new house barn red, which was apparently scandalous at the time, when every other house was gray or white. My father once told me that the house cost them $7000, which seems hard to grasp, until you factor in his weekly salary of forty-five dollars. Despite the expected nepotism in a family-owned company, the Dietz boys couldn't just barge in and take over a factory run by others for half a century. They had to start out at the bottom and work their way up. By the time I was paying attention, my Uncle Gerry was President, my father was Vice-President, and my grandfather, who had long since relocated from New York, was Chairman and semi-retired.

When Robert and Barbara joined their middle sons and their families in Syracuse in 1950, they had Charles Umbrecht, a talented local architect, build them a suitable house at 301 Sedgwick Drive. V-shaped, set on an awkward sloping wedge-shaped lot at the juncture of Sedgwick Drive, Farmer Street, and Wendell Terrace, the house was both small and grand. Its $50,000 cost in 1950 was a family scandal (given that my parents would spend $30,000 on a house twice the size in 1951), but spoke to the architect's attention to detail. A ranch house designed for an elderly couple (my grandparents were sixty and sixty-one when the house was built, younger than I am as I write this), it was built of clinker brick and stained shingles, a modern house in Colonial costume. It was shaped like a V to suit the contours of the property, with the dining and service rooms in one wing, bedrooms in the other, and an elegant living room and library at the apex. A row of French doors opened from the library onto a long screened porch that faced the small garden, which was dominated by an old apple tree that we kids all climbed and fell out of periodically while the adults drank and smoked on the porch.

At the front, facing the point of the lot, the beautifully proportioned living room, had a barrel-vaulted ceiling designed to make room for two large tapestries from the Murray Hill house. The only window in the room was a large semi-circular bay facing out onto the parabola-shaped lawn that sloped down to the wide intersection formed by the meeting of the three streets. You could fit a three-person sofa, my grandfather's wing chair, and my grandmother's bergère in that bay window. From there we could watch the neighborhood during our daily cocktail hour and, when necessary, pass judgment.

In 1951, after my sister Edie (Edith Root Dietz) was born, my parents sold the little red Cape Cod on Mertens Avenue and moved up Sedgwick Drive to number 402. This was a twelve-room Spanish style stucco house built in 1929. The thirty-year, $30,000 mortgage was a major commitment for a young couple with two small children. It was also across the street and a block away from my grandparents. With my birth in 1955 and the arrival of my little brother, Edward Johnson, called Ned, a year later, the family was complete. Ned and I shared a room next to my parents, and my earliest memory is lying in my crib in that room—with its pink and blue wallpaper depicting animals—watching my father pour water into the humidifying tray at the top of the metal radiator cover. The sound of the clanking pipes that ran from the boiler in the basement to those radiators still echoes through my memories.

Although I was happy at 402, the house itself made me unhappy as I grew older and gradually understood just how profoundly my parents had ruined it in the name of a half-hearted post-War modernism. The alterations they made in the late 50s and early 60s, stripping nearly all of its Spanish-inspired detail, made no attempt to match the style or quality of the original house. In retrospect, this was all very typical of the insensitive modernizing done to old houses at the time all across the country.

I have to wonder if my parents were irritated by my adolescent expressions of dismay at our house's aesthetic shortcomings. These bothered me increasingly as I moved from childhood to teen years. If Julia and Sandy had committed to serious modern design, I might not have minded so much; but they never really did. Having bought "moderne" style furniture from W. & J. Sloane when they moved from New York to Syracuse, they gradually let the

Sedgwick Drive house evolve into a hodgepodge of 1940s black lacquer and inherited Colonial Revival mahogany.

Aunt Ethel followed her brother and sister-in-law to Syracuse, purchasing a big Georgian-style house at 1650 James Street. Built of a rich plum-red brick, it had crisp white trim and dark green shutters. There was a large garden and an oddly elegant garage of white painted stucco. Ethel settled into 1650 James with her Irish cook, Nelly O'Fletcher, and her German maid, Maria Schmidt, who would be prominent figures in my childhood. Maria had worked for the Dietz family since she was sixteen and newly-arrived from Germany. She wore different uniforms for different times of the day: light blue or green for daytime. Mauve-gray silk for routine dinners. And black silk for special dinners. I loved Maria, who was both forbidding and kindly. She cared for Aunt Ethel with a relentless devotion. Maria and Nelly would drive Ethel's big green Mercedes up to Kennebunkport every year to open Ethel's house, called Windy Brae, for the summer. Even in Ethel's unhappy later years, her mind lost to dementia, Nelly and Maria stayed with her. I would visit them in the kitchen rather than see Aunt Ethel, whose diminished state made me terribly sad. Nelly, who was a wonderful traditional cook, became increasingly eccentric as she got older, developing a propensity to drink and fall down the basement stairs. Maria, on the other hand, aged, but her energy never seemed to waver. She would ultimately spend fifty years in Ethel's service, retiring to Germany in her eighties with a tidy fortune in unspent salary to enjoy during her last years as a rural matriarch.

James Street in the fifties and sixties still clung to its status as the most elegant boulevard in the city. Starting at the bottom of a long hill that terminated in Clinton Square, in downtown Syracuse, James Street offered a chronology of American domestic architecture from the Greek Revival of the 1830s—when the grand houses looked out over the Erie Canal that went right through the city center—through the Gothic and Italianate villas of the Romantic era; to the larger, more ornate, and more eclectic mansions of the city's Gilded Age millionaires. As James Street approached Sedgwick Farm, where I grew up, the mansions had become more sedate, larger versions of the Tudor, Spanish, and Colonial houses that filled our subdivision. By the time I left

home for good in 1976, nearly every one of those great houses had been demolished and replaced with wretched low-rise modernist office buildings. To
my teenage soul, it was an act of long-term desecration that would confirm my
love of the past and ultimately steered me into my career.

CHAPTER FOUR

LEAVE IT TO BEAVER

W hen, in my mid-twenties, I thought about my childhood in Syracuse, I recalled it as idyllic. My boyfriend Gary and I would move to Maplewood, New Jersey in no small part because of my memories of my childhood. Eventually, I would come to recognize the shadows in the corners of that life, but I've never stopped feeling that it was a happy time, because I was a happy child. I was loved, I was safe, I wanted for nothing. I was more or less oblivious to anything else right up to the point when I wasn't any more.

Our life in our small upstate city was, I'm sure, pretty much like life for privileged folks anywhere across America at the time. The center of my existence was our big, faux-Spanish house at 402 Sedgwick Drive. My grandparents were installed in their custom-built Cape Cod ranch down the street at number 301. My father's brother Gerry and his wife Cynthia were settled in their newly built, shingled Colonial at 111 Burlingame Road, just a few blocks away. My great-aunt Ethel Nichols was ensconced in her grand brick house up at 1650 James Street. From our tidy family hub in Sedgwick Farm, the social spokes that radiated outward to structure my life were church, school, the family firm, and in the summer, the country club, and the lake.

It seems odd, looking back, that church was so central to our life, since my family has never, in my own mind, been a very religious one. Yet I am still an active Episcopalian, probably even more devout and involved than either of my parents were. My family, on both sides, was filled with Episcopalians of long standing, but few of them were affiliated with any congregation in New York City, and neither Sandy nor Julia attended services as young professionals before World War II. My father told me that his grandmother, the redoubtable Olga, attended St. Bartholomew's, across the street from her duplex apartment at 333 Park Avenue. I remember my mother confessing sheepishly to me once that, to her parents, church was something poor people did on Sundays. My mother wasn't baptized until she was seven years old, while Edith and Ulysses were living in San Francisco.

I can only imagine that, in the mid-1940s, as a young couple new to a small city, my parents must have cast about for ways to anchor themselves socially in Syracuse. There were clubs, both city and country, and there were churches. My aunt Cynthia was from a strong local Presbyterian family, who attended the big downtown congregation, Park Central. Her parents, Susan (known to us as Susu) and Hugh (known as HH) Goodhart were pillars of Park Central. Cynthia Goodhart Dietz was born in 1919 in a house all of two lots away from my grandparents' new house, her father the head of advertising for Franklin Automobiles. By the time I came along, Susu and HH had moved to the shores of Skaneateles Lake, a couple dozen miles to the west. I loved them, and it was years before I realized that they were not, in fact, related to me by blood, but only by their daughter's marriage to Gerry Dietz.

When faced with the reality of choosing a church, Sandy and Julia went with what they knew, and began attending St. Paul's Episcopal. It was a grand, if somewhat grim, Victorian church of rough-cut granite with a tall, pointed stone spire, located just a few blocks from Park Central Presbyterian in downtown Syracuse. At some point in the 1960s it became the Cathedral of Central New York, and the rector, Dick Hutton, who lived across the street from us, ascended to the title of Dean. I always loved that church for its grandeur, its stained glass, and the polished mahogany woodwork. The pews had maroon velvet cushions, and the apse that framed the great Eastern window depicting St. Paul was covered in gold leaf. I suppose that living in a relentlessly off-white house from which all Spanish character had been stripped made me hungry for color and texture. It occurs to me that possibly it was St. Paul's that seeded my passion for the visual opulence of the Victorian world that would become the centerpiece of my professional life.

St. Paul's had a substantial school building attached to it, and I remember a decade of Sunday school within that wood-floored warren of classrooms. The presence of children before the age of confirmation was not encouraged in the main church for Sunday services. We had our own large room, in a 1940s addition, which served as the Parish Hall. Here we had our weekly devotions, and here we all watched terrible movies about the Nativity and the Resurrection and learned to sing the wonderfully-named Lesbia Scott's celebrated children's hymn, *I Sing a Song of the Saints of God*. My mind still reels at the thought of all those classes, taught by mothers of the parish, including special projects and homework—all the better to inculcate into our malleable heads the tenets of Episcopalianism.

The Episcopal church in the 1960s was still not the Eucharist-based denomination it would later become, as it reclaimed its liturgical and theological ties to both the Church of England and the Roman Catholic Church. Post-

War Episcopalians tried hard to be Protestant, and thus Communion Sunday at St. Paul's was relegated to once a month, just like the Presbyterians down the street at Park Central. The other three weekends made do with Morning Prayer and the Apostles Creed. We did not cross ourselves or genuflect; we did not say "mass." This was before the 1979 revision of the Book of Common Prayer, and thus the language of our services, both for child and adult, was rich with the English of King James. Our rector, then dean, had a voice not unlike Richard Burton's, and I remember his rich baritone rolling across the cavernous interior of St. Paul's on those Sundays when I accompanied my parents once I was confirmed and could receive communion.

Secular life in Syracuse revolved around school for the children and work for the fathers. For my family, work was the R.E. Dietz Company, where my grandfather, father, and uncle all went every morning. Sandy and Uncle Gerry drove American cars—generally Ford station wagons—while my grandfather always drove his own Cadillac, a make of car he had owned since he rode the rutted mud streets of Albuquerque in 1913. Great Aunt Ethel scandalized the family by purchasing a little Mercedes sedan in 1960, an act of sedition that ended with her storming out of the family cocktail hour in tears after Grandfather all but called her a Nazi sympathizer.

The Company (known in the local vernacular as the "Dietz Lantern Factory") was a sprawling four-story brick building from the end of the nineteenth century, with a central sky-lit court that served as a staff lunchroom. The executive offices and boardroom were in a small painted-brick addition to the east side of the main factory. Located slightly west of downtown, in what had once been a prosperous neighborhood in the Civil War years, the Company was convenient to the two main city clubs where my male relatives lunched: the Century Club and the University Club. Those clubs were also places that figured into our social lives, when we gathered for festive family meals. The Century, which still exists, adhered to strict gender-based rules and the women in the family (Aunt Ethel had an honorary widow's membership) could only enter through a long exterior staircase at the side, and eat in dining rooms at the rear of the club reserved for females and children. It never dawned on any of us to question this arrangement, even though it forced my grandmother to climb a staircase despite her lameness and her need to use a cane. Obviously, there were no ADA regulations back then, either. I didn't see the grand nineteenth-century rooms at the front of the club—which was in an 1840s Greek Revival mansion that had originally backed onto the Erie Canal—until I was a teenager and my friend Margy Amos purposely took me in the front door so that I could see the waiters freak out at her boldness.

My strangest memory of the more business-oriented University Club was a slightly surreal evening where my father took me and my little brother Ned to a dinner, the point of which was to meet a group of Syracuse University football players. I recall rather numbly getting autographs from a lot of large, broad-shouldered men who meant nothing to me at all, including the legendary Syracuse football alumnus Jim Brown. I suppose my brother was more excited than I was, and while I wasn't bored exactly, I didn't quite get the point.

As far as I knew, mothers in Syracuse didn't have jobs, except in cases of duress. The vivid exception was the Rulison family, whose eight children (including two sets of twins) were childhood friends of my siblings and me. Their father, Larry, who I remember as tall, handsome and gentle, was a rising star in the local legal and political world and a state senator. He died young of lung cancer (having never smoked a cigarette), leaving the community shocked and his family stranded. His widow, Betty, who in my memory was unfailingly cheerful and welcoming, not to mention astonishingly patient, returned to nursing and raised all eight of her kids into upstanding adulthood. Betty was always something of a heroine in Sedgwick Farm.

For the most part, however, the mothers I knew made breakfast, got their husbands and children off to work and school respectively, and then went about their days. In the summer there was the country club for golf and lunch. In what might have been an upstate quirk, the winter alternative to golf embraced by my mother's golfing buddies was bowling. When bad weather closed the Onondaga Country Club for the season, the ladies of Sedgwick Farm gathered at Erie Lanes, a sprawling red-brick bowling center on Erie Boulevard (where the Erie Canal had run) on the eastern edge of town. Mother had a black and blue marbled ball, and all her friends, whom I knew from both the country club and the neighborhood, were in this league. They would chatter and smoke and bowl and enjoy themselves, and sometimes I got to tag along and eat snacks. Oddly enough, the men in my parents' social circle didn't share this enthusiasm for bowling. When I went away to prep school and met New York City and Boston WASPs, they were uniformly horrified at the idea of ladies bowling. But I suppose Upstate winters were long, and one needed to pass the time.

Committees were another important part of my mother's life. Honestly, I don't really remember the PTA at our schools having a very strong presence when I was a kid, though maybe that was just my parents' disinterest by the time Ned and I came along. There were plenty of other committees to keep these smart, educated women busy. Mother was on the board of Memorial Hospital, where all her children were born, and was part of a herculean merger process between that hospital and another one—Crouse-Irving—during my childhood. It was a big deal to have women in positions of such power, often at loggerheads with businessmen who had other ideas. In the years before corporate healthcare conglomerates, hospitals merged to survive and grow, and this merger had far-reaching impact in the community, including newspaper articles with photographs of my mother. In these pictures she invariably wore one of her signature tweed suits, including a skirt, not pants, at the negotiating table. Even to my naïve mind back then she was a hero.

The local art museum, originally called the Syracuse Museum of Fine Art, was another focus of activity for my mother. In the 1950s, my father had been involved, but ceded his place to her in the 1960s. Mom was on the board of the museum when they chose I.M. Pei to design what would be a Brutalist jewel-box, completed in 1965, in a reclaimed wasteland downtown. Renamed the Everson Museum of Art after an important donor, it would play a major role in my life for the next several decades. Through my family's support of the Everson, and the Syracuse Symphony, my own future interest in cultural institutions was fostered.

I haven't mentioned housework, because, in my neighborhood at least, mothers had maids. This sounds idiotic, and I know that many of my school friends did not have household help. Their mothers were housewives in the full-on June Cleaver mode. They cleaned. They shopped. They cooked. Sometimes they lunched. But in that little pond of Syracuse, in the fifties and sixties, there was help for those who had the means. If many families in Syracuse were *Leave it to Beaver,* my family was *Hazel.*

My great-aunt Ethel's household was exotic, because she had two servants and they were both European. More typically, families had maids who were general housekeepers and laundresses, as well as cooks for dinnertime. Live-in maids were becoming less common during my childhood, although both of our immediate neighbors had them. Many, but not all of these maids were African American.

On one side of our house was Mattie, a soft-spoken Black woman who lived in at Mrs. Henninger's. Susan Henninger had an elegant Tudor house with a secluded, fenced garden. Shyly friendly, Mattie would let Ned and me into her employers' kitchen and give us cookies. Sometimes she'd take us in to greet Mrs. Henninger, whose late husband, Anthony, had been mayor of Syracuse, and after whom a new high school was named in the mid-1960s. Mrs. Henninger was sweet and grandmotherly, although she and her husband had lost the only child born to them. This we knew because, to our wide-eyed horror, Mattie knew where the post-mortem photographs of the baby were kept. Once, when her mistress was out, she pulled them from a cupboard in the front hall: large black and white images of the tiny baby, laid out on folded satin. It was something we never forgot. Mrs. Henninger also had one of the first color televisions in our neighborhood, and I remember going over there to watch *Mutual of Omaha's Wild Kingdom* with Marlin Perkins.

On the other side of our house was Leona, a white woman who cooked and cleaned for Mr. Charles Brannock. She would give us cake. Her bachelor employer's claim to fame was the Brannock Device, a clever and ubiquitous gadget that measured one's feet for shoes, still in use, as far as I know, in shoe stores all over the country.

One of my best friends growing up was a pretty blond boy named Windle, and his family's maid was Sarah. I have lots of fond memories of Sarah's humor, her exuberance, and her kindness to all the children who roamed Brattle Road, playing hide-and-seek and other games while trampling through everyone's back yards. Sarah also worked with Rita, the one caterer who seemed to do all of the "special" parties in Sedgwick Farm. WASP foodways were not as varied then as they are now, and veal Marengo was the dish that always appeared for any party involving a crowd large enough to need a caterer.

My grandparents sort of employed a couple. Frances was an impressive, slightly terrifying, Black woman who cared for Robert and Barbara Dietz with a ferocity that kept us in awe. She was a fabulous cook and maintained their household with all the care she could muster. Her husband, Floyd, was a gentleman, soft-spoken and rotund, who could barely fit into the narrow pantry the architect had designed next to the kitchen. He was retired, but took on the role of butler when Frances needed him, wearing a snug short white jacket. He also drove my grandmother around now and then and purchased my grandfather's Cadillacs after he finished with them every two years.

When I was a baby, in our house at 402 Sedgwick, there were two young Scottish women imported under what, in retrospect, seems like an awful sort of indenturing program. The way it was explained to me as a child was that poor girls from places like Glasgow were given passage to the U.S. and a green card, paid for by a prospective employer. In return, they had to work for the family who paid their way for a set amount of time. The first of these was a young woman called Stewart, of whom I have no memory at all. To be honest, I don't really remember much about the second one, Maria, either, but my older brother does. The central piece of family lore related to her time at 402 Sedgwick was getting into a battle royal over my little brother's first haircut. Maria was outraged at the shearing of his golden curls in favor of the 1950s crewcut that we all wore as children. She lasted until Martha's Vineyard one summer, when she left my little brother and me, both toddlers, alone at the beach with some other children.

Next came Amaza Taylor, Maza for short (with a long a, as in amaze), who left a warm, though indistinct impression on me. I can see her face, and I can hear her voice, but little else remains. She did warn us that the maid who worked for the old lady across the street was a witch, and I remember standing on the front steps watching this sinister person, in her white uniform, walking up Sedgwick Drive toward the bus stop on James Street, with Maza looming behind us protectively.

Maza was replaced by Bessie Johnson, a rotund African American woman with a large smile. Like Maza, Bessie was only with us for a few years, but she left a big impression. She would iron in the sunroom-turned-library while watching soap operas. She talked with us, chided us, encouraged us. She and my mother got along very well. Bessie had a friend named Ceola, who was sharp-tongued and funny. Now and then, presumably with my parents' permission, Bessie would pile me and Ned into Ceola's huge pale turquoise Mercury Monterey and take us to bingo nights at her church. We'd sit at the back, each of us with our cards, and use big red ink markers that fascinated me. I've never been a gambler, but bingo was fun.

Bessie also gave me my first lesson in careless racism—my own. We were in the sunroom/library one afternoon, watching television while Bessie ironed. I was possibly five. Maybe Ned was napping or playing with a friend, but we were alone. No doubt to please me, we were watching Bugs Bunny cartoons, and specifically the great *Barber of Seville* spoof. At one point, as Bugs sang the name Figaro repeatedly, I chimed in, and then—with no thought at all—changed the initial F to an N.

Bessie stopped ironing, and said my name, softly but somehow harshly: "Grant." Then she gave me a short, succinct lecture, no more than a sentence or two, on the evil of that word and the fact that she was hurt and never wanted to hear it from me again. I honestly had no idea what I had said, nor what was going on. But I learned two things in that moment: The N-word was bad, and that words had power to hurt the people you cared for.

Then Bessie died, giving me my first experience of death close at hand. My grandmother Grant died in 1963, but my memories of her are so distant and few that it didn't have a great impact on my eight-year-old psyche. Bessie, on the other hand, was in my life every day, and her sudden death from a kidney ailment, complicated by her weight, blindsided me. This is my first memory of real grief.

Finally came Vernice. A native of North Carolina, she was born Rebecca Vernice Branch, and moved north with the Great Migration of African Americans from the South during World War II. She was married to Charlie Curry, who was a "puddler" at Crucible Steel (meaning he dealt directly with molten steel, a dangerous job). Vernice and Charlie had two sons, Terry and Bruce. Vernice would live through the turbulent sixties with my family, remaining until she retired in 1977, when my parents moved to Cazenovia, a small lakeside town twenty miles East of Syracuse. My mother continued to pay her salary until she died.

None of this seemed remarkable as I was growing up, but I confess it all seems a little bizarre looking back. Like most children, I was paying no attention to the world that concerned my parents. Like all of my childhood peers, I felt valued and cared for. I never gave a moment's thought to children—or families—unlike my own.

On the other hand, when I read Kathryn Stockett's *The Help* in 2009, I was shocked to see the echoes of that Jim-Crow-era Mississippi world in my own, cozy upstate youth. Of course, we were never so cruel and overtly racist as *those people* were. Still, all those Black women in their pastel uniforms walked up the hill to James Street every day to catch the bus to *their side of town.* We thought little of their lives, especially us children. I like to think that my parents' interest in the Curry family, evident to me in any number of ways, such as Dad's lending his Oldsmobile Cutlass convertible to Terry Curry for his wedding, made a difference to them. Of course, the truth is that we'll never know what they really thought of us. I'm pretty sure Vernice loved us, and I know I loved her; although I'll never know if her affection was mixed with resentment. This occurred to me when I read the flawed but fascinating *Go Set a Watchman,* the posthumously published 2016 "prequel" to Harper Lee's *To Kill a Mockingbird.* In it, the grown-up Scout has a horrifying realization that Calpurnia, the gentle and caring Black woman who all but raised her, might in fact have always hated her and her family.

My mother paid Vernice's salary after 1977 as a kind of pension. I know she did this in part because Mom was a kind and generous woman; but I also think it's possible she did it in part because she felt guilty.

Why would my mother feel guilty? She herself had grown up knowing Black people only in menial roles, as servants, railroad porters, waiters. She had very little first-person experience with African Americans in positions of authority. This was something she said to me reluctantly once, as I was telling her about an African American colleague with whom I was working on a major museum project. Behind this sense of embarrassment at her own ignorance, my mother also knew that her own beloved father, Ulysses S. Grant III, grandson and namesake of the man who freed the slaves and saved the Union, had embraced a deeply racist view of the world. While I would guess that he never spoke harshly to a person of color in his entire life, that tall, gentle, white-haired man, whose name I bear, was a believer in eugenics, and in particular the idea that African Americans were genetically inferior to whites. My mother told me that her father had, to her dismay, given her a copy of one of his favorite books on the subject during her career days in New York City. She never read it, and from that time on began to quietly rebel against his conservative opinions, to the degree that she voted for Franklin Roosevelt during his controversial third election in 1940. My grandfather was actually related to Franklin Roosevelt, through a common genealogical link to Mayflower passenger Richard Warren by way of the Delano family. Grandfather also worked for Roosevelt in his various military roles throughout FDR's time in office. The fact remained that my mother's family saw FDR, the great progressive, as a traitor to his class, as did most Republicans at the time. My mother never told her father of her rebellious vote.

My mother also knew of her father's ill-fated role in the Civil War Centennial Commission in the early 1960s. This is something I knew of solely through a widely published color photograph of him that appeared in *National Geographic*, sitting in the parlor of the McLean House at Appomattox. I never knew that my grandfather was unable (or unwilling) to moderate the aggressive pro-Confederate, pro-Jim-Crow attitude of the Southern states as the Civil War Centennial geared up in the late 1950s. Grandfather believed firmly in states' rights, which suggests that segregation didn't trouble him as much as it troubled my parents. In any case, he was quietly replaced on the commission by historian Allan Nevins.

Behind these truths, which were left unspoken during my childhood, was the reality that Ulysses S. Grant's own children were probably less embracing of racial equality than their big-hearted, permissive father, who had thought long and hard about the way people of color were treated in his country. My great-grandfather Fred and his siblings all grew up with slavery around them, and had a mother who kept enslaved house servants even as her husband led the Union Army to defeat the Confederacy. This irony was never mentioned when I was a child, being cared for by a series of African-American women in upstate New York at the height of the Civil Rights Movement. Slavery, needless to say, was not a topic that ever came up at my family's dinner table, other than to acknowledge that General Grant's winning the Civil War resulted in the ending of slavery.

What was never talked about was that Ulysses S. Grant had witnessed slavery firsthand in his wife's family, and had worked alongside her father-in-law's slaves in the fields at White Haven outside of Saint Louis. We were never asked to wonder about the fact that Grant tolerated slavery as part of the American system, and allowed his wife to keep the enslaved people assigned to her by her father at the time of their marriage in 1848 (because Fred Dent knew that his underpaid son-in-law would never be able to afford paid help for his family). We were never told that Julia kept her enslaved servants with her until the Emancipation Proclamation of 1863 made it too embarrassing for her husband.

I think I would have liked to know about the one slave that U.S. Grant owned himself, a man named William Jones, whom he acquired from his father-in-law, Colonel Dent. It would have been good for me to learn that my great-great-grandfather emancipated this thirty-five-year-old man, despite the fact that Ulysses and Julia were all but broke, and that Jones's value was more than the family's income for that year. Why, in the mid-1960s, did my family not talk about the way Ulysses S. Grant committed himself to racial equality and civil rights in his years as commander of the army from 1865 to 1868, which saw some of the bloodiest assaults on record against Black voters in the former Confederacy? Or that he continued that commitment, known as Reconstruction, throughout his eight years as president? Why did my staunch Goldwater-Republican parents never mention that the Republican Party turned on Ulysses S. Grant almost as completely as the former Confederacy did, despite the magnanimity with which General Grant treated the Army of Northern Virginia at Lee's surrender in 1865? Why did I grow up not knowing that Grant's fight for civil rights for people of color died with the dubious election of Rutherford B. Hayes in 1876, and that, in the end, equality for Black people was sacrificed for a new union between North and South, and U.S. Grant's reputation along with it?

The answer to all these rhetorical questions is probably that my parents didn't in fact know anything about it, having themselves been deprived of any accurate story of the Civil War and Ulysses S. Grant's role in it. During my parents' childhoods, the Lost Cause mythology became the accepted truth for many Americans, including Northerners. Also remember that, when I was born in 1955, U.S. Grant's reputation was at its nadir, steeped in negative mythology relative to Grant's generalship, his drinking, his intelligence, and his presidency. I shake my head at the shockingly inaccurate and biased way that Civil War history and Reconstruction were taught to me and my fellow classmates in Syracuse, New York in the mid-1960s. We elementary school kids were all oblivious to the way history had been recast to support the national status quo, even as the Civil Rights Movement took center stage and bussing was instituted in Syracuse to integrate the public schools. None of us had a clue that it was in fact Ulysses S. Grant who spearheaded America's Civil Rights movement in the 1860s, only to have it buried under the myth of the Lost Cause and the racist laws of Jim Crow. These things we were not supposed to know.

It wasn't until William S. McFeely's Pulitzer-Prize-winning biography of Ulysse S. Grant appeared in 1981 that historians began to seriously reconsider the life and career of the man whose name I carry, and it would be another decade before I began to learn the truth I'd missed out on all along.

CHAPTER FIVE

THE WONDER YEARS

The educational tradition in my family was public school through ninth grade, and then boarding school. My cousins on Burlingame Road all went away after finishing Salem Hyde Elementary and Lincoln Junior High. My siblings and I followed suit. The 1960s, whatever else they may have been, were good times for public schools in Syracuse. We walked to and from school twice a day until junior high. We didn't have crossing guards, we had student patrols, and I remember getting to wear that heavy white canvas belt/sash as one of the high points of my sixth-grade year.

Another great tradition of the prosperous post-war years that my family embraced was the epic cross-country vacation. One of the largest and most vivid memories of my childhood idyll was the trip we took in the summer of 1964, when I turned nine and Ned turned eight. Somehow, my father was allowed to take a month off (well, he *was* the vice-president of the Company by this point).

As if all four children weren't enough, Sandy and Julia invited a friend of Jed's, then sixteen, to join us. Johnny, whose sister Margy was my close friend, and whose mother was one of Mom's golf buddies, was in a rough spot at home, and Dad thought it would be good to get him away from Syracuse. My teenaged cousin Claire was added to the gang, supposedly to help look after Ned and me. Thus, eight of us piled onto an airplane in July 1964 and flew to Chicago, where we boarded a transcontinental train that took us to Helena, Montana. Being the babies of the group, Ned and I were assigned sleepers, while everyone else made do with sitting up all night in the coach cars. I remember getting the upper bunk in our tiny mobile bedroom, and waking up the next morning looking out over the Badlands of South Dakota to see pronghorn antelopes running through the scrub.

We then piled into a massive white Dodge station wagon with a rear gate-door and three rows of seats. With all of us stuffed inside, most of the luggage (including three trunks) was strapped to the roof. We drove from Helena to Yellowstone National Park. Aside from Old Faithful, I remember little of this great national park other than my own carsickness, probably from gorging myself on waffles at breakfast. It is at this point that this summer trip begins to get surreal, if only for its ambitious itinerary. The whole crew continued the long desert drive to Jackson Hole, Wyoming, and to the Triangle X Ranch. I was in the way-back during our drive (probably to prevent any further barfing on my part), and I got to watch as my cousin Claire's suitcase flew off the roof rack and bounced happily down the highway. Amazingly, it didn't split open. Maybe it was American Tourister, although all I remember is that it was red.

For two weeks we pretended to be cowboys, taking over a couple of big comfortable log cabins and eating in the communal dining hall. Triangle X was a working cattle ranch at the foot of the Grand Teton Mountains, and had recently adapted its brand to Triangle X2, to make altering the brand on an animal more difficult. More than half a century later it's still operating.

We were assigned horses for the daily trail rides. Mine was a gentle sorrel female named Pecos. Broad of back and slow of gait, I learned the basics of riding with a Western saddle on her. Mostly we just walked along the desert trails around the ranch, but there were times when our leader would move the horses collectively into greater speed. The shift from the bumpety-bump of the trot to the startlingly smooth roll of the canter blew my little mind. The teenagers in our group were assigned newly broken horses, still a little skittish but manageable enough for young adults. Cousin Claire got a black pony she named Gypsy. Jed got a horse whose pale color suggested the name Goldwater (this was 1964 and we were Republicans, after all). The ranch hands demurred at this request and gave the horse the less political name of Yellowstone.

Jackson Hole was a small town then, a far cry from the glamorous watering hole for the glitterati it has since become. We outfitted ourselves with cowboy boots and hats, and those nifty plaid shirts with snaps instead of buttons. Ned and I were pretty cute in our little buckaroo ensembles. I diverged from my siblings in that I developed a fascination with tiny china figurines of animals, which I collected determinedly during our two weeks at the Triangle X. There is one picture that both charms and mortifies me, taken by my mother before we packed up all the ranch-related stuff and shipped it back to Syracuse. I'm sitting in the sun outside our log cabin, staring adoringly into a corral made from the lid of a boot-box. In it I've scattered pebbles and grass, and on that landscape I've carefully arranged my little china menagerie. I sent home all my porcelain animals, carefully wrapped in toilet paper, and stuffed into a cardboard ice bucket. I'm pretty sure this was not an interest that my parents anticipated.

From Jackson Hole we flew to Salt Lake City, whence we boarded a train to San Francisco. Settled into a grand old hotel in Oakland, Sandy and Julia decided to divide up the children into age-appropriate camps. Sandy got me and Ned and decided that a nice movie would be the thing for a quiet evening. Quite innocently, he took us to what was billed as a comedy. *Yesterday, Today and Tomorrow,* starring Sophia Loren and Marcello Mastroianni, was indeed a comedy, and Ned and I both enjoyed the first two stories in the three-part film. At the third act, in which Loren plays a fancy prostitute in Rome, the disapproving stares we were getting from other audience members forced my embarrassed father to hustle us, protesting loudly, out of the theater and back to the hotel.

My mother's plans went similarly awry. She had pegged a nice comedy club for Jed and my cousin Claire, leaving the other two adolescents at the hotel. After all, she could have a nice scotch on the rocks, and what harm could come from an evening of jokes? Turns out, the star of the show that night was Lenny Bruce, then in the middle of his New York State trial for obscenity. Bruce, a legend in stand-up comedy circles for his blunt language and criticism of the status-quo, was often under police scrutiny, in this era when freedom of speech was subject to a great deal of conservative interpretation. He was convicted in November of that year.

We rode the famous cable cars that hauled office workers and tourists up and down the steep hills in San Francisco, and visited Chinatown as well, whose main street, Grant Avenue, was named after Ulysses S. Grant. Mom shopped at Gump's and I. Magnin, and we had tea at the Fairmount Hotel. I remember a kind of wax-museum that had a display about the great earthquake of 1906 featuring both movement and sound effects. Then we carried on to Los Angeles, stopping at San Simeon, to see what we all called "Hearst's Castle." I don't know what everybody else felt, but I think my nine-year-old life was changed that day. I have never been back, but images of that sprawling estate, from fifty-plus years later—the eye-popping swimming pools to the gilded doves serving as faucets in the kitchen, to the saffron-yellow satin bedspreads in the Celestial Suite in one of the towers—burned themselves into my mind. My own suspicion is that a decorative arts curator was born that day.

Somehow, we plowed onward, heading almost as far as we could go, ending in San Diego, where I took blurry pictures of the famous zoo. And then it was over. We flew home to Syracuse, and life returned to its normal rhythms. My family never took another vacation like this again.

Life changed dramatically in seventh grade, when the other kids from my neighborhood and I walked in a different direction to the ancient brick pile of Lincoln Junior High School on the hill above James Street. I don't think anyone ever pointed out the obvious source of the school's name, nor did anyone ever connect that name with me. My parents' plan had succeeded. Grant Dietz was well below the radar as a name, and I was more notorious for having a surname that appeared on a big factory downtown.

Early each morning we listened to a program called *Mack and Maude* on the local radio station to hear what the school lunch would be, and either carried brown bags or took lunch money and ate there in the low-ceilinged lunchroom on the bottom floor of the turn-of-the-century building.

Junior High should have been a nightmare for me, but it wasn't. I was the archetype of the sissy nerd: awkward, bad hair, ugly glasses, braces. Somehow, I managed to charm people into making me into a friend rather than bullying me. Some of this was surely because I was part of what was referred to as the Excel class, a group of kids who, I suppose, were seen the way "gifted" students were in the early 2000s. We were kept together throughout seventh, eighth and ninth grade, at least for the key classes such as English, science, social studies, and math. We were all white, which, at the time, never registered in our minds. Looking back, I can't believe that our uniformity reflected any sort of reality other than the racial divide that was only just being addressed in the Syracuse public schools.

Another reason I might have avoided being targeted was that I was gregarious and, as I recall, funny. I was the top male student in the class, but I was also something of a class clown. Making people laugh is something I've done all my life. I got the kids to laugh, and I got the teachers to laugh. I'm not sure if it was wit or just a desperation to be liked, but it worked. I always managed to be friends with what passed for the popular kids, even if I was never quite at the center of the group. The most popular girls (Rita, Patty, Diane) were genuinely pretty and liked me enough to fuel my delusions that I liked them "that way." Those delusions kept me nicely compartmentalized regarding sexuality until high school. The popular boys—the athletes and the sexually precocious boys who already sported facial hair and muscular bodies (Tom, Joe, Danny)—all tolerated me with good humor. In retrospect, I was enormously lucky, not to mention oblivious.

A case in point was a new arrival in junior high: Janice. She was not one of the kids I'd known at Salem Hyde Elementary. She was a handsome girl with long brown hair and a strong Roman profile. She was tough as nails and happened to be seated in front of me because her name came just before mine in the alphabet. Instantly she began to pick on me, and my response was instantaneous: I cracked jokes. I made her laugh. By the end of the day, we were friends and would remain so. Not close friends, but close enough to avoid any friction. She dubbed me Dietzel, a nickname that stuck with me through middle school.

In retrospect, I can see clearly that I was never part of the extracurricular social life of most of these kids. My circle of friends were the same kids I'd known all my life, particularly Larry Bousquet and David

Moynihan. Occasionally I'd be part of a larger social event, and of course there were the school dances that managed to cause confused boys like me profound emotional trauma, as we shuffled around the gym floor to the strains of songs like "Cherish" and Bobby Goldsboro's unaccountably popular tearjerker, "Honey."

In fact, the only social dark spot I can dredge up from Junior High is the day that, walking home from Lincoln to our neighborhood in Sedgwick Farm, two of my best female friends, Marion and Jerelyn, told me casually but bluntly that they were no longer going to spend time with me. They were done, and I was out.

Why these two girls decided to "dump" me as a friend I can't quite say. My guess, from all these years later, is that somehow I must have seemed inappropriate to them. After all, in my generation, this was the time when boys stopped having girls as best friends—straight boys at least. Maybe these two girls saw something in me that embarrassed them; something I didn't see myself. Oddly, I can't remember feeling particularly crushed or demoralized by this event. I suspect that I was really hurt, but that, most likely, I just locked it away with the other things I didn't think about.

A very distinct social divide happened during the shift from Salem Hyde Elementary to Lincoln Junior High. This was the moment when a subset of my childhood friends and neighbors moved to a private school called Pebble Hill in the suburban town of Dewitt. These were the kids who, like me, had mothers who neither worked nor did their own housework. I didn't know Pebble Hill well, other than having taken two years of dance class there with my Sedgwick Farm peers. On those evenings, in the school's semi-rural setting, we wore coats and ties, the girls wore gloves, and we learned to waltz, fox-trot, rhumba, cha-cha, polka, and something called the *schottische*. It was fun, believe it or not, partly because everybody had to dance and no one got left out. This was a setting in which I was gregarious rather than shy, because I knew all the kids and loved the dancing. There were no wallflowers; nobody was ignored. The only negative was that dancing class fell on the same night as *Batman*, forcing me to miss it almost every week. I had to catch up in the summer re-run season.

Life in Syracuse from this vantage point seems strangely distant, like a slightly faded home movie. We rode our bikes around the neighborhood, knowing exactly where the safe boundaries were. We roamed in little packs, playing versions of hide-and-seek, and games that were gleefully described as "boys against the girls," but which seem to have had no purpose other than allowing us to run around screaming and laughing. David and Larry and I could take the bus from the start of Sedgwick Drive down James Street to shop in whatever stores we felt like exploring. Syracuse was big enough to boast three department stores and plenty of specialty shops, including a great toy store called Ed Guth's. There were three big movie theaters for us to choose from. The Loew's and the RKO Keith were on Salina Street, the main drag. Then there was the Eckel, which was right next to my church, St. Paul's. It was smaller and somewhat less reputable than the other two. One Easter Sunday I went with my friend Larry to see Christopher Lee's *Dracula has Risen from the Grave* at the Eckel. Such blasphemy apparently hurt neither of our souls. Larry, whom I'd known since pre-school, ended up the principal of a large Syracuse law firm and managed my mother's estate for years.

All of our fathers worked somewhere downtown. Our mothers shopped downtown and went to meetings there as well. There were Saturday swimming lessons at the YMCA downtown, tucked in between St. Paul's Episcopal and the Catholic Cathedral of the Immaculate Conception. After school in the warmer months there were tennis lessons at the Sedgwick Farm Tennis Club in the middle of our neighborhood. I spent a decade being relentlessly mediocre at tennis, in spite of the endlessly patient tennis pro Al Romeo's attempts to improve my skills. I carried that mediocrity into prep school. My lack of interest in tennis was the first major manifestation of a lifelong aversion to organized sports. I didn't like to sweat. I had no sense of competition or drive to win. Sure, I liked winning, because I think we're hard-wired to appreciate victory, but to win for the sake of triumphing over someone else never held any appeal.

Summer also meant golf for my mother, which meant being dropped off at the pool at the Onondaga Country Club. My little brother and I, and sometimes my sister, would spend hours splashing around and getting snacks at the pool's grill, which we just signed onto our mother's account. Both Ned and Edie (and probably Jed before them) were on the club swim team. Competition never appealed to me; nor, for that matter, did anything remotely athletic. I was a good swimmer, but that never translated into wanting to swim competitively. My parents were surprisingly supportive of my lack of interest in the sporty things my siblings did. It was only much later that I learned what might have been the reason why: they had been forewarned that I might be different from my siblings in other ways.

A part of each summer was spent away from Syracuse. Being transplanted New Yorkers, my parents had tried to make Martha's Vineyard our summer spot, recalling their younger years in New York City; but after a few memorable seasons renting an ample, shingled house in Oak Bluffs, they threw in the towel. The Vineyard was a long way from Syracuse, and I was particularly prone to carsickness. In any case, the Finger Lakes were close by, and the picturesque town of Skaneateles became our summer place. For much of my childhood we rented a series of houses on the east side of Skaneateles Lake. Robert and Barbara Dietz rented a tiny cottage on the west side of the lake, with extensive lakefront and a huge lawn. The family would gather there on weekends, and often the cousins from Albuquerque and Denver would come East to visit the grandparents.

During the school year, and any time we were in town, the family gathered for cocktails every day at 5:30 at Robert and Barbara's. Great Aunt Ethel would inevitably be there. Uncle Gerry, Aunt Cynnie, my parents, and whichever of the eight Syracuse Dietz children were home would be present too. Friends and the occasional neighbor would drop in, although for the most part it was just family. The cocktail hour was a near-sacred ritual. My little brother and I would make the drinks (even at eight I knew everybody's brand of liquor and could mix a martini) and help Frances prepare rye crisp, cheddar cheese, sliced kielbasa, and little dill pickles on a tray. Then we would sit and talk, covering whatever was in the air that day, and also commenting on whomever passed within sight of the big semi-circular bay window where we were clustered in my grandparents' living room. This is where we learned what adult conversation was. This was where we learned about Syracuse politics and our own family history. The cocktail hour at my grandparents was more important than the Sunday dinners we ate there or at Aunt Ethel's, just as enduring a memory for me as Thanksgiving or even Christmas Eve. This was our daily WASP Shabbat. It punctuated our routine and tied us together as a family. When I wrote a eulogy for my father's funeral many years later, a central theme was the cocktail hour at my grandparents.

CHAPTER SIX

Speculation #2
THE PROPHECY

S andy parked the Oldsmobile station wagon on the wide macadam apron in front of the Cranstons' garage. The house sat low and sleek, its cedar-sided horizontality perched on the edge of a wooded ravine.

Everything was quiet. This felt far from the noise of the city.

Mrs. Cranston answered the door as soon as they'd rung the doorbell. Actually, her real title was *Doctor* Cranston, since both husband and wife were psychiatrists. Mrs. Cranston smiled warmly up at Sandy and Julia, her eyes bright beneath the curled bangs of her ash-blonde wig. She was petite, stylish. Not motherly, she was instead kind and calm.

"The boys are still with Bob," she said, referring to her husband, the *other* Dr. Cranston. "We can wait in the consulting room." She ushered them into the small, simply decorated room, which had a sofa and several chairs lining the walls. Everything in the house was modern, sleek. Neutral colors dominated. It was restful.

Julia clutched her purse and her gloves. She wore no hat, and had on a tailored blue and white tweed suit with a short skirt and low-heeled navy-blue pumps. Sandy was dressed for work, a gray suit and dark narrow silk tie. As the fall day was still warm, he'd worn no hat or overcoat.

Sandy and Julia had come to the Drs. Cranston because Sandy, at forty-seven, was stressed out. Maybe it was work. As vice president of the R.E. Dietz Company, which made kerosene lanterns and construction lighting in downtown Syracuse, Sandy worked with his elder brother, Gerry, who was president, and their father, Robert, the company chairman.

Whether it was work, or the anxiety of middle age, or worries about his family, Sandy and Julia had decided they needed to talk to someone, and it had been suggested they bring their two youngest children, Grant, ten, and Ned, nine, to participate in some family sessions. And, while they were at it, the two youngsters could be evaluated individually and given IQ tests, just to see that everything checked out.

The two older children, Jed and Edie, were away at school. Edie was in her first year at Shipley, a girl's boarding school in Bryn Mawr, Pennsylvania, where Julia had gone. Jed was a sophomore at the University of North Carolina, Chapel Hill. Somehow he'd managed to pull off a Morehead scholarship, designed to bring good students from Northern prep schools to this great Southern university. This was a full, four-year free ride. So, whatever it was, at least Jed's college costs were not part of Sandy's stress.

Dr. Cranston made polite small talk with Sandy and Julia until her husband quietly opened the door and slipped into the room. Perhaps "slipped" isn't the right word because Bob Cranston was stout and jowly. His warm smile and gentle manner made up for a slightly intimidating appearance. His graying black hair was Brylcreemed neatly in place.

Having shaken the younger couple's hands, he sat in the chair next to his wife. Then they looked at each other, as if for cues. It was apparently decided that *Mister* Dr. Cranston would speak first.

"I've left the boys playing in my study," he said. "I thought we could chat for a bit."

"Is everything alright?" asked Sandy.

"They're both fine boys," reassured Bob, flashing a toothy smile, as his little wife beamed alongside him.

"And Grant?" asked Julia, softly.

"Grant is a very happy young man, Julia," answered Bob. "As you know, he's very bright. He has a vivid imagination, full of daydreams."

Julia and Sandy said nothing, but the attentive looks on their faces made it clear they expected him to go on.

"Grant's a shy boy. He's a little timid about new situations, about things he doesn't know. But he's very content, and it's important you understand that. He's not lonely. He feels he has plenty of friends. He loves school."

Bob looked at his wife for affirmation. She merely smiled again and repeated. "He's a happy kid."

"Ned's happy too, right?" Sandy interjected, a furrow of concern creasing his high forehead.

"Of course," both doctors said almost in unison. Bob chuckled and smiled at his wife as she patted his knee.

"Ned's fine," she assured the parents. "As you know, he's also very bright, outgoing and highly social."

"But he's more of a loner than he seems," Bob continued, following his wife's train of thought. "He's not nearly as introspective as Grant, and is more dependent on others. There's a restless spirit there."

"And some anger," his wife added. "Being the youngest can be frustrating, even with Grant being so close in age."

"But it's nothing to worry about, you understand," Bob said. "Nothing at all outside the normal range we see in boys this age."

Julia and Sandy exchanged looks with each other, tacit relief reflected in their faces—that is, until they noticed the doctors were looking at each other, an unspoken question being telegraphed between them. They saw Bob nod at his wife, who then turned to the couple, her hands folded in her lap.

We've been wondering whether to bring this up at all." She hesitated, as if gathering her thoughts. "It is very conjectural, to be honest, but we both feel that you two are such good, strong parents, that it would be useful for you to hear this."

"What in heaven's sake do you mean?" asked Julia, puzzled. "You said nothing's wrong."

"No, no, nothing's *wrong*," the petite doctor continued, apparently with some effort. "It's just that we've both studied the boys quite closely these past weeks and have had a chance to see them together and apart."

"And?" Sandy asked, a note of impatience in his voice.

"It would be our opinion that Grant, according to what we've observed, is quite likely to be homosexual."

Sandy and Julia stared at the doctors. Julia glanced quickly at her husband and saw an odd look of fear, as well as surprise, etched into his face.

Sandy found his voice first. He managed a husky whisper. "Well, um, what do we do about it?"

Both the doctors Cranston raised their eyebrows at the younger couple.

"Do about it?" Bob said first. "Why, nothing. There's nothing you can do about it."

"It's the way he is," interposed his wife. "Nothing you do will change the outcome. All you can do is support him. Look out for him. And be ready when the time comes."

"If the time comes, of course," added her husband, nodding sagely.

Mrs. Cranston rose and moved to the door. "I'll just go get the boys."

Sandy and Julia stared at Bob Cranston in dumbstruck silence for the few moments until Ned and Grant came clattering into the room for their final family session.

Little did Grant know that from this moment on, his parents would never see him quite the same way again.

CHAPTER SEVEN

MY ROOTS

In my dressing room, there are half a dozen framed photographs of my dead relatives. Some of these I knew personally, some are simply ancestors. I see these people every day, and their presence is not accidental. I began gathering these pictures and getting them framed when I was in college. In recent years, I've realized that it's an odd thing to be able to find Wikipedia pages about so many of one's antecedents, much less published biographies about them. I was not always aware of this fact about my family. That knowledge began to solidify during my prep school years; but the truth is that snippets of conversation throughout my childhood had begun to plant seeds of an awareness that my family was not entirely like the families of my friends.

If there was a physical center point for my emerging sense of my wider family, it was my *other* grandparents' house at 101 College Hill Road in Clinton, New York. I suppose this was the house that germinated the obsession with domestic architecture that would be well in place by the time I hit puberty. Grandmother and Grandfather Grant's summer place had a long history before my grandmother's family acquired it. Built in 1816, it started as an elegant, seven-room Federal house on five acres set at the top of the long steep hill that rose from the village of Clinton to the Hamilton College campus. The house was expanded in the mid-nineteenth century when a large wing was added to the back, creating space for a long common room and four additional bedrooms upstairs. A Hamilton professor by the name of Upson and his wife ran the place as a boarding house for Hamilton students.

Next door to the Upson House was another pretty federal building, built in the early 1800s, that had started life as the Root Tavern. By the mid-1800s it had become the home of Oren Root, professor of mathematics at Hamilton, a descendant of John Root, one of the founding settlers of Farmington, Connecticut in 1640. The Roots had made their way west from Connecticut at the end of the eighteenth century, where they had married into a local family called Buttrick, and had been settled into their tavern soon after the founding of a small college across the road named for the first Secretary of the Treasury, Alexander Hamilton.

This is important because Oren Root had a son named Elihu, born in 1845, who would leave his family's home and college and set out for New York City after attending Hamilton during the Civil War. Graduating New York University Law School in 1867, Elihu Root would go on to become a founding figure in modern corporate law and was, in his day, seen as the most powerful lawyer in private practice in the nation.

In the 1890s, Elihu Root would return to Clinton and purchase the Upson house, by this time owned by a family named Darling, and add yet another wing at the back, to house servants. Elihu and his wife Clara Frances Wales Root would spend their summers at 101 College Hill Road for the rest of their lives. Clara's father was Salem Howe Wales, publisher of *Scientific American* and a founding trustee of the Metropolitan Museum of Art. He had been one of the initial developers of the potato farms in Eastern Long Island in the 1880s, naming his Victorian summer house there *"Ox Pasture."* Elihu and Clara had Carrere and Hastings build them a large, shingled summer house in Southampton in 1896. At the same time Salem's farmhouse was remodeled by the same firm. However, the social whirl in Southampton never really suited Elihu and Clara's more bookish tastes, and by the time Salem and his wife Frances Elizabeth had died (he in 1903, she in 1905), the Roots had sold the Southampton house and renovated the place on College Hill Road as their summer retreat from the cares of New York and Washington.

Frances and Salem Wales had two children. Clara Frances, born in 1853, would meet Elihu Root in New York in the early years of his legal career, when as junior defense counsel he made his name by failing to successfully defend the infamous William "Boss" Tweed. Elihu and Clara married in 1877. Clara's brother Edward Howe Wales was born in 1856 and would end up as the personal secretary to Frederick William Vanderbilt and have his own house on the Vanderbilt estate in Hyde Park, New York. Edward's only child, Ruth, would carry on the family tradition of summering in Southampton, where she would meet Henry Francis duPont and end up as the chatelaine of the great Winterthur estate outside of Wilmington, Delaware. Ruth duPont and my grandmother Edith were first cousins and shared a love of things literary. Harry duPont and my grandmother shared a love of gardening.

When Elihu Root died in 1937 at the age of 92, the house on College Hill passed to his daughter, my grandmother. Both of Edith's younger brothers, Elihu Jr. and Edward Wales Root, lived in adjacent houses on College Hill. Edward and his wife Grace Cogswell Root lived in the original tavern, now known as the Homestead, while Elihu and his first wife Alida had Carrere and Hastings build them a colonial style wooden house a bit further up the hill, past the collection of farm buildings that linked all the properties together into what amounted to a family compound.

Although Elihu Jr. was a lawyer like his father, both he and his younger brother Edward were avocational painters. Edward was an art history professor at Hamilton, and a serious early collector of modern art by American painters. Elihu Jr.'s second wife was Nancy Root, a cousin and an artist as well.

My grandmother Grant, born Edith Root in New York in 1878, was Elihu and Clara Root's eldest child. Being female, she was educated at home, and served as her father's hostess during a good part of his political career. Clara, who by all reports was a vibrant and intelligent woman, probably couldn't manage the press of social activity her husband's political and legal success demanded and turned some of it over to her beautiful and strong-minded daughter. It was Edith who, while Elihu was Theodore Roosevelt's Secretary of War, was assigned to chaperone and help manage Alice Lee, Teddy's famously defiant daughter by his first wife. Alice and Edith became good friends, although Edith was six years older. In 1903 they traveled together, but otherwise unaccompanied by either secret service or maids, to New Orleans, to enjoy Mardi Gras. They stayed with the McIlhenny family of

Philadelphia who had rented a house on Louisiana Avenue for the festivities. My grandmother kept a diary of the journey, which offers up vivid images of them smoking illicit cigarettes and doing up each other's hair, while they gossiped about young men.

Soon after the New Orleans adventure, Edith was at a White House event with her father. She was introduced to a strikingly handsome young Lieutenant, a recent West Point graduate, with brown hair and bright blue eyes. He was working as an aide to President Roosevelt, most likely through the influence of his father, Frederick Dent Grant. Fred Grant was the eldest child of Ulysses S. Grant and had followed Roosevelt as Commissioner of Police in New York. Thus it was that Elihu Root's beautiful daughter met Ulysses S. Grant III, grandson and namesake of the Civil War general and Reconstruction-era president.

Edith and Ulysses married in Elihu Root's rented Victorian pile on Rhode Island Avenue in Washington, DC in 1907. Alice Roosevelt Longworth and her husband attended the wedding, and Ruth Wales, the future Mrs. Henry Francis duPont, was her only attendant. President Roosevelt and his wife Edith toasted the newly married couple, and the son of Mexico's president, a former suitor who was still smitten with Miss Root, sent thousands of gardenias to add to the floral decoration of the house for the wedding. My grandmother and grandfather, twenty-nine and twenty-six respectively, spent their wedding night at Friendship, the estate of John R. McLean on Wisconsin Avenue.

My grandfather, like his father and grandfather, was career army. He graduated West Point in 1903 ranked number six in his class. Ever mindful of his own dubious history at the Military Academy, Ulysses' father Fred constantly reminded him that he couldn't just coast by on his famous name. The irony here is that both Fred and his son were haunted by the myth that Ulysses S. Grant was a poor student at West Point, which was not remotely true. Grandfather learned his lesson, although it must have smarted that Douglas MacArthur was number one in his class and would be forever both his competitor and colleague in the army.

Grandfather Grant would take part in both world wars. He was present at the Treaty of Versailles that ended World War I (but also set the stage for

World War II due to conditions imposed on Germany, thought by them to have been unduly harsh) and would be appointed by Franklin Roosevelt as the head of American Civil Defense during the second war. Ulysses and Edith and their growing family moved around the country, from New York to San Francisco to Washington to Wilmington, Delaware and back to New York. For them and their three daughters (Edith, 1908; Clara Frances, 1912; and Julia, 1916) the Root clan and their houses on College Hill Road in Clinton would become a constant in their lives, as close to a permanent home as any of them knew.

My Grandmother Grant died in 1962, and when my grandfather died in 1968, the house became the shared property of his three daughters, each of them with children of their own. My mother and her sisters loved that house and tried to hold onto it in spite of the impracticality of a twenty-five-room frame house with two furnaces and no insulation. My mother was the only Grant girl who lived within spitting distance of College Hill Road, and I remember listening hopefully to conversations between my parents over the idea of moving to Clinton and my father commuting the forty-eight miles to Syracuse every day. Needless to say, I was all for it, being a teenager with grandiose notions of living in such a big house. The Clinton house represented in my mind the ancestral stately home of the forebears I only vaguely understood. However, my parents were not me, and fully grasped the issues of maintaining a ramshackle mansion fifty miles from all their friends. Ultimately the family sold the property to Hamilton College in 1978. Today it is Hamilton's admissions office, and my grandmother's peony garden behind it has been restored to reflect my family's many summers there.

CHAPTER EIGHT

Speculation #3
LEAVING THE NEST

C lara leaned back in her chair, closing her eyes for a moment to rest. A small pile of correspondence sat on the desk in front of her, neatly divided into notes of thanks, invitations to be answered, and letters to her family and friends. She was halfway through her morning tasks, but she couldn't entirely push away the feeling that, at the age of fifty-four, it was all more tiring than it once had been.

She opened her eyes and let them wander to the open window. Below on Rhode Island Avenue the sounds of passing carriages and the occasional motor car disturbed the shimmering quiet of the hot Washington morning. A faint breeze stirred the embroidered muslin vitrage curtains but did little to alleviate the oppressive warmth. Clara thought to herself how glad she would be to return to Clinton and her shaded garden once the government recessed for the summer.

A quiet rustle behind her drew her attention to the open door that lead to the shadowed upstairs hall. Clara's daughter Edith, looking fresh and cool in white linen, came into the room, smiling as she kissed her mother and then moved to sit on the edge of the daybed. A furrow on Edith's brow contradicted her smile, and Clara was instantly on the alert for whatever was troubling her eldest child.

"Has Father gone to work?" Edith asked.

Clara knew her daughter was stalling. Elihu was always out the door by eight o'clock when he was in Washington. President Roosevelt was energetic and expected his lieutenants to be at his side throughout his long days. Though her husband was thirteen years older than his friend and employer, Mr. Root was never one to let the young president outpace him.

"Don't be ridiculous, my dear," she answered her daughter, her voice gentle but clear. "Just tell me what's on your mind and I'll order some iced tea for us.

Edith snorted softly in a rather unladylike way. "Gad, mother, I can never fool you for a minute, can I?" Her smile broadened to a grin, and Clara noted how beautiful Edith was, as she felt relief fill her heart. This wasn't something bad, then.

"Ulysses has asked me to marry him, Mother."

"Lieutenant Grant?" Clara asked, knowing full well that there was only one Ulysses in Washington that she was aware of.

Edith was all earnestness. "Yes. Just yesterday."

"And did you answer him?" Clara's tone was purposely dry, but she was hard-pressed to keep from smiling at her daughter's obvious happiness. Edith chuckled again. "Really mother, you're spoiling my presentation. Of *course* I said yes."

Clara allowed herself to beam at Edith's smiling face. Her Edith was so serious, so smart, so bookish—and like her mother—so patient. Her daughter's large dark eyes glittered with emotion.

"You know he doesn't have any money." Clara arched her eyebrows, hoping this gesture added a comic effect to the not-entirely-purposeless words. She knew that playing the protective dowager was a gambit that Edith would see through immediately.

"Oh, I know that, Mother." Edith couldn't stop smiling, even as she played along. "All they have is the money the old general made writing his memoirs. His parents are up in Governor's Island, where his father is the commandant. I suppose a general makes a good salary."

Edith smirked at her mother. "Anyway, we have more than enough money, don't we?"

Clara couldn't help chucking herself. "I suppose we do. Do you love him?"

"Oh, Mother, don't be absurd, how could I *not?*"

"Well, he is an attractive young man. And quite well-mannered."

"Mother," Edith scoffed, "you adore him. You told me so yourself."

"Be that as it may, my dear, you are my only daughter. I shan't just cast you away carelessly after all these years."

Edith's expression instantly sobered. "That's exactly it, mother: *all these years.* I'll be thirty next year. I've been biding my time. I managed to keep Alice mostly out of trouble until she married Mr. Longworth. There are so many impossible young men these days, and I have always loved my life here with you and Father. But Ulysses is more than just handsome. He's smart. He's curious about the world. He's serious about his career in the army, and there's not a frivolous bone in his body."

Clara couldn't hold back the beginnings of another smile. "That's rather an unromantic declaration of love, but it suits you to a tee." She stood up from her desk and moved to sit beside her daughter, taking Edith's slender, pale hands in hers.

"It is time you married, and it seems you've found someone who fits your unique outlook on the world. I have never worried that you'd find someone someday, but I am glad that it is young Lieutenant Grant who found you."

She leaned in and planted a gentle kiss on Edith's cheek. "I will speak to your father when he gets home this evening."

"Do you think he'll object?

"I think he'll be very sad at the idea of losing his baby girl. But your father is a fair man. He's had you all to himself for quite a while, and I rather suspect he'll be willing to share you at last."

Edith put her arms around her mother and embraced her. Despite the heat, Clara returned the hug, her heart soaring and breaking at the same time. Clara pushed away gently and looked into her daughter's eyes.

"Have you told anyone else?"

"No. Not yet. Not before I talked to you and Father."

"Good. Once your father and I have talked, I think we should probably tell Mrs. Roosevelt first, and let her tell the President. Then we can work out a time to announce it."

Clara stood and went back to her writing desk, sitting down in the gilt chair and sighing slightly.

"Meanwhile, I must finish my letters, and you have to begin packing for the trip to Clinton. Father has engaged a Pullman car for the journey, so we'll at least have some privacy."

Edith jumped up from the daybed and, giving her mother another quick peck, disappeared down the hall to her room. "I'll go see about that iced tea," she called out, as her voice diminished into the gloom of the old house.

Clara picked up an invitation to a dinner at the McLean's, shaking her head at the thought of sitting through another elaborate meal and listening to all that inconsequential chatter. But, she reasoned, John and Emily were good-natured and more fun than many here in the capital.

So, reaching for a piece of her engraved stationery, she opened the inkwell, dipped her pen and began to write, careful not to blot her words, and trying not to dwell upon the idea of life without her daughter.

CHAPTER NINE

THREE WEDDINGS
AND A FUNERAL

Clinton, New York, is a quaint nineteenth-century town not far from Utica—another of the once-thriving small industrial cities that were the chief ornaments of Upstate New York. Clinton has a central town green, and it's no accident that it resembles such greens found all over New England. On that green was once the Hayes National Bank, actually run by a family named Hayes. The Hayes bank, like so many local and regional financial institutions in the nineteenth century, printed its own federal currency, and the Hayes family also oversaw the Root family's finances. Once Elihu and his progeny became citizens of a wider world, the Hayes family continued to be the summer bankers for the family while they were in residence up on College Hill. The street at one corner of the Clinton village green heads west out of town and gradually rises up the steep incline toward Hamilton College.

I have only vague memories of going to the village of Clinton, since my family generally approached my grandparents' house from the west—the Syracuse side. I do remember staring out the car window at the charming houses of the village, noting as they gradually gave way to substantial old Federal and Italianate style homes set on large lawns. They were not splendid; they were gracious. They were genteel, possibly elegant, but not grand. As one neared the crest of College Hill, the tree-filled Hamilton campus opened to the right, the tall, boxy outline of its stone chapel drawing one's gaze as other buildings, constructed later, hunkered down around it. The Root family land spread along the left side of the hill across from the college, above one of the Hamilton fraternity houses. By 1910, there were three family houses on this stretch of College Hill Road: the Lower House, occupied by Elihu and Clara, and their oldest child Edith, with her husband Ulysse S. Grant III; the Homestead, occupied by the Roots' younger son Edward and his wife Grace; and the Upper House, built by the elder Root son, Elihu, Jr., and his wife Alida. The houses were connected by the acreage that ran behind them, consisting of farm fields and outbuildings linked by red shale drives. For my mother's generation, the Root compound on College Hill was the place where the family gathered for holidays and summer vacations. For my mother and her sisters, who were army brats, the Lower House was the only real home any of them ever had.

My own family rarely went to Clinton more than a few times a year, and it was always a big deal. We might go for an afternoon to have lunch in the yellow-papered dining room, or possibly for dinner and an overnight stay. My little brother and I would, in that case, sleep in painted iron bedsteads in one of the smaller bedrooms, known as the nursery, in the 1850s wing, over the pantry. The nursery had a connecting door to one of the older, larger front bedrooms. This was called the "Blue Room" because of its pale blue wallpaper and blue and white gingham curtains. Our parents would be stationed there to keep tabs on us.

For me, the Lower House was something like Hogwarts must have been to Harry Potter, but without the moving staircases. When I was a child, it seemed vast and mysterious, and captured my already-romantic imagination. It was so unlike our prosaic 1920s suburban house in Sedgwick Farm, where you could see every room from the front hall. The Lower house *rambled.* There were whole wings not visible from the front hall. There was also my grandfather's housekeeper and cook, Emily Ryder, who was as warm and friendly as an upstate farmwoman. She made cupcakes for us and was endlessly patient while my little brother and I hung around in the strange old kitchen, its disused wood-burning stove long since replaced with a modern electric model, and with massive glass spring-water bottles in wooden stands lurking in the larder. Emily and her husband Colen lived in an apartment on the ground floor of the servants' wing, which could be reached by going through a servants' sitting room and then the laundry room. Ned and I rarely saw Colen, and he rather terrified us. Being the sort of general handyman and gardener for the house and its five acres, he seemed to spend most of his time lurking out of sight in the labyrinthine basement.

As I grew older and smarter, my sense of the house's vastness began to dwindle, but its effect on me never diminished. Essentially unchanged after Elihu Root's death in 1937, the house evoked the early twentieth century in its décor and furnishings. According to my mother, a good amount of the fancier furniture came from my great-grandparents' apartment at 998 Fifth Avenue in New York after Elihu Root died. The more summery furniture, such as wicker armchairs, had long since been banished to the basement. Nonetheless, stepping into the long, narrow front hall at 101 College Hill Road was like stepping back in time for me.

Overall, the Lower House was big but not grand. Like the rest of the houses on the hill, it was not built for show, but to hold family and guests. The house's prim 1816 street front, with its butter-yellow paint, white trim and dark black-green shutters, disguised the actual size of the building. The Upsons' boarding house wing, invisible from the street, doubled the size of the house, stretching more than fifty feet back from the 1816 section. Beyond that, Elihu and Clara Root's service wing extended another forty feet or so. When the Roots acquired the house in the early 1900s, they left the original part intact, and upgraded the 1850s wing to suit their social position and the taste of the time. The boarding house common room became a long living room, with room for two large bedrooms, a bathroom, storage and dressing rooms on the floor above it. The living room, called the Big Room by the family, had an over-scaled Federal-style fireplace mantel with columns. Outside the room, facing east, the Roots built a two-story columned portico topped by a pediment. This one grandiose detail provided functional spaces for outside living and (upstairs) sleeping. By the time the Roots were settled into the Lower House, it had seven family bedrooms, an upstairs boudoir for Mrs. Root, five servants' rooms, and an apartment for their full-time caretaker and his wife. There was also a new three-car garage behind the house.

Elihu and Clara Root made an interesting kind of Gilded Age couple. Both of them were from old New England families, but with new money. The house on College Hill Road pretended to be modest, but afforded its owners large living spaces and numerous bedrooms to suit their Gilded Age status as a quiet, socially unambitious power couple. This was a place where Andrew Carnegie (Elihu's client and friend) and William Howard Taft (Elihu's colleague and friend) would visit. The Roots did not like the social whirl of Southampton. Nor were they suited for Newport or Lenox or Bar Harbor—or any of the high-powered Victorian summer places to which people they knew flocked. Clinton was where Elihu Root had come from, and it became the only place he and his wife always went back to, year after year.

My obsession with this house has perhaps given it more emotional weight in my memories than the actual time I spent there might warrant. The fact is, however, there were significant moments in my family history that occurred there, thus cementing its importance in my psyche. The very first event was one I didn't attend: my parents' wedding.

In the summer of 1945, after the war in Europe was over, a twenty-five-year-old Sandy Dietz was granted leave and came back to the United States. As far as Sandy knew, he was to be sent to Japan to carry on his duties there after his furlough. He and Julia were determined to get married before he was reassigned to the Pacific Theater, and in anticipation of Sandy's return Julia took off on a cross-country journey to Albuquerque to get Robert and Barbara Dietz's blessing. Julia and Sandy must have felt the end of the war in Europe was enough for them to move ahead with their plans.

My Dietz grandparents had been living in Manhattan again since 1937, but they still spent their summers at Nassau Farm on Rio Grande Boulevard in Albuquerque, which was being overseen by their eldest son, Robert E. Dietz III (my Uncle Bob). Julia, having been bumped off a commercial flight in Dallas, called her mother, who would have been settled in for the summer on College Hill Road, to let her know that she would be getting married there in two weeks' time. She bought her wedding dress in

Albuquerque, presumably helped in selecting it by her soon-to-be mother-in-law, Barbara Dietz.

Grandmother Grant must have been at least a little frustrated: three daughters and not a single big wedding. Not only had all three of her daughters refused to "come out" in the traditional way in either New York or Washington, but my Aunt Clara Frances, known as Hansy, had stirred up scandal by eloping to Long Island with a handsome lieutenant in 1935, throwing the family into a tailspin. My uncle Paul Ruestow (Rusty) was in fact under my Grandfather Grant's command at Fort DuPont in Delaware and had waited until a promotion (and its attendant salary increase) before confronting his new father-in-law with what he and Hansy had done. Julia's oldest sister, Edith, had married more conventionally, to a dashing colonel, also under Grandfather's command, who was a widower with two adolescent children. Deedy and David Griffiths were wed in the Episcopal chapel on Governor's Island, off Manhattan, where my grandfather was stationed as a colonel by 1936. Their wedding had to wait until the reverberations from Hansy's elopement died down.

The first atomic bomb was dropped on Hiroshima on August 6, 1945, Sandy's twenty-sixth birthday, just as Edith Grant was pulling together a small wedding in the garden of the Lower House on College Hill. The second bomb hit Nagasaki on August 9th. Nine days later, on a beautiful day in Clinton, Julia married Sandy on August 18th (aged twenty-nine and twenty-six respectively, just like her parents). August 18 was also three days after the Japanese surrendered, unofficially ending World War II, although the formal declaration wouldn't happen until September. It's hard to imagine that two atomic bombs and the end of the war didn't come up during my parents' simple summer wedding on the east lawn at the Lower House. On the other hand, WASP protocol might simply have decreed that such unpleasantness not spoil the happiness of the day.

Robert and Barbara Dietz couldn't travel to the wedding due to wartime restrictions, but they were represented by Sandy's three siblings, his sister Olga acting as Mother's maid of honor; and by Barbara's sister, Edna Caulkins, known as Edgie, and her husband Hugh. There is a wonderful photograph of the wedding party and guests assembled in front of the east porch at 101 College Hill Road. My parents look impossibly young and thin—not to mention happy.

Two other family weddings involved the Lower House, but these I attended, and both came after my grandfather's death, during the years when Julia, Hansy, and Deedy owned the house jointly. My much-beloved cousin Claire Ruestow—daughter of my Aunt Hansy and her husband Rusty with whom she eloped—was married in the austere beauty of the Hamilton College chapel. The reception was held in the Big Room at the Lower House. Claire married a man who was not only a lot older, but European. George Telecki, a Hungarian of Serbian ancestry who left his homeland for the United States, ended up serving in the U.S. Army after the end of World War II during the American occupation of Japan—where Claire's father, now a major general in the Air Force, happened to be posted in 1952. George put up with a lot of good-natured teasing for his foreign-ness from the American Protestant Grants and Roots, but ultimately everyone loved him. They loved him because he made Claire happy. I was an adolescent at the time of their marriage and was charmed by him and his surprisingly numerous American émigré relatives, all of whom were, to my youthful eyes, both exotic and elegant.

My cousin Nancy, youngest child of my Aunt Deedy, was also married in the Lower House. This time, however, the ceremony itself was in the Big Room, and I remember Nancy and her older sister Frances entering the room, wearing simple and pretty full-skirted dresses with floral trim. Nancy's groom, Brian Price, was shortish and attractive and blond. I will always remember him as I saw him, but I never saw him after the wedding. This is my last memory of a significant family gathering at the Lower House. Only when it had been sold to the college, did I wander its rooms one last time, choosing things to take with me for my first apartment with Gary Berger in New Haven.

Because Ned and I, the eleventh and twelfth grandchildren, were the youngest on our side of the family, we had never attended the great New Year's Eve parties that my grandparents hosted at the Lower House. I think it was possibly 1965, when Ned and I would have been respectively nine and ten, that we were allowed to come to Clinton for New Year's Eve. My parents rightly suspected that this might be my widowed octogenarian grandfather's last hurrah, and they figured we should experience this event.

It was fantastic. A hundred people, consisting of family, neighbors, and Hamilton faculty, packed into the old rooms, the Big Room's floor shifting alarmingly under the weight of the throng. Ned and I were in wool trousers, tweed jackets, and skinny neckties. We ate and talked and generally behaved ourselves. There were our Root cousins, and our Ruestow cousins, and our Griffiths cousins (counting Deedy's two stepchildren, Marian and Dick). There were also local characters, such as Digger Graves (aka Professor of History Edgar Baldwin Graves) and Sylvia Saunders, whose father Percy was a celebrated hybridizer of Chinese tree peonies (including one named Julia Grant after my mother when she was sixteen). This party was the only time I ever got a really good look at the world in which my mother had spent her summers as a young woman.

As the evening wore on and some guests began to go home, Ned and I were included in the charades competition assigned to the younger generation for the amusement of the elders. We pretty much had no idea what any of the titles we were acting out meant, but we collaborated with our teammates, while sequestered in the old parlor at the front of the house. We enjoyed ourselves and relished staying up late with the grownups. It would be the last time Ned and I slept in the nursery together.

My grandfather Grant died in late August 1968, while my family was in Bermuda on vacation. Aunt Hansy and her husband were staying with the general on College Hill Road, and he had been suffering from a kidney ailment. It was something that, today, would have been treated and taken care of. However, in 1968, it killed him at the age of eighty-seven, leaving his three daughters bereft. Both his father and his presidential grandfather had died in their early sixties of cancer, so my grandfather's long life was a triumph in more than one way. He had just submitted for publication the manuscript of his own biography of his grandfather: *Ulysses S. Grant, Warrior and Statesman* (William Morrow, 1969). Like his grandfather's memoirs, my grandfather's book would become his legacy, the first important addition to truth-telling about Ulysses S. Grant in over a generation.

Grandfather's pride in his name doesn't diminish the fact his three daughters, to whom he dedicated his book, had felt cherished and honored their whole lives by this man. In a generation that didn't often value female children, Ulysses S. Grant III treated his daughters, and his wife, as intellectual equals. As my mother told me, the Grants were not huggers. They were not casual. They were truly Victorians, but they loved their girls, and the girls' sadness at his passing was proof of it.

Although there was a memorial service in Washington, Grandfather's funeral was held in the Hamilton Chapel, and I remember a lot of lurid floral arrangements and wreaths in red, white, and blue presented by the wide world of military, political, and social acquaintance my grandfather had garnered during his long career. His casket was simple and sleek, all modern polished mahogany, without any visible hardware. An olive-green military hearse waited to carry him the short distance to the Hamilton College Cemetery, where grandfather's grave had been prepared beside his wife's, and next to those of Elihu and Clara, and various other Roots. Grandfather could have been buried in Arlington or at West Point, but he chose Clinton. His parents, Fred and Ida, were interred at West Point, while his grandparents, Ulysses and Julia, lay eternally in state in their red granite sarcophagi on Riverside Drive in New York City. The smart young woman he had met at the White House during Teddy Roosevelt's presidency would remain by his side for all time.

Not everybody in the family had attended the memorial service in Washington, but everybody gathered in Clinton for the funeral. There were at least sixteen of us packed into the Lower House, and even the long-unused servants' rooms in the back wing were dusted and occupied. My little brother and I were not put in the same room. Ned got the nursery and I was allowed to sleep in my grandfather's room at the front, in the 1816 part of the house, in the small four-poster twin bed that would later go into my room in Syracuse. Looking back, I'm not sure why. Did I get Grandfather's bedroom because my name was Ulysses, the only one in my generation? Did Ned simply not care, and I wanted the big room with the fireplace? In any case, I didn't sleep in the bed my grandfather died in; he died in the canopied four-poster in my grandmother's pink bedroom across the hall, which opened directly into one of the two bathrooms that served the seven bedrooms.

The point of this is that, after the interment service, but before Grandfather's casket was lowered into its gold-painted concrete vault, my older brother Jed asked the undertaker if he could see his grandfather. Our sister had not lingered, but since Ned and I were hanging around, we got to see him, too. Jed was twenty, a student at the University of North Carolina, Chapel Hill. I was thirteen, and Ned had just turned twelve. The casket's upper lid was opened, and the funeral director stepped back to give us privacy. My grandfather was dressed in his best blue military uniform, his campaign ribbons on his chest. His white hair was neatly combed, but the funeral parlor makeup looked luridly pink in the daylight. Oddly, there was a number two in red on the back of his left hand, which lay on top of the beige velvet blanket that matched the casket's neutral lining.

At the time, I didn't have much of a reaction, but as I lay in bed later that night, in my dead grandfather's big, empty bedroom, I quietly freaked out. I don't know if I had nightmares or simply couldn't sleep well. At one point I woke up in a panic, and became vividly aware of a dark figure standing in the far corner of the room, near the folding screen that shielded the marble-topped sink from view. It was probably a shadow, but in my own mind, it was my grandfather watching over me, or trying to send me a message. Whatever it was, it terrified me, and I lay there trembling until I finally drifted back to sleep.

CHAPTER TEN

I ONLY MET THE
PRINCESS ONCE

The day we learned of my grandfather Grant's death, my family was at the end of a month-long vacation in Bermuda. My parents had rented a white-roofed pale pink villa that came complete with a taciturn Norwegian housekeeper and a big brown mutt named Bumpsa. The house was by the Belmont Hills Golf Club, and a picture window in the living room looked out over the Great Sound and its scattering of little islands. A large, framed neo-Impressionist landscape on one wall slid down into its frame to reveal the bar. It was a fantastic place for my brother Ned and me. There was a miniature coral reef off the little concrete jetty at the foot of the property and we played there endlessly. My parents had to tote us around on the padded back seats of their motorbikes, since then (as now) outsiders weren't allowed to rent or drive cars in Bermuda. I can remember getting dressed up in seersucker jackets, with Bermuda shorts and knee socks (seriously, even my father wore those) and riding on motorbikes into Hamilton for dinner at the Princess Hotel.

The house had five bedrooms, but my parents, my sister Edie, and Ned and I only occupied three of them. This news got out to the rest of the family, and the increasingly disgruntled housekeeper had to deal with an endless stream of relatives who came to visit and messed up her kitchen. My older brother Jed was only there intermittently, but at one point brought his girlfriend Julia along. I think this was the second time I'd met her—a beautiful blond girl from Southern Pines, North Carolina. Having a Julia with Confederate antecedents in the house with our mother Julia, née Grant, must have caused some comment, although I only remember it coming up when Jed finally married her in 1974 and she decided to keep her maiden name, McMillan.

Our grandfather's death didn't deeply affect my little brother and me, even though seeing his body in a casket would send me into a tailspin after his funeral. As the babies of the family, we had only known Grandfather Grant distantly, from the infrequent visits to the house in Clinton. We had never visited him in Washington, DC, and I really had no idea what he had done for a living. I had cousins well into their thirties by 1968, and they had known our grandfather in an entirely different way. My Aunt Deedy's stepdaughter, Marian, was only seven years younger than my mother, and my Aunt Hansy's two older children were both born in the 1930s. Even my closest Grant cousin, Claire Ruestow, was a decade my senior, and had known Grandfather far more intimately than Ned and I ever did.

Until well into my adult life, I had no idea that I had something in common with my grandfather other than our shared name. Trained as an engineer, he had been part of the Army Corps of Engineers and ultimately became the Director of the Office of Public Buildings and Public Parks in Washington—meaning, he was essentially the landlord of the White House and its tenants during the Coolidge, Harding, and Hoover administrations. He oversaw the design and construction of the new third floor on the White house built for the Coolidges. He headed the commission that built the Arlington Memorial Bridge and the Mount Vernon Parkway in Virginia. Later in his life, after his military career was over, he rejoined the planning commission for the National Capital, and collaborated with President Truman in establishing the National Trust for Historic Preservation. I knew none of this during his lifetime, however, but like to think that my love of historic preservation and my obsession with old buildings comes from him. It saddens me that he never sat me down, his young namesake, and told me about himself. Perhaps I wouldn't have been terribly interested at the time; but I would have remembered.

I look back on that summer, despite my grandfather's death, with a special nostalgia, because it would be the last summer that would see my family intact and unbroken, the perfect image of American post-War excellence. Of course, none of us had any idea what was coming.

We trooped back from Bermuda to the United States and Syracuse, unpacked from our truncated holiday, and then headed to Washington, D.C. for a memorial service planned to honor the general. Ned and I simply followed the rest of our family, unclear as to what was about to happen. We probably stayed in the Dupont Plaza Hotel on Dupont Circle, which at the time was not the chic locale it is now.

The memorial service was held at the still-unfinished National Cathedral on its hill above the capital, just four months after Dr. Martin Luther King Jr.'s final sermon there. King had been assassinated less than a month after that sermon, sending the city into a convulsion of grief and violence. My grandfather had been involved with the Cathedral for a long time, probably stemming from his years as Director of the Office of Public Buildings and Public Parks of the National Capital.

I was unaware of King's historic sermon at the National Cathedral, although we all had witnessed the national mourning at his death. All I remember taking note of from this memorial service is the vastness of the cathedral's gothic interior, along with the puzzling fact that tourists continued to walk through the building during the memorial itself. As my family hovered at the main entrance, a customized silver and black Cadillac limousine pulled up to the curb, and two old ladies were helped out by the driver. One of them, stoop-shouldered and swathed in black silk, was my great aunt, Julia Grant Cantacuzene. She was my grandfather's older sister, his only sibling, and my mother was her namesake. At that time my great aunt was ninety-two, having been born in 1876 in the White House during Ulysses S. Grant's second term of office. All I knew about her—other than her name—was that she was a Russian princess. I had never laid eyes on her before.

Holding firmly onto Aunt Julia's arm was eighty-one-year-old Marjorie Merriweather Post. Straight-backed and beautifully coiffed, she towered over her old friend. Mrs. Post and my grandparents had been good friends for years. After my grandmother's death in 1962, Mrs. Post, having long since sworn off husbands, found my grandfather to be the perfect "extra man" at her dinner parties. Perhaps more significantly, Aunt Julia's grandson (thus, my grandfather's great-nephew and my second cousin) Rodion Cantacuzene had married Mrs. Post's granddaughter Melissa MacNeille in 1960. Of course, I didn't know any of this at the time. Mrs. Post and the princess swept past us with the briefest of greetings. They were seated in the first pew, right in front of me, and I was aware of Mrs. Post's height and her tidy little black hat, which blocked a good deal of my view of the service.

Once it was over, we did what WASPs do after funerals: we went to Aunt Julia's little apartment in an old apartment building called the Dresden and drank sherry. I may have had ginger ale, but I remember little of the event, other than summoning my best manners at meeting various Cantacuzene cousins, including her eldest son Misha, generally known as Mike, heir to the family titles should the Communists ever be overthrown. Mike was retired, having managed the Palmer House Hotel in Chicago for much of his career. He was also married to his third wife by the time I met him and was the father-in-law of Mrs. Post's granddaughter Melissa.

My Great Aunt Julia had divorced the prince in 1934, after thirty-five years of marriage. He remarried and lived out the rest of his life in Sarasota Florida, working in the Palmer Bank, until his retirement. The Prince-turned-banker, known as Uncle Mike to my mother, died in 1955, the year I was born.

The critical moment of that awkward post-service party is burned into my memory of that day: I was sitting on the floor next to Aunt Julia, who had settled onto a French settee in her little parlor. I tried desperately to chat with her, since she was very interested to meet the boy named for her little brother. She and my grandfather had been very close and had both been present at former President Ulysses S. Grant's deathbed in 1885. I knew this, because I had seen copies of Julia Cantacuzene's memoirs, and in them the famous picture of the entire Grant family sitting on the porch of the cottage at Mt.

GROWING UP GRANT · 75

McGregor, surrounding the dying patriarch. My grandfather, then four years old, had long blond ringlets and wore a wide-brimmed straw hat. Aunt Julia was already a pretty nine-year-old.

By 1968 I was already deeply fascinated by great houses, and I might possibly have asked a lame question about whether or not Aunt Julia had memories of Peterhof, the great yellow palace outside Saint Petersburg. She said yes, and our conversation fell rather flat after that. Never in my life had I been so aware of what I didn't know. Like the ignorant child in the Passover Haggadah, I was too uninformed to even know what to ask. Julia's history was taken for granted by the family around her; and nobody had thought to tell me much about that history. In an odd way, it was akin to my ignorance about Ulysses S. Grant's life and career—something acknowledged by the adults, but never discussed in front of the children. Having lost forever the possibility of learning about Ulysses S. Grant from his own namesake, I now had come face-to-face with another family legend, and had no idea what to say to her. I felt stupid and embarrassed. I was also disappointed, keenly aware that I had missed an opportunity to learn something important. I think a switch was flipped inside me that day. From that moment on, I was keenly aware that my family story didn't conform to those of my peers in Syracuse. Soon after we got back home, I started reading my mother's copies of the princess's three books about life in Russia before the Revolution. It was the beginning of the end of my ignorance.

Julia Grant Cantacuzene died on October 4, 1975, aged ninety-nine. I had turned twenty that summer and was a junior at Yale. I was also a student researcher for a big Bicentennial project at the Yale University Art Gallery, and thus did not attend her funeral. Great Aunt Julia's death came just ten days before I met Gary Berger, who would change my life in a completely different way.

CHAPTER ELEVEN

Speculation #4
THE PROPOSAL

A cool breeze blew in off the Mediterranean, billowing the curtains and bringing with it the mixed scent of salt air and spring flowers. Vases of fragrant hot-house roses filled the sitting room with their own sweetness. Bertha sat reading, deeply ensconced in the floral chintz cushions of the sofa as she concentrated on the latest French translation of *Anna Karénine*. In spite of her fluency in French, she found Tolstoy rather tough sledding, and had grown to thoroughly dislike Mrs. Karenin and her bourgeois lack of will power. Bertha soldiered on nonetheless, enjoying the quiet and the breeze and the soft cushions of the canapé as her husband Potter napped in the adjacent bedchamber of their airy suite of rooms.

The noise and constant social whirl of Rome had worn on her husband, even though she had spared him most of the strenuous activity. In the best of times, Potter was not given to large parties and big crowds. Even back in Chicago, Potter liked home life more than society, and was never happier than when closeted with a few close friends in their library on Lakeshore Drive. His recent illness had worried her, and she felt enormous relief that the weather in Cannes seemed to have instantly improved both his health and his spirits. Marrying a man twenty-three years her senior had seemed inconsequential back in 1871, when she herself was but twenty-two. Now, twenty-eight years later, her gentle spouse's frailty seemed ever more apparent.

As Bertha tried again to focus her mind on Mrs. Karenin's unhappiness, the parlor door clicked open. Rather than a maid, it was Bertha's niece, Julia, who peeked her head around the door and broke into a smile upon discovering her aunt alone. Julia had been traveling with the Palmers in Europe since the fall of 1898, when her father, Fred Grant, had been posted to Puerto Rico, and taken her mother with him to San Juan. With Potter's ill-health, and her two sons recently graduated from college, Bertha had invited her sister Ida's smart and vivacious older child to join them.

Having no daughter of her own, and seeing her own dark good looks reflected in her niece's features, Bertha had grown very fond of this energetic young woman. Born in her grandfather Grant's White House, and raised here and there according to the whims of her father's military career, Julia had thrived as a thirteen-year-old when Frederick Grant was posted to the American legation in Vienna. There he had served as the United States Minister to the court of Franz-Josef, and Julia had benefited from the experience of spending four years in the heart of one of the greatest imperial cities. She had even danced with the Emperor himself before her family's return to New York City in 1894. Ida and Bertha had kept up a busy correspondence over those four eventful years.

Julia quickly crossed the room and unceremoniously plopped herself onto the settee next to Bertha. Bertha studied her niece's face, noting that she was rather pink, and that a mischievous smile was playing across her pretty lips.

"I have the most exciting news, Aunt," Julia began, reaching out to grasp Bertha's wrist.

"Whatever could it be, child?" Bertha asked, putting her book on a table. A jolt of concern ran up her spine despite the evident pleasure on her niece's face.

"Prince Cantacuzene has asked me to marry him!" Julia declared, her voice rising with emphasis on the word "marry."

Bertha was startled, to say the least. Whatever her plans for her sister's fortune-less daughter might have been, she hadn't been aiming at this. At least not so quickly.

"I don't understand. You just spent the other evening at dinner declaring to anyone who would listen that no foreigner would want you, if I remember your exact words."

"Well, the other evening I believed it." Julia sat there, beaming at her aunt as if enjoying the most ridiculous joke. "Why would anyone over here want me? I have no money, and I'm too outspoken on top of it."

"Yet apparently he wants you?"

"Yes! He followed us from Rome expressly to propose to me."

"Do you mean, when we found him reading in the lobby of the hotel a few days ago, it was part of a *plan*?" Bertha was both amused and horrified. She had no idea that Russian princes could be so simultaneously calculating and impulsive, especially without prior indication. Julia had met Prince Michael years earlier in Vienna when still a girl and they had rekindled their acquaintance in Rome just a few weeks ago. He had been friendly and unattached and had played the tourist with them around the Eternal City. Bertha had thought nothing of it, and now felt quite dim-witted at her lack of insight.

"Julia, dear," said Bertha softly, placing her free hand over her niece's, "how do you really feel about this? I know it must be exciting, but have you *thought* about it?"

Julia sobered immediately, letting go of Bertha's wrist, taking her aunt's hands in her own. She turned to face Bertha more fully.

"I have, Aunt. Michael is charming. He is handsome. He seems to like me quite a lot. I find the idea of moving with him to Russia and being a princess quite attractive."

Bertha stared briefly at Julia's face. There was no guile in it. She was stating the facts as she saw them.

"Shan't he have to tell his family? And your parents—we'll have to communicate this great news to them."

"We shall, Aunt. We'll take care of it all, and I know you'll help me."

"And you're quite sure there's no issue of a dowry? It is a Russian custom, I believe."

"Michael tells me it matters not a fig. They have lots of money, and eighty thousand acres, with a chateau in the Ukraine!"

Bertha almost rolled her eyes at what was either her niece's calculation or naiveté, but resisted the temptation. Julia was no fool, but she had also suffered through her grandparents' humiliating bankruptcy in 1884 and had lived in suburban obscurity in New Jersey with her mother and father for perhaps a bit too long.

"Well, your uncle and I will give you a dowry in any case," she continued, raising her hand to still Julia's objection. "I won't have those Russians resenting you for bringing nothing into the marriage but your wit and your great American name. A hundred thousand should do it. It is the least one could expect for the granddaughter of a great American general and president."

It was Julia's turn to be dumbfounded. Her big dark eyes were wide with wonder.

Bertha patted her hand. "My darling child, you are, for all intents and purposes, my daughter. What joy you bring me! Your mother is my dearest friend and sister, and I know she will let me do this for you and for the family. Your mother has her pride, but she is practical, and she knows my heart."

At this, Julia threw herself forward, wrapping her arms around her aunt and letting herself be embraced in turn.

"Oh, thank you, Aunt!" she sobbed, her happy tears muffled in Bertha's shoulder.

Bertha said nothing, but held her niece, her mind already leaping forward to the summer, when, assuming that Potter's health continued to improve, they could return to Newport and begin to make plans in earnest. This was a chance that Mrs. Potter Palmer wasn't going to let slip by.

CHAPTER TWELVE

DANCING ON THE EDGE
OF THE GILDED AGE

I can't avoid it any longer. It's time to talk about Ulysses S. Grant, the most famous of my eight great-great grandfathers. The failure-turned-hero was the first of eight men with that name spanning seven generations in my family. Interestingly, Ulysses Jr. (Buck) was the second son, not the eldest, who was Frederick. Ulysses III and IV were first cousins, and the sons of Fred and Buck, respectively, while Ulysses V was a grandson of Jesse, the youngest child of Julia and the general's. There is today a Ulysses S. Grant VI, a generation younger than mine, grandson of Ulysses V. The only Ulysses in the current youngest generation is French, a descendant of the Grants' daughter Nellie. I am, as I've said, the only Ulysses in my entire generation of forty-one great-great grandchildren born between 1925 and 1956. Even in the family, it was not a popular name.

If you find this confusing, you should know that I only figured it out for myself when I hit my fifties. It is a big family that has grown more complicated with each passing generation.

By the time President Grant brought his First Lady Julia to the White House, they had four children. First came Frederick Dent, named for his slave-owning grandfather and born in 1850 at the Dent farm, White Haven, west of Saint Louis on Gravois Creek. Next came Ulysses Jr., known as Buck, born in 1852 (on what would be my birthday, as it happens). Buck was born in Ohio, where his father was born, and thus was a Buckeye. According to family lore, it was the enslaved workers on the Dent farm who gave him his nickname. Third was Ellen Wrenshall, born in 1855 and forever called Nellie, named for her grandmother Dent. Nellie was born in Wish-ton-Wish, a romantic villa on her grandfather's farm. The baby was Jesse Root, named for Ulysses's father in 1858. Jesse was born at Hardscrabble, the log house on the Dent farm that Ulysses built himself and that Julia despised (but never aloud to her husband). Each of these children grew up in the shadow of their famous father, and each of them handled his complicated reputation in a different way.

Jesse wrote in his memoir, published in 1924, that each of the four children felt that they were their parents' favorite, something they didn't discover until they were all adults. The fact is, all four children were adored by their parents, and were indulged by Julia and Ulysses in a way that would seem permissive by the standards of my own childhood. Even as their famous parents came to dance at the edge of the Gilded Age, Fred, Buck, Nellie and Jesse became participants in the family's newfound celebrity. They lived up to it; they lived it down; they suffered its humiliations and enjoyed its benefits. None of them became as famous as their father, and I suspect that only two of them, Fred and Buck, were ever as happy as their parents.

It is now so impossible to extricate myself from Ulysses S. Grant and his story that it's hard to reconcile my adult knowledge with the truth that, up until my teen years, all I understood or cared about was that I was named for my mother's father and that I was descended from a president. Because my parents called me Grant and kept my mother's lineage discreetly tucked away most of the time, my presidential heritage was a background shadow. It had no direct impact on my childhood and youth. It is a great disappointment to Grant buffs and Civil War scholars that my family did not sit around and swap stories of the great General-President's exploits; nor did we have reunions with the other three lines of descendants. My grandfather, U.S. Grant III, knew all his first cousins and was very close with some of them; but by the time my mother's generation came around, all of those relationships were tenuous at best. By the time I was born in 1955, we barely knew our own second cousins, and those only in our line of descent from Fred.

You don't need a biography from me; the general's life is very well documented. Ulysses S. Grant and his wife, Julia Boggs Dent, were married in the Dent townhouse in Saint Louis in 1848. Ulysses was four years older than Julia, and they were both born on the American frontier in the 1820s. The S in Ulysses's name was a typographical error, and never stood for Simpson, which was often assumed because it was his mother's maiden name. His middle name was really Hiram, but that disappeared with the flick of a bureaucrat's pen when my great-great-grandfather was seventeen and entered the U.S. Military Academy at West Point.

Much has been made of Ulysses and Julia's differing social statuses, but this is exaggerated, especially in the context of the American West. Ulysses was the eldest son of an entrepreneurial striver who made good money tanning leather and selling leather goods in small-town southern Ohio, Kentucky, and later in Illinois. Julia was the eldest daughter of a slave-owning farmer who was often land-poor and had a large spread on the outskirts of Saint Louis, Missouri, in an area referred to as Gravois Creek. Jesse Grant saw himself as a hard-working, self-made American. Frederick Dent saw himself as a gentleman. Both men were typical of their era and geography, and both of them gave Ulysses a hard time. Jesse Grant loved his son, but not always in a supportive way. Frederick Dent came to grudgingly admire his son-in-law.

Much has also been made of Ulysses' rise from obscurity to international fame in the course of five years between 1860 and 1865. What interests me, however, is the fact that the life Ulysses and Julia led together from 1848 until his death in 1885 captures the entire great sweep of the American story of the nineteenth century. These two young people are farmers, and they are a military family; they are obscure frontier people, and they are celebrities in the greatest political and financial cities in the country. They are poor, then rich, then poor again. With their four children, Ulysses and Julia experience every kind of educational system available in America at the time, from one-room schoolhouses to private tutors and Ivy League universities. History tends to focus on the biggest successes—the John D. Rockefellers and the Cornelius Vanderbilts of America. What Ulysses and Julia experienced is probably far more typical of what happened to a lot of Americans; except, of course, for the presidential part, which is what makes their story extraordinary.

In New York City, when Ulysses and Julia were in Galena, Illinois, my great-great-grandfather Robert E. Dietz tapped into America's industrialization by inventing the flat-wick kerosene burner. This useful little gadget would revolutionize American lighting technology and would give Robert Dietz's family access to the benefits of the burgeoning industrial world of the post-Civil-War years. My great-great-grandfather Grant, by contrast, happened upon the one non-commercial skill that would matter in the years between Lincoln's election and General Lee's surrender: that of warfare. Having had to pawn his gold watch to buy his children Christmas presents because of his failure as a farmer, Ulysses would buy his wife a $30,000 house in 1865 as a direct result of his success at being a general. Somehow, Ulysses had fumbled forward into the Gilded Age despite a lack of business acumen that would haunt him to the end of his life.

Ulysses S. Grant was certainly taciturn when it came to talking about himself. I have long admired his modesty for not blowing his own horn. His bitterest enemies were not, surprisingly, former Confederates, but members of his own party such as Senator Charles Sumner, who thought far more highly of themselves than they did of this quiet, thoughtful, westerner. It is clear that Grant considered himself a westerner despite his old New England lineage. His self-confidence lay in things military and literary. He knew he was educated and literate and could write. If he cared what others thought of him, he hid it well.

Julia, on the other hand, was probably less introspective than her husband, although she knew that she was no beauty. I love Julia for her homeliness, because I know that her personality must have been what attracted Ulysses to her. You can't see it in those rare early images of her as wife and mother; all you see is that inward-turning eye and her plain features. However, she must have been smart and funny and quick-witted. Julia saw herself the way her father treated her: as an American frontier belle. She was a romantic, and Ulysses was not, although he read lots of novels. Julia's strabismus made reading problematic for her, but she loved being read to by her beloved Ulys, whose voice by all accounts was melodic and clear.

The marriage of Julia and Ulysses is one of the great love stories of the American nineteenth century, on par with England's Victoria and Albert. The fact that Queen Victoria herself thought both Julia and Ulysses to be common as dirt only makes it better.

Post-Civil-War America was full of striving middle-class housewives whose husbands had suddenly made money because of the war. A lot of the pre-war wealth in America had been locked up in the slave economy of the South, though there were certainly rich people all over the country before 1860. However, even the grandest houses, North or South, before 1860 were still haut-bourgeois villas by the standards of European aristocracy. Americans wanted comfort and elegance and maybe even some luxury; but there were limits to what was considered appropriate for an American family to live in. It was only after the cataclysm of the war that the country's newly rich men finally decided that they should just *flaunt it*. I'm not sure anyone has ever figured out exactly what sparked the explosive mansion-building of the post-Civil War years; but once it got going, it spread like a wildfire across the country. All of the proscriptive and prescriptive cautions of the pre-war writers and tastemakers were pushed aside, and the mad rush to build big and build fancy was on.

The way American wealth was spent in the years from 1865-1914 (before another war put a stop to it) came to be known as the Gilded Age, after Mark Twain's remarkable 1873 novel of American politics and self-reinvention, published with co-author Charles Dudley Warner. For Samuel Clemens, the term "Gilded Age" was pejorative, seen in opposition to the Golden Age when Americans and their leaders were supposedly paragons of integrity. Mark Twain might in fact have realized that the Golden Age was nothing more than myth, and that the Gilded Age he witnessed was a truer expression of the American character. This period, as it happens, would become my specialty as a decorative arts curator, and so my ancestors' role in this phenomenon holds a special fascination for me.

Because Julia and Ulysses had no significant family money of their own, and always counted on Ulysses's salary, they seem to have depended on the kindness of friends and strangers to advance in their tentative *pas de deux* with Gilded Age America. During the war they had been given a fine house in Philadelphia by rich friends. Their house in Georgetown was heavily subsidized by the General's supporters in the Washington area and also paid for with his substantial salary as head of the American military. In the 1880s, their big brownstone on East 66th Street in New York City would be underwritten by others, too. Only the Grants' summer house in Long Branch, New Jersey, and the family farm in Saint Louis would be funded through their own resources. Even their final resting place, the towering granite and marble mausoleum on Riverside Drive in New York, would be paid for by public subscription. The White House, during Grant's two terms as president, ended up being the house where they lived the longest.

Not surprisingly, it was in the White House where Julia was happiest. It was, after all, a symbol of the nation's love for her husband and an acknowledgement of what he had done for his country. The First Family's living expenses were, at this period, out of pocket, and paid from the president's salary. Julia took whatever allotment Congress was willing to offer towards renovation and redecoration during each of her husband's two terms, and made the most of it. The great old building, whose walls, at least, had been seen by George Washington, filled her with a joyous sense of her place in history. Julia is seen as the first First Lady to really love the White House and to truly enjoy living there.

During Ulysses' years in Washington before the election of 1868, Julia had settled into a world of comfort and social prominence beyond anything she had known as the daughter of a low-end planter on the Western frontier. By the time the Grants entered the shabby President's Mansion in 1869, George Washington's dream house had become a hodgepodge of styles and furnishings. The Monroes had intended in the rebuild of 1817 to give the house something of the aristocratic glamour of its size and original intent, by importing piles of gilt Parisian furniture and ormolu. Since then, however, the term-by-term changes had really reflected the middle-class perspective of the first ladies who had spent four or eight years trying to figure out how to live within its cavernous walls.

The White House was, until at least 1870, the largest private residence in North America. L'Enfant's grandiose presidential palace, though severely toned down by James Hoban, was still clearly modeled on a mid-sized English nobleman's country house. Very few Americans had ever encountered one of these great houses in person, and even Abigail Adams, who had been to London and Paris, was defeated by the task of living in such an echoing pile. It was only Andrew Jackson who finally finished and decorated the East Room in 1829, which at forty-by-eighty and twenty-two feet high, was the largest private room on the continent. My personal theory is that Jackson's decorator (whoever that was) used as his model the lobbies of the new luxury hotels being built in the 1820s in America's largest cities.

Julia Grant, at forty-two, entered a White House whose décor was largely the result of Harriet Lane (James Buchanan's niece) and Martha Patterson (Andrew Johnson's daughter). I am sure she was entirely undaunted by its eighteen-foot ceilings and massive spaces. Her own memoirs suggest that she was immediately at home and set about rearranging the furniture and ordering new draperies. This, clearly, was a house worthy of the man she loved so unquestioningly.

I particularly like the fact that it was Julia who got to bring the Gilded Age into her White House, using Congressional appropriations to mold the place into her version of the American dream. In the first term, it was largely curtains and carpeting, since Congress didn't allot much in the way of funding. She did put a huge crystal-hung gasolier in the Blue Room, and placed a massive, life-sized family portrait by William Cogswell on the east wall of the Red Room. This was Julia's way of marking her territory. In the painting, she sits, the matriarch, at the center, with her four children (Fred, Buck, Nellie and Jesse) gathered around her. Her husband, in uniform, stands meekly to her left. It is such a powerful statement of American self-perception at the time: the mother, the housewife as the centerpiece of the American home. Her husband may have been the president, but she was the chatelaine of the president's house.

Julia and Ulysses also built a billiard room onto the west side of the house, next to the greenhouses and up against the State Dining Room. This became a place where her husband could socialize in good Gilded Age form with his new political and military friends—and smoke his ever-present cigars. The Billiard Room is a tantalizing mystery, as it was demolished soon after the Grant administration ended, and no image or drawings of it survive. It became a sort of family room for the Grants and their friends. In the first term, Julia also redecorated the president's cabinet room upstairs at the east end of the house, replacing the worn furniture dating back as far as Jackson's presidency with modern pieces from New York's Pottier & Stymus.

It was in her role as First Lady that Julia got to know the newly-rich of the postwar era. One example was Alexander T. Stewart, whom the president famously asked to be his Secretary of the Treasury. This set off a scandal, because Stewart was "in trade" and thus not appropriate to hold a cabinet position (a stance that seems quaint in light of recent history). Fueled by profits from his department store, Stewart and his wife Cornelia had completed the first great Gilded Age urban palace in America in 1868, on New York's Fifth Avenue. Julia and Ulysses would visit this palatial house, worthy of France's Second Empire, during their Washington years from 1865 to 1876. Its art collection, its scale, and its French-accented, eye-popping opulence would have set a very high bar.

Julia didn't get a chance to test her mettle as a Gilded Age homemaker until her husband's second term, when Congress allotted a much larger amount for improvements and redecoration. While she didn't get the money to redo the entire house (no first lady ever did until Edith Roosevelt), she made three important changes that brought the old place into the Gilded Age in a major way. She got rid of all the old furniture in the Red Room, last refurnished by Sarah Polk in 1847. The Red Room served as the First Family's good parlor, and they used it every day. Julia turned to a New York firm called Herter Brothers in 1874, for a large custom suite of rosewood furniture in the modern style. She also removed Hoban's original neoclassical double staircase at the west end of the cross hall and replaced it with a grandiose single-flight stairway that both suited modern taste and allowed for a sitting area on the second floor.

(Remember that since the president's offices were in the White House proper, they took up nearly half of the second floor's bedroom space.)

Julia's greatest triumph at the White House was the setting she created for Nellie's wedding in 1874: the reimagining of the East Room, transforming it from the slightly dowdy lobby of a big 1850s hotel into a merchant prince's glittering ballroom. She and her architect added columns and massive beams, monumental mantelpieces with towering overmantel mirrors. Picking up on James Hoban's classical details of the 1817 rebuilding, she amplified these with gold leaf and added enormous prism-hung gasoliers that dwarfed the Andrew Jackson era fixtures. Julia covered the original pinewood floorboards with half an acre of floral wall-to-wall carpeting and added a large suite of silk and velvet upholstered modern furniture, eliminating the remaining furniture from the Monroe and Jackson administrations. By the time she was ready to stage her daughter's wedding to Englishman Algernon Sartoris, the East Room was easily the flashiest ballroom in America. Within a decade it would be eclipsed several times over, but in 1874 it was unsurpassed for over-the-top modern American opulence. Julia had come a long way from the six modest rooms of White Haven.

Nellie's marriage to the stylish and debonair Brit made for great headlines, but it would not end well, something that Ulysses himself seemed to fear from the very start. Algernon was, sadly, both an alcoholic and a philanderer. Henry James would write of Nellie in 1888: "She is illiterate, lovely, painted, pathetic, and separated from a drunken idiot of a husband. The Sartorises don't like her much, but they like her more, I suppose, than they do their disreputable 'Algie.'" James, being an ex-pat, was probably a worse snob than the English among whom he chose to live, but it is a sad image of Ulysses' favorite child, and an all-too-familiar Gilded Age story of a young woman trapped in a miserable marriage. The president wept at his only daughter's wedding—the first White House wedding—an eerie foreshadowing of the unhappiness that would haunt Nellie's life.

Another family wedding that year, however, told a happier tale. Fred Grant, my great-grandfather, who had followed his father to West Point immediately after the Civil War, fell in love with a ravishing dark-haired beauty from Chicago named Ida Honoré. Ida was the younger daughter of a successful real estate developer in that fast-growing city. Fred courted her after meeting her at a dinner party with General Philip Sheridan at her sister's house in Chicago. Her sister, Bertha, had married Potter Palmer, a family friend twenty-three years her senior. Palmer had met Bertha Honoré when she was only thirteen, because her father, Henry Hamilton Honoré, was a fellow real estate developer. Palmer, a handsome, taciturn Quaker from New York State, was just two years younger than his father-in-law, having been born in 1826— the same year in which Julia Dent Grant was born.

Fred and Ida were married at the Honoré summer house in semi-rural Chicago in October 1874, now part of Chicago's south side. It was a big deal. The President and First Lady were there, as were Bertha and Potter Palmer, who had been married in 1871, the year of the great fire that changed Chicago's landscape.

Fred and Ida settled into married life, and in due course had two children. The third presidential grandchild was born in the White House in 1876 and named Julia after her grandmother. Her little brother, Ulysses S. Grant III—my grandfather and the third grandson—was born at the Palmer's country house in Chicago on July 4, 1881, sharing his Aunt Nellie's birthday. The younger Ulysses and Julia, strategically named for their famous grandparents, would lead the third generation of Grants in the dance of the Gilded Age.

It has always felt to me that the General-turned-president and his wife never quite made it to the center of things during this fabled time, even when they were in the White House. Though they knew people, and went places, and were famous in their own right, they didn't have the money to be full players in the competitive social game that had emerged in post-Civil-War America. Moreover, Ulysses was as asocial as his wife was enamored of public life. His well-documented taciturnity only fell away when in the company of a few like-minded individuals, when his intelligence and his wit became apparent. Ulysses' fame, his international renown as a hero and a warrior, gave him a peculiar status that didn't quite make up for his lack of a large fortune. They lived in houses that they didn't pay for, furnished with things purchased with a government paycheck (albeit a large one; the president earned $25,000 a year up to 1873 and $50,000 thereafter, the equivalent of $519,000 and over a million dollars in 2020). Ulysses and Julia straddled the line between the salaried upper-middle-class and the social world of the self-made *nouveau-riche*.

Grant's military brilliance and logistical genius at managing armies didn't translate into the kind of business shrewdness that made men rich in the Gilded Age. Or, perhaps, it was simply his strong scruples. Honesty was as much a hindrance as a help in the financial free-for-all of the post-Civil-War years. Ulysses never played the stock market, although he sent a large portion of his presidential salary to New York investor Joseph Seligman in 1876, and presumably this was wisely invested on his behalf[2]. Having been nearly conned about the gold market by Jay Gould and Jim Fiske in 1869 (thanks to the interference of his own brother-in-law Abel Corbin), Ulysses seems to have nonetheless maintained a naïve trust in rich men. Possibly, with his Calvinistic Methodist roots in southern Ohio, he believed that such men and their wealth were a sign of divine benediction (i.e. they were rich, so they must be good men). Indeed, there were rich men who would be good friends to Ulysses, including William H. Vanderbilt and Alexander T. Stewart; but Ulysses had been cheated more than once in his early years, and his lack of good fortune in business must have felt at times like a curse. It's understandable that he should revere men who, unlike him, were wealthy beyond his own wildest dreams.

The fact that Ulysses and Julia decided to spend all their money on a two-year global voyage at the end of his presidency, despite there being no presidential or military pension waiting for him after 1876, speaks volumes about their financial innocence. The voyage they took, which has been well documented, actually made them better traveled than even the richest Gilded Age Americans, and surely made Ulysses the best traveled president in the history of the nation to that point, and for many years after.

My great-great-grandparents returned home triumphantly in 1879, working their way east from San Francisco, celebrated every inch of the way

---

[2] The check, dated 1876 and drawn on a Washington bank, is now in the collection of the U.S. Grant Presidential Library at Mississippi State University.

as if they were conquering heroes. They settled into a big modern brownstone house just off of Fifth Avenue on the north side of East 66th Street. Once again, rich friends had gotten together and raised not only the money to buy them the house, but to create a fund to support them in their life there. By this time, I wonder if Julia and Ulysses hadn't rather come to believe that this was the way their world worked. Julia wrote of the house in her memoirs: *"It was a much larger and a more expensive house than we had intended (or had the means) to buy, but it was so new and* sweet *and* large *that this quite outweighed our more prudential scruples."*

And so began their brief life on top of the social pyramid, ensconced in a fashionable house in the most socially prominent enclave of the most financially powerful city in North America. For four years Ulysses and Julia lived the dream. I can't imagine that Caroline Schermerhorn Astor (Mrs. William Backhouse Astor Jr.) would have thought much of the Grants or ever invited them to mingle with the famous 400 in her 34th Street ballroom. But people with newer money—including the Vanderbilts, who would be building heavily on Fifth Avenue in the early 1880s—were probably more open-minded than their old-money predecessors. William Henry, eldest son of Commodore Vanderbilt and father to a family of insatiable house builders, would do the former president a great favor in his hour of greatest financial need. Vanderbilt turned out to be one of those rich men in whom Ulysses S. Grant wisely placed his trust. In the end, however, it didn't save Ulysses and Julia from humiliation.

For a brief, innocent moment, Ulysses actually believed that he was a Wall Street player, and that he was rich to boot. How his second son, Buck, convinced his father and older brother Fred to lend his name to Ferdinand Ward's investment firm is hard to fathom; but is the lure of easy money ever easy to resist, especially when you have known poverty yourself and everyone around you is getting rich? Ferdinand Ward was reportedly both handsome and charming. It's easy to criticize Grant and his sons for their shocking lack of interest in the actual workings of Grant & Ward's finances, but then again, Bernard Madoff fooled a lot of rich, smart, sophisticated people, too, until his house of cards collapsed in 2008. There was nobody nodding sagely when the

Ferdinand Ward's scheme collapsed in 1884, leaving Grant, his family, and many of his friends with nothing.

The real revelation about Ulysses' involvement with the Grant & Ward scandal is his reaction to it: his shame and guilt over the people who were hurt, including virtually everyone in his family. Having asked for and received a $150,000 loan from William Henry Vanderbilt—the very asking of which must have shamed him incredibly—he scrambled to do what he could to salvage things. Ultimately, as was all too familiar to him, Grant failed to save the firm to which he had attached his name. The money he lost was real enough. As if shame and penury were not enough, Grant discovered the same year that he had inoperable throat cancer. This would be quite a plot arc for an opera set in America in the 1880s; although Grant's well-known tone-deafness would seem to make an opera about him rather ironic.

The silver lining in this mess was the fact that, forced to find a way to make money other than by waging war, Grant turned to the one thing he did as well as military strategy: write. I find it wonderful that Samuel Clemens, to whom Grant was an overt symbol of American corruption in his novel, *The Gilded Age*, would become his savior, befriending the stricken general and arranging the astonishing book deal for Grant's memoirs that would give his widow over $400,000 in cash by the time her husband died in 1885. More heroic still was the fact that Ulysses wrote what would be a two-volume, 800-page memoir while in constant pain in less than a year's time. He saved his family and his pride and left a legacy that set a standard for memoirists for generations to come.

My great-grandfather Fred had left the army in 1881 to work as his father's secretary and ended up being his closest aide during the last months as he worked desperately to complete his memoirs. Before the bankruptcy, he and Ida and their children had moved to Morristown, New Jersey, lured there by his friend, the political cartoonist Thomas Nast. He commuted into New York from Morristown, using, coincidentally, the same train line I would later take to my job in Newark for thirty-eight years. When the Grant & Ward scheme failed, he and his family moved back to 3 East 66th Street, both to economize and to support his shattered parents.

Fred was the dutiful son, and like most firstborns was probably closest to his father, or close to his father in different ways than his siblings, all of whom were educated and married by the time of their father's death. Fred looked like his father and eventually cultivated that similarity with a neatly trimmed beard. After the former president's death, he and Ida and their two children continued to live with the widowed Julia on East 66th Street until 1889. Then President Benjamin Harrison appointed Fred to be the American Minister to Austria-Hungary. It was a plum post, bringing with it not just a $17,000-a-year salary, but a rambling apartment above the American Legation in Vienna.

Ida Grant began writing letters to her mother and sister in Chicago as soon as their Austrian adventure began in 1889. Over the next four-and-a-half years, she would write 138 letters home, many of them extensively cross-written, and some numbering a dozen or more pages. I inherited this pile of correspondence and got to know my great-grandmother Ida through her distinctive view of diplomatic life at the Austrian court. My grandfather Ulysses was eight and his sister Julia thirteen when they sailed for Vienna in May 1889. In addition to appreciating the income, Ida knew that this was a unique opportunity for her children to see a larger world than they had known, but also to meet influential people who could help them become adults and make their way without the benefit of family money. Ulysses was enrolled in the Theresianum, the elite school founded by the Empress Maria Theresa in the eighteenth century. There, alongside the son of the Khedive of Egypt, he learned German and French. It was an experience very far from his namesake's childhood in western Ohio.

As Minister (the title Ambassador was only given to representatives of monarchies; democracies could only have Ministers) Fred took to his duties happily, while Ida took to her role as the American Minister's wife even more happily. She groused a little that he looked like a waiter at court functions, because he didn't have his military uniform and only wore formal evening dress. All men in the Austrian aristocracy wore military gear all the time for official functions and for parties. Ida, with her fluent French and her beauty, was readily welcomed by both the diplomatic crowd and the clannish Austrian nobility. She was well aware that being the daughter-in-law of the great

American general and president was a card she could play to her advantage. She loved the fact that people bowed to her and Fred on the street, and that their carriage was given priority when in line for cultural events in Vienna. However, Ida didn't develop any real interest in Austrian history or culture or have any wish to know the Austrian people outside the tight-knit circle of diplomats, nobles, and rich Americans, for this was where she felt most at home.

Comparing her Viennese life and her American life, Ida candidly reported to her sister in 1889 that "we really will be spoiled, and find it very hard to go back where we have scarcely enough to live on or buy our shoes." Unlike her mother-in-law in 1881 in New York, Ida knew that her time in Vienna was limited, and she clung to it with all her might, reveling in a life far more luxurious than she could have lived in New York at the same time.[3]

Back in New York in 1894, Fred became a police commissioner, and through that job met Theodore Roosevelt, who was appointed President of the Board of Police Commissioners in 1895. It was probably also at this time that Fred met Elihu Root, a friend of Roosevelt's and a powerful corporate lawyer. Root would follow Roosevelt into Washington politics, while Fred returned to the army in 1898, becoming a Brigadier General as the Spanish American War unfolded in the Caribbean.

I've often wondered if my grandfather Ulysses ever dreamed of doing something other than following his father and grandfather to West Point. He was just fifteen when he attended the dedication of Grant's Tomb on New York's Riverside Drive on April 27, 1897, exactly a century before I gave my speech at its rededication in 1997. Throughout his childhood, the press watched Ulysses III, the handsome, slender boy who carried the name and the blue eyes of his nation's savior. His mother constantly worried about money, while his father worried about the family's reputation, probably still burdened by the memories of humiliation suffered after his own father's financial disgrace. Julia herself had sold the East 66th Street House and moved back to

---

[3] Ida's letters home from Vienna are now in the archives of the Ulysses S. Grant Presidential Library at Mississippi State University.

Washington, where for the rest of her life Nellie, separated from her husband at last, served as her companion.

My poor grandfather never had much choice. Three months before he died, Ulysses S. Grant wrote a poignant letter to whoever was president when the time came, beseeching him to guarantee a place at West Point to his three-year-old grandson and namesake. The request was seconded in 1887, on the letter itself, by none other than William Tecumseh Sherman. In 1898, it was President McKinley who granted the appointment, adding his inscription to the sacred epistle, and thus launching my grandfather on a lifelong career in the army.

The young Ulysses would represent his father, absent in the Philippines, at his sister's wedding to the Russian Prince Michael Cantacuzene in Newport, Rhode Island, in 1899. Eight years later, he would play his own role in the Gilded Age, marrying Edith, the cherished only daughter of Elihu Root, Teddy Roosevelt's Secretary of State, and purportedly the most highly-paid lawyer in America. Bertha Palmer had done right by her sister Ida's child. With Ulysses' marriage to Edith Root in 1907, Fred and Ida had succeeded as parents beyond their wildest dreams. The real miracle is that both Ulysses and Julia adored their mother and father and would be close to their parents until Fred's death in 1912, and Ida's in 1930.

My mother, named Julia after her father's big sister, found her regal, silver-haired Victorian grandmother Ida slightly terrifying, although Ida was never anything but gentle with her. As the youngest available child in the mid-1920s, little Julia would accompany her grandmother Grant to church at Saint John's Episcopal on Lafayette Square, known as the Church of the Presidents. This was a memorable event on Sundays, as Ida was the last private person in Washington to use a carriage rather than an automobile. Mother would be taken to her grandmother's house on New Hampshire Avenue, and from there the horses would pull the old-fashioned carriage through streets crowded with automobiles and trolleys to the little yellow church near the White House where so many presidents had prayed before.

When I was a little boy, I envied my mother when she told me stories like this. She, however, only remembered being an embarrassed child riding in a carriage when everybody else was in cars.

Ulysses S. Grant and his family gathered at Mt. McGregor in Wilton, New York, shortly before his death on July 23, 1885. From left to right: Ulysses Jr. (seated), Julia, Nellie (standing), granddaughter Julia, the General, grandson Ulysses, (my grandfather, in the hat and ringlets), Ida, Fred (standing), granddaughter Nellie, Jesse's wife Elizabeth, Jesse (on the railing). From the Bultema-Williams Photograph Collection, Ulysses S. Grant Presidential Library.

CHAPTER THIRTEEN

Speculation #5
FRED AND IDA

Ida dozed as a warm breeze blew across the fields from the distant lake. Shaded as she was by the deep, ivy-draped verandah, she found the August heat quite bearable, as long as there was no need to move. She luxuriated in the silence, punctuated only by the hum of insects and the occasional rustling of the ivy overhead; her poor body was relaxed and almost free of pain.

The faint sound of wheels on gravel gradually entered her reverie, heralding the approach of a carriage on the drive. Ida tried to ignore it, but finally admitted defeat when, from within the house, she heard the excited cries of "Papa's here!" accompanied by the futile shushings of the nurse as two pairs of shoes came rattling down the stairs. Even as the sounds of the carriage grew louder at the front of the house, the faint sound of a baby wailing from the direction of the nursery added itself to the rising commotion. Ida could hear her sister's voice giving orders to the nurse while attempting to calm little Julia's enthusiasm.

In spite of her aches and pains, Ida smiled as she struggled to a more upright position, adjusting the fastenings of her dressing gown. Fred had been away for weeks, and she was as pleased at the prospect of seeing her husband again as her rambunctious five-year-old was.

Ida could hear the tumult reach a crescendo as the maid opened the front door and Fred greeted his elder child with a hearty salute. Her squeals of delight suggested that he had lifted her up and swung her about, an action of which Ida disapproved but little Julia adored. Fred loved his daughter no less now that he also had a son.

A few moments later and Fred had been pulled by tiny hands across the parlor and out onto the verandah, where Julia crowed "Mama! Look! Papa's here!" as if she had brought him all the way from New York herself. He let go of Julia's hand and went down on one knee by the chaise longue, taking both of his wife's delicate hands and leaning in to kiss her on her cheek. Fred looked stout and ruddy, the long trip from the East having done nothing to lessen his vigorous good health.

"How are you, my dear?" he asked, his blue eyes full of questioning concern.

"Much better, now that you're here," Ida replied. The sparkle in her large dark eyes echoed the smile on her face.

Julia whimpered with quiet impatience, aware even at the age of five that her mama and papa deserved this uninterrupted moment. The spell was ultimately broken by the arrival of the two young Palmer cousins and Ida's sister Bertha, holding in her arms the swaddled baby Ulysses.

As Fred lifted himself to his feet, his sister-in-law kissed him on the cheek and unceremoniously handed the infant to him. "Here, hold your beautiful son. Both he and his mother are doing well."

Bertha gestured to her sons and her niece, "You should be most proud of Julia, Fred. She defends her baby brother nearly every day from the predatory envy of my boys." She smiled, her eyes twinkling with amusement. "They keep trying to convince Julia that the baby rightfully belongs to them, since it was born in their house."

She turned and smiled indulgently at her sons Honoré and Min, as Potter junior was called. "Now boys, why don't you take Julia back upstairs with Nurse, and let Julia's mum and dad have a little conversation?"

At the grumbling from all three children, Bertha grew imperious. "No arguments, you three. Do as you're told, and we can all have lunch out here together."

That seemed to appease them, and they obediently trundled off with the nurse.

Bertha turned back to her sister and brother-in-law. "I'll leave you two be for a bit. I'll send out some lemonade for you, if you'd like."

Fred beamed at his sister-in-law, who was as carefully gowned and coiffed, out here in the country, as his own dear wife was casually dressed owing to her convalescence. "That would be lovely, Bertha. Will you join us in a little while, before the children descend upon us again?"

"Of course," she smiled back at him. "I've got some letters to write, and I'll return when I've finished them." With that, she turned and disappeared into the parlor, the lace curtains fluttering in her wake.

Alone, Fred settled himself on the chaise longue next to his reclining wife and took her hand.

"So, my love, how are you *really* doing?" There was a joking tone in his voice, but his expression couldn't hide his anxiety.

"Sis believes that a positive attitude is all I need to feel myself again," Ida responded, her smile genuine but tinged with melancholy. She squeezed Fred's hand. "Of course, she's quite right, and I *am* feeling much improved since you last saw me. It's just that, Ulysses is a very large baby and even at birth he was even larger than Julia was."

"And you're such a little thing." Fred's voice was almost a whisper. "I had hoped…you were so well, right up to the lying-in."

Ida's eyes glimmered with unshed tears as she took a deep breath. "The doctor came the other day to speak to me. He says I shouldn't have any more children. This last birth was very difficult. It damaged me." She took a deep breath before continuing. "He's afraid another like this could cost me my life."

Fred put Ida's fingers to his lips, then placed his forehead on the back of her slender hand. He held it there for a moment, as if gathering strength from it, then straightened himself. He looked at his wife of seven years.

"Then we are most fortunate that we have two such beautiful babes, aren't we, sweetheart? We have both a Julia and a Ulysses to cherish."

Ida nodded, but silent tears began to trail down her pale cheeks. Fred pulled her into a gentle embrace, letting her cry into his shoulder.

"How lucky my little ones are to have you as their mother. You are so strong and brave. You will be well soon, and then we'll go back to New York. Mother and Father are settling nicely into their new house on East 66th Street. It's very large and there will be a whole floor set aside for our use."

Ida, leaving Fred's embrace, repositioned herself against the cushions, while sniffling softly. She took his proffered handkerchief and wiped her eyes."

"I had so hoped to have a home of our own." She studied her hands. "It probably is the best, especially now. Mrs. Grant will be so happy to have the children with her, and it will give your father a chance to get to know his namesake."

Fred couldn't help grinning at his wife's diplomacy. "I know my mother can be a bit overbearing, dear heart. She frets and fusses; that's just her way. You know she loves you very much. She's just so used to bossing Father around that she forgets sometimes that the rest of us are quite grown up."

Ida laughed, her face lighting up with genuine amusement. She playfully slapped her husband's arm. "I know, I know. And I am sincere. It will be nice to live comfortably without worries while the children are so small. Perhaps when I'm back at one hundred per cent..." She didn't finish her thought.

"I think I am ahead of you on that point," Fred said. Ida looked at him with curiosity. Fred shifted a bit closer to her, as if about to take her into his confidence. "I've been talking to Tom Nast about taking a house next year in Morristown, New Jersey. Ever since he and Sarah moved there in seventy-two, he's been extolling its virtues."

"But what about your work with your father?"

"That's the beauty of it. There's a train line that runs directly from Morristown to the main station in Jersey City. It takes only an hour, and then I can catch the ferry across the harbor to Wall Street. It's hardly more cumbersome than a carriage ride from 66th Street."

"Is it a big town?" Ida asked, excitement filling her now-dry eyes.

"Very much a country town," Fred answered, "but prosperous and bustling. There are many elegant houses and people from New York and Newark have begun to establish themselves with country seats in the neighborhood. We would find ourselves a nice society there."

"And it would be so good for the children to have grass and trees around them."

"And we could of course still visit Mother and Father in New York whenever we wish."

They both paused, looking at each other and absorbing the promise of their brief conversation in companionable silence. The breeze shifted off the fields that surrounded the house and enveloped them with its warm embrace in the shadow of the veranda, bringing with it the scent of mown lawn and fresh-cut hay.

It was Ida who broke the silence first. "I feel so much better. The oppression that has been weighing on me seems to have lifted." She paused, sighed deeply, then took her husband's hand. "Thank you, dear Fred. What a lucky wife I am."

Her husband's only response was to smile broadly at her, and to raise her hand once more to his lips and give it a gentle kiss. At just that moment a maid arrived from the depths of the house, bearing a silver tray laden with tall glasses and a gently tinkling crystal pitcher of iced lemonade.

[4]

---

[4] It has always been a mystery to me that Fred and Ida only had two children, given child mortality in the late 1800s. I know that the babies were both very big, and know that Ida was unwell after my grandfather's birth in 1881. The rest of this is, as the title suggests, speculation.

CHAPTER FOURTEEN

THE END OF THE WORLD

When I was very small, I attended a nursery school behind a big old Presbyterian church on the west side of downtown Syracuse. My memories of this place are both intense and dim. A lot of kids from my neighborhood with whom I would spend most of my elementary years were my classmates. I remember long hallways, and big light-filled rooms with polished linoleum floors. The rooms were large enough that we could ride tricycles and other wheeled toys up and down their length. I guess children are taught to categorize and covet early on, because the hierarchy of riding toys was well established. There was a sort of tricycle, but more fully developed, with streamlined fenders and an odd storage compartment behind the seat and between the rear wheels. It was painted a metallic ruby red and was unquestionably the great prize whenever it was made available for the riding portion of our morning. Snagging the red tricycle was a high point for the successful child.

Somewhat more esoteric was the very high status placed on a particular petticoat in the dress-up box, valued as I recall for its sturdy elastic waistband. It was a simple, white, A-line petticoat, with a couple of horizontal bands of boning to help it keep its shape, and small enough for four-year-old children to wear. Maybe it was just me, but my impression is that this dress-up garment was as highly prized as the dark red tricycle. Was I the only boy who cared about the petticoat? I have no memory that I was somehow odd or different because of it. I can only assume that, at the age of four, the point of it all was learning to lay claim to what one wanted in life. I distinctly remember at least one occasion when I somehow captured *both* the red tricycle and the elastic-waisted petticoat, which I carried proudly in the storage compartment behind the seat as I rode my way around the room. I would become much harder to please as I got older.

An incident from those two pre-school years was relayed to me many years later by my mother. Perhaps she told me this during the months in 1976 after I came out to her and my father, and my mother and I were talking about early signs of my latent orientation. Aside from the forewarning given to them by the Dietz Company's psychiatrist when I was ten or eleven, there was one image fixed in my mother's memory from very early in my childhood.

Mothers took turns dropping off and picking up the neighborhood children from nursery school each day. Five or six of us would be piled unceremoniously into whichever station wagon was on call. Of course, nobody ever thought of seatbelts. We would fight for space in the "wayback" which for whatever reason was deemed more desirable than one of the regular seats. More than likely, the maternal chauffeur was smoking as she drove; all my mother's friends smoked. On the day in question, my mother was at the wheel. When she arrived, we were at the end of our morning session, and everybody was out on the playground—at the center of which was a massive unpainted steel jungle gym set into a dirt play yard, along with swings and a seesaw. Pulling into the nursery school parking area, my mother scanned the crowd for her various charges and located all of them but me. As she steered the car— probably the huge black 1959 Ford station wagon I remember so vividly—into a vacant space, she spotted me. I had wandered away from the ruckus my peers were causing in the playground and was squatted at the edge of the parking area, contentedly picking up gravel and putting it into a plastic bucket at my side.

I was wearing the petticoat. Apparently, it had been a good day.

Looking back at my childhood from my mid-twenties, when Gary and I bought our first house in New Jersey and started the careers that would see us into retirement, my memories were bathed in the golden light of remembered happiness. Much of what I wanted in my life in the 1980s was colored by my memories of Syracuse in the 1960s. In the 1990s, as Gary and I struggled to become fathers as a gay couple, I realized that I had a strong instinct to keep the good things in the forefront of my mind while pushing everything else back into the shadows of memory.

Julia Grant Dietz, John S. Dietz and their four children were the perfect, prosperous model of a small-city Episcopalian family for all of thirteen years. Then, in 1969, in a perfect storm of domestic cataclysm, my family's *Leave it to Beaver* life began to implode. Only when I became a father did I finally understand that I had used that baker's dozen of happy years as a sort of shield, suppressing memories of all that was unhappy in order to reassure myself that all would be well.

My adult memories of childhood happiness usually filtered out the repercussions of the anxieties that filled me as a kid. Learning childhood skills was troublesome, but somehow I managed to achieve these things in spite of my fears. Swimming, which was essential because we spent part of every year at a lake, was terrifying. Ned, a year younger, learned everything ahead of me, all at once, being fearless like our older brother Jed. I fretted and struggled. Eventually, in the shallow water by a rented shingled boathouse on East Lake Road in Skaneateles, I managed to turn dog paddling into actual swimming. Subsequently, there were Saturday swimming lessons with friends at the YMCA in Syracuse, but it began at the Laphams's boathouse when I was seven.

Bicycle riding was another trauma. I was maybe eight. My father's attempts to teach me to ride a bike had failed, but I had been left with a bribe firmly in my mind: if I learned to ride a bike, my father would buy me a Steiff toy. Steiff toys were those beautifully made little velveteen and mohair animals produced in Germany since the early 1900s. Steiff was the inventor of the Teddy Bear in the early twentieth century, and they were one of my obsessions as a child, along with little cars by Corgi and Dinky and Matchbox. The lure of a new Steiff animal inspired me one afternoon when my parents were out and our maid Vernice was ironing and watching television at the back of the house. I stood, straddling my bicycle (which was a small size, perfect for seven-year-olds) by the porte-cochere of our house at the top of our slightly sloped driveway. It was only a dozen or so yards to the street, so my trajectory meant I had to turn sharply as part of my launch. The surprise is that I did it in one take. I shot down the rough pavement of the driveway and turned right, pedaling madly so as not to lose momentum or allow myself to think about what I was doing. I didn't fall over. I kept pedaling. When I had gone entirely around the block, sweating feverishly, and returned to our house, I stopped. Then, minus the downhill launch, I started riding again, triumph surging through me. I got a Steiff zebra for this accomplishment.

For two of these idyllic childhood summers Ned and I were sent away to summer camp instead of going to the lake. Adirondack Woodcraft Camps was a big, expensive, highly regarded camp up near Fourth Lake. It was a huge complex, with a couple hundred boys divided into three age groups ranging from eight-year-olds to high-school seniors. Each group came with its own level of oversight and coddling. I think I was eleven and twelve the two summers Ned and I attended Woodcraft. I only saw him in passing during those eight-week stints away from home. The only other person I knew at the camp was Charlie, one of my childhood friends from Sedgwick Farm, whose parents knew my parents. He was a mischievous redhead and was the camp's biggest fan. I didn't see any more of Charlie during those two summers than I did of my brother.

I didn't hate camp. After all, I went for two years. We slept in cabins named after the tribes in the Iroquois Nation, and the bathroom facilities were in a separate building that was used by all of the cabins. I seem to remember long troughs to pee in and toilet stalls with no doors. None of this bothered me then. We had teenaged counselors whom we had to call "sir." First year (I was a Tuscarora) we had Dick Sir. Second year, when I was a Seneca, and we had Gary Sir. Both young men were nice to us, but Gary was cuter and more cheerful, so he merited an adolescent crush that I didn't fully acknowledge at the time.

I'm not sure if I had the same cabin-mates both years. What I do remember is that it was a more diverse group of boys than I'd ever met before. There was Baldy, who appeared from whatever Deep South state he came from in a chauffeured Cadillac convertible. There was Bob, a plump redhead from the Midwest who was dubbed "Fats" on the first day and suffered under that unkind nickname the whole time. Then there was Dick, from New Jersey, who professed his distaste for camp in general with a snide, defensive attitude that provoked the latent cruelty of the other boys and must have made him even more miserable. Henry, a sweet, attractive boy, taught me that Versailles was pronounced differently when it was a town in Kentucky. Mark, a gregarious, charming Jewish boy from Long Island, was enough of a friend that I sent him an embarrassing holiday card for "Honica" after our first year. Finally, there was Kim, a precocious, handsome blond boy from Manhattan who spoke with dubious knowledge about intimacy with girls. I was rather obsessed with him, even though I never really believed his talk of girlfriends.

I had never been remotely interested in sports, unlike all my siblings and most of my cousins, who swam and rode horses and skied and sailed and played tennis, soccer, or golf with some level of seriousness. My mother was more athletic than my father, but both were far sportier than I. Nonetheless, at Woodcraft I learned that I enjoyed canoeing (never good enough for stern, but adequate for bow position), and swimming was something I had mastered already. The reward for competent swimming was a green badge, which meant one could swim outside the U-shaped dock that defined the protected swimming area for the younger campers. I managed to get this status without too much trouble by completing two full lengths of the enclosed swimming area. I took to horseback riding because I loved my horse—a big buckskin gelding named David. Surely, I remembered the dude ranch in Wyoming from when I was eight, but in spite of a spill off David's back during a racing exercise, I always loved being on horseback.

Interestingly, I loved both archery and riflery—twenty-two-caliber rifles, which I shot left-handed, lying on a mattress in a protective shed. Admittedly, part of my interest was actually in the riflery instructor, a thirty-something man named George, who wore tight red polo shirts and horn-rimmed glasses. He made me fairly faint with inexplicable longing. There wasn't, I swear, anything remotely sexual in this—or, not that I understood. I never felt any shame or embarrassment in my crushes. It is only in retrospect that I can see what was going on. Understanding would come later.

Well into the first summer at camp I came down with strep throat – something I would be prone to until I reached adulthood. The result was spending a week in the infirmary, sleeping on a comfy bed with soft sheets. I read twenty-five Hardy Boys books during that week, and was cared for by the two young female nurses, who were pretty and friendly and smelled nice. It was lovely.

The only real sadness I remember from camp was the night, during an overnight trip to Blue Mountain Lake, when my tent-mates and I wouldn't stop talking, and Gary Sir knocked our tent down and made us sleep under its collapsed canvas. This upset me, not out of fear, but because I had made my counselor angry. I cried myself to sleep that night, the rain drumming down on the soggy tent as it rested on my face, while out on the lake loons called to each other.

Junior high school was fine. I was a happy adolescent, although I know that sounds like a contradiction. I liked my teachers and they seemed to like me. I was a star student and basked in the validation that getting high grades provided. I didn't know that I wasn't popular, and I had my comfortable social niche, a few good friends like Larry, David and Margy, with whom I could spend time. I wore appalling clothing that I thought was totally cool. I had braces.

Gym class, segregated by gender, was the one uncomfortable place in my adolescent routine. Because it was such an old building, there were no showers, so at least I didn't have to deal with locker-room issues and fears of being unclothed in front of my classmates. I was scrawny and non-athletic. Lincoln Junior High's gym teacher was a big burly man who did not shy away from paddling a student who displeased him (and I mean literally, with a long wooden paddle). He was not cruel or sadistic, but he kept his boys in line. Looking back, I think I suspected that the gym teacher went easy on me because of my family's name (Dietz, not Grant, because, remember, my "famous" name was still largely unknown).

On the other hand, I couldn't avoid the misery of dodgeball, where I was lousy at throwing but great at dodging, and thus frequently ended up all alone as people pelted me to end the game. I was always picked last. Neither could I miss the public humiliation of (not) climbing the rope to the gym ceiling, although I don't remember failing too badly at the pommel horse.

I think the secret to my happiness was that I was oblivious—a blessing I cannot overstate. My ability to not see the bad side of things, to see the glass half-full as it were, has been my superpower throughout my life; second only to my ability to compartmentalize and isolate anything negative to avoid dealing with it.

Because of my academic prowess, in eighth grade I was required to do a presentation at the local science fair on the history of linear measurement. I remember being terrified at the thought of this, because, at thirteen, I suffered from terrible stage fright. I had even negotiated for a piano teacher who would allow me to skip any sort of recital, so fearful was I of public performance. I was the only child in our family with this anxiety. My sister and brothers were all gregarious and popular. They reveled in public attention as much as I shied away from it. In 1965 we had traveled to the Deerfield Academy in Massachusetts to see my brother on stage, in drag no less, perform in a production of *The Man Who Came to Dinner.* My brother will be the first to admit that he was never a great actor, but he was fearless. In his blond wig and high heels, on stage at this elite all-boys school, he was mesmerizing to me.

Despite my churning fear, I lovingly created a twenty-minute program based on my own hand-drawn and crayoned illustrations inspired by my research on the topic of linear measurement in our set of World Book Encyclopedias. Decades later, in her late eighties, my mother returned those drawings, still carefully mounted on cardboard so they would rest on an easel. They are not very good, but at the time they served their purpose. I was placed in a classroom in whatever high school hosted the Syracuse Junior High Science Fair that year and was given a mixed audience of adults and students. I gave my little talk, quaking in fear. I am sure that I embellished my presentation with clever asides as I put each drawing on the easel, adding entertainment value to the facts and distracting myself from my anxiety. Humor was my go-to defense against my insecurity. It was the ending, however, that ingrained itself into my eighth-grade psyche. When I was done, the captive little audience burst into applause, and not just polite clapping to spare me shame. It was enthusiastic applause. They were clapping for me. They had enjoyed the way I took a possibly tedious science report and amused them with it for twenty minutes. In retrospect, those absurd drawings of Egyptians measuring cubits on their forearms were the harbingers of the thousands of slides and PowerPoint images that would later fill my professional life. I had discovered the joy of positive public attention, and I have never lost my taste for it.

As anyone of my generation can tell you, the sixties didn't end well. The assassinations of Martin Luther King Jr. and Robert F. Kennedy in 1968 knocked my adolescent world off the rails. I had been too young to really comprehend President Kennedy's assassination in 1963, but by seventh grade the impact and the implications of this pair of political murders was deeply felt. A year after the Detroit and Newark riots, the summer of 1968 was rocked by a second wave of urban riots all over the country. It never dawned on me at the time that perhaps this was why my parents decided to take us to Bermuda for a month that year, instead of the usual setting of the Finger Lakes.

In the midst of the tumultuous summer at home, my grandfather Grant's quiet death at eighty-seven in August of 1968 was, unknown to any of us, a harbinger of worse to come.

Nineteen-sixty-nine started off all right. My brother Jed was a senior at the University of North Carolina in Chapel Hill. My sister Edie was at the Shipley School in Bryn Mawr, Pennsylvania, which both our mother and my father's sister Aunt Olga had attended. My little brother Ned and I were both at Lincoln Junior High in Syracuse, growing apart even as we were growing up. Spring saw my eighth-grade class trip to Washington, a ritual undertaken to this day by middle-schoolers across the country. My memories of the trip itself are fuzzy, other than having a lot of fun with my classmates in a third-rate hotel where in gleeful horror we watched the rats playing in the dumpsters outside our ground-floor window. I have no doubt that we were edified by what we saw in Washington—including President Kennedy's grave at Arlington—although I have no memory that my ancestral ties to Ulysses S. Grant ever surfaced during our visit. I was, after all, Grant Dietz, and not inclined to drag my lineage out for inspection.

More engrained in my brain are some memories of the eight-hour bus trip back to Syracuse. Two things stand out in vivid detail, especially with fifty years of hindsight to sharpen them. At some point, during a lull in the general hilarity, I can clearly remember watching two of the most popular couples in the eighth grade making out at the back of the bus. I knew these boys and girls, and could give you their names, even now. What I realized, to my dawning horror at the time, was that I was not remotely fascinated by the girls, or where the boys' hands were on those girls. The closest I had ever come to touching a girl was during a slow dance at one of those angst-ridden school dances during seventh grade. What I remember from that bus ride is the bulges in the boys' trousers, and the sharp sense that I wasn't supposed to be looking at, much less caring about them.

The counterpart to this realization, at a much livelier moment on the trip, was the decision by some of the girls—the ones I liked best—to put makeup on me and tie my hair up in a ribbon. Photographs were taken. It was, at least to me at the time, all done in good fun. I laughed along with them. These were my friends. We were just goofing around. In retrospect, I wonder if perhaps they weren't making assumptions that I had not arrived at myself. All along I had been safe in my role as court jester. It had never occurred to me that perhaps I was also a joke.

As we got older, my younger brother and I became very different boys. Only thirteen months apart, we had long been treated (and dressed) as if we were twins. For me, there had been no life before Ned, and so shared the odd birth position in our family of being stuck between the baby and the middle child. Jed was the eldest, with all the advantages and pressures of being the First Boy. Edie was the angel, the only girl, pretty and smart, popular at school and well-liked by everyone. Before heading off to boarding school, our sister had been moved into the big bedroom that Ned and I had shared since infancy. Her former room became the guest room, and Ned and I were moved into the back of the house into what had been maids' rooms during our early childhood. As we hit puberty and our differences became more obvious, someone wisely figured that we should have more privacy. The service suite consisted of two little bedrooms opening into a tiny sitting room off of which was a bathroom, which was renovated for our occupancy. Ned had his room painted a dark forest green. I chose what I called a jade green but was really a sort of turquoise. Mother made white dimity curtains for the two windows in each of the bedrooms, trimmed with a fluffy cotton fringe that matched the wall color. Ned hung the dayglo poster for the film *Endless Summer* in his room (a film he enjoyed for the surfing, and I enjoyed for the surfers). I put brightly colored pop-art flower stickers on my walls and dragged a big French ormolu clock out of the attic. My toy cars were displayed on a badly-stained wooden shelf I'd made in seventh-grade shop class. (The French clock, by the way, had been purchased by Elihu Root in Paris as a young man, and had been left to my father by my mother's uncle, Elihu Root, Jr., as a joke, since my father always made fun of it.)

There is a snapshot of Ned and me taken in late 1968, no doubt by Mother, who was ever the shutterbug. We are standing in the doorways of our rooms. Ned is bare-chested, looking tall and muscular at the age of twelve. He seems to be preparing to throw darts at a dartboard on the wall opposite his bedroom doorway. I, next to him, am leaning on my door jamb in what I'm sure I thought was a comical pose. Shorter and skinnier than Ned, I am wearing pale green paisley pajamas.

Me with my younger brother Ned, early in 1969.

For whatever reason on a warm Tuesday in spring 1969, I decided to drop in on my grandparents on the way home from school, rather than wait until the cocktail hour, when the family normally gathered at their house. The elder Dietzes were both in their library, along with my great aunt Ethel Nichols. I kissed them all and sat for a while, having a ginger ale and chatting comfortably. I've no idea why I decided to change my routine that day. Having spent what seemed like the right amount of time with my grandparents, I kissed everyone goodbye and headed home, where I did my homework, and settled into my father's faux-Eames easy chair in front of the television in our study. Later that evening, I found myself on my own in the house. Ned was off goofing around with his friends somewhere after school. My father was at work. My sister and mother were in New York City. The significance of this would become apparent soon enough, but in all honesty, nobody had talked to me or Ned about it and it wasn't something I'd paid any attention to. I just remember that it was me in the front of the house, while Vernice, our maid, was puttering in the back of the house, probably ironing or making dinner.

Suddenly, Vernice appeared in the front hall, spied me, and headed down the living room toward the study. The only thing she said to me as she got closer was "Your grandmother's dead." She came into the study and turned off the television. I don't remember if we talked, but presumably her friend Frances, my grandparents' maid, had called her with the news. I don't remember much of anything about the rest of that day.

Barbara Bancroft Johnson Dietz, at seventy-nine, had led a sedentary life for half a century. Crippled with a chronic joint disease, she was stout, although I never thought of her as fat. She smoked and drank, every day. She liked Jack Daniels on ice, and always kept a big silver Ronson table lighter next to her French bergère on a little carved Chinese table. Apparently, her great old Bostonian heart had given out as she was writing Frances's paycheck at the desk in the library. In that moment a central pillar of my childhood had been pulled away.

Their matriarch fallen, the Dietz family gathered from all over the country. My Uncle Bob Dietz came from Albuquerque with his wife Ann. Aunt Olga flew in from Denver with her husband Jake Turner. Uncle Gerry and Aunt

Cynnie were just a few blocks away. There were sixteen cousins, counting us four, and I think we were all there, signaling this seismic shift in our reality. Barbara and Robert had been married since 1914.

The following week is a blur but two moments unrelated to the funeral preparations remain crystal clear. At one point Jed, who had returned from wherever he was spending his summer, brought me and Ned together in my room at the back of the house and explained to us, in his most serious big-brother-at-college way, that he was going to drop out of school, and was going to refuse the draft. Vietnam was a bad war, but he said he couldn't claim conscientious objector status on religious grounds. He was pretty sure he would probably go to prison because of it. Ned and I were wide-eyed at this turn of events. My parents, needless to say, were beside themselves.

The other moment simply added a surreal quality to the unfolding events as our placid upstate life began its death spiral. My mother had returned from New York for the funeral without my sister. Apparently, Edie had been feeling poorly and tired for much of the second semester of the school year. A visit to Fred Weber, our family doctor, and a close friend of my parents, had produced worrying results. Thus, Edie had thus been taken to Sloan-Kettering Memorial Hospital in New York, where she was diagnosed with leukemia. She was seventeen.

I don't remember Grandmother's funeral, other than seeing my grandfather in church, looking suddenly diminished, a shadow of himself after fifty-five years of marriage. Saint Paul's Episcopal Cathedral was full. The funeral came and went. A substantial catered reception at my grandparents' house provided ample if uninteresting food and plenty of liquor. Later that year, all four of Barbara Dietz's children, raised on horseback on the farm in Albuquerque, would ride up into the wilderness of the Hamilton Mesa and scatter her Bostonian ashes across the landscape that had become her home at the beginning of the twentieth century.

A week after my grandmother's death, I was once again sitting at home watching television. It was evening, and *The Doris Day Show* was on. Vernice had gone home for the evening, picked up by her husband Charlie and whisked back to the Currys' comfortable two-family house on the other side of town. My father was reading his newspaper in the living room, just a few feet away from me. Mother was back in New York with my sister, presumably meeting with doctors and making plans for her treatment.

Ned was out with friends—again. He was the one with a busy social life. I neither had one nor felt its lack. It's not that I didn't have any friends, but we would hang out after school and then head home to our families at dinnertime. Ned had a more loosely knit group of acquaintances, and his time spent with them was more spontaneous and, now that I think of it, far less supervised. It was a warm, drizzly evening, and in my typical bossy, ineffectual big-brother way, I had chided him for planning to go out barefoot. This was a city, and although we had run around the neighborhood barefoot in warm weather most of our lives (because you had to toughen up your feet in preparation for summer), I didn't think it was right for this evening. Maybe I was just annoyed that Ned didn't seem to be taking our grandmother's death, or our sister's illness, as seriously as I was. Maybe I was just jealous that he had friends to go out and run around with. Having spent so much time together since infancy, Ned and I now moved in separate circles. Whatever my motivation, Ned had long since stopped caring what I thought, and after dismissing me, he disappeared into the spring evening to meet his buddies. His bare feet were, at the age of twelve, already size eleven.

That night, halfway through *Doris Day,* the front door burst open, and my cousin Tim Turner from Denver rushed into the hall. Tall and gangly, Tim spotted my father and me and said, his voice breaking with panic, "Neddy's hurt."

My father threw down his paper and, still in his white shirt and suit pants from the office, ran out the front door. I got up and followed, but only made it as far as the front steps. Down the street, in front of my grandparents' house, a small crowd had gathered. The police cars were flashing their red and blue lights across the placid facades of this quiet, affluent neighborhood. There was no noise, other than that made by my father, who with his arms outstretched, was already halfway down the block, running toward the ominous tableau. I could hear him keening with the anguish of a parent expecting the worst.

I went back inside and turned off the television, but I didn't leave the house. The thought of following my father into whatever horror awaited was impossible. I didn't want to think about what those flashing lights implied. I think my cousin Tim might have stayed with me. We would have talked, but my mind is a blank. When, two hours later, my father returned, Tim must have asked if Ned was all right.

My father's exhausted, defeated answer was simply, "Neddy's dead."

Somehow, I went to bed. Decades later, my father told me he had always felt terrible guilt over not staying with me that night to comfort me. I told him to let go of any guilt, since I have no memory of how I made my way to my room, and certainly no recollection of feeling neglected. I must have brushed my teeth and put on my pale green paisley pajamas and climbed into the little four-poster bed in my turquoise room with the clock and the toy cars and the flower stickers on the walls. When I woke up in the morning, I thought immediately of the empty room next to mine, and the unalterable truth that my world was now off its axis.

By the time I made my way downstairs, various family members, minus my mother and sister, were gathered in the living room. Even though it was early, Vernice was already there, long before her regular time. She wore her starched light blue uniform and served coffee to the gathered family, tear tracks staining her cheeks.

I was never shown a newspaper, was never supposed to see the headlines in the morning's *Post-Standard* or the evening *Herald Journal* about my brother's death. Somehow, my shattered father managed to tell me that Ned and his friends had been hanging around next door to my grandparents' in front of Dr. Farone's house (Tony Farone was in my grade, but he was Ned's friend more than mine). Ned had been climbing on one of the cast-iron, green-painted streetlights that lined Sedgwick Drive. On this one the baseplate that concealed the inner workings had not been properly reattached, and when Ned's wet bare foot made contact with one of the exposed wires, he was electrocuted instantly. He was not pronounced dead until the ambulance, my father at his side, arrived at Memorial Hospital. Father had been told that, had he lived, Ned would probably have suffered severe brain damage from the waves of electricity that surged through him when he completed the circuit with his foot.

My mother returned home with my sister. Another funeral was held at St. Paul's Cathedral, this time packed to the rafters with people who knew my family and shuddered in sympathy at the shocking suddenness of my little brother's death. Ned was cremated, but there was no burial. My family drove to Clinton to scatter his ashes in the Root Glen, a garden behind the old Root Homestead on the Hamilton Campus. Back then, my great-aunt Grace Root still owned the Glen, but had turned the Homestead itself over to the college. She had taken up residence in her husband Edward's painting studio behind the house. The Root Glen was nothing more than a wooded declivity with a creek running through banks of myrtle-covered red shale. One little valley of the glen had been heavily planted by Grace Root with Asiatic primroses. Every spring, their funny geometric flower clusters peppered the fern-covered banks with rainbow colors. This would be our first pilgrimage to this place to scatter ashes.

I had always been a model student, beyond struggling with my penmanship because I was left-handed. Ned, on the other hand, had never been as focused on his schoolwork, and had never had the consistent high grades that I made each semester. When we went through family counseling with our parents a few years earlier, we had also been given IQ tests. My score was, not surprisingly (at least to me), high. Ned's, however, was only one point behind mine, which threw all of us for a loop, including him. I remember marveling at the idea that my goof-off little brother was just as smart as I was. It was a weirdly comforting notion that, despite our increasing differences as we entered puberty, we were still alike in this invisible way.

Mom showed me Ned's final seventh-grade report card when it appeared in the mail a few weeks after his death. He had made the honor roll for the first time.

That summer, after a typing class in an office building downtown on County Courthouse Square, I stopped in at the grand old Carnegie library. It was a place, redolent of old books and well-waxed terrazzo floors, that I had only visited to do research for some local history paper at some point in my childhood. I went right to the periodical room and requested back issues of the Syracuse papers, and I found those front-page stories about my brother's accidental death. The papers had used his seventh-grade class picture. There was a slight smirk on his face. He was wearing the same mustard-colored sports coat and wide green floral silk tie in which he had been cremated.

I had no idea that during that same June in 1969, while my family was falling apart, a group of angry drag queens and other assorted gay folk had fought back against the police during a routine raid on a bar called the Stonewall Inn in a place I'd never heard of called Greenwich Village. I don't think I even knew what the word "gay" meant at the time.

CHAPTER FIFTEEN

RECONSTRUCTION

S omehow, as my muddled adolescent brain tried to make sense of what had happened to my brother, I lit upon the idea that God had taken Ned in order to spare us pain later. At twelve, he was already experimenting with girls and pot and booze; this I knew from the middle-school rumor mill. Who knows what might have happened in the future? From where I sit now, it's hard to fathom what sort of tortured logic led me to the conclusion that God decided to kill my brother to keep him from getting into trouble and causing his family grief. I must have been desperate to give some meaning to what had befallen us, to hold onto the notion of a loving, benevolent deity. My years in Sunday school at Saint Paul's hadn't prepared me for this—things like this didn't happen to my family.

We achieved a sort of broken normality the summer I turned fourteen. Edie and one of our parents would spend time in New York, developing protocols with the Sloan Kettering doctors for treating her especially pernicious form of leukemia. My parents began to remake the relationship with Manhattan they had abandoned in 1945. Jed was sent back to Chapel Hill to finish out his degree. My parents, unhappy as they must have been, didn't argue with his stance on the draft, but insisted that he was not going to throw away a four-year Morehead scholarship at the last moment. He got his degree.

That summer we were given the use of a tiny cottage on Skaneateles Lake some twenty miles to the west of Syracuse. Jean and John Amos were old friends of my family, and their daughter Margy was a longtime friend of mine. The Amoses lived in the big cottage up the hill from ours, part of a cluster of early-twentieth-century shingled houses on the lake known as The Colony.

The guest cottage had one room with a fieldstone fireplace and two built-in beds under the big windows that faced the lake. My father and I slept in these. An even tinier cottage, a shack really, served as a separate bedroom for my mother and sister. There was a rudimentary bathroom in the cottage, but the little shack was a dozen yards from the back door.

That summer, Mom and Dad decided I should go to Denver to visit my Turner cousins. I suspect it was so that I wouldn't be at home during the first week of August, which included not only my father's, but my grandmother Dietz's and my brother Ned's birthdays. August is a big month for birthdays and anniversaries in my family. I've never known if Sandy and Julia were trying to spare me, or spare themselves, the sadness of my being present on these birthdays; or simply thought a change of scene would be good for me.

The weeks I spent in Denver turned out to be a blessing for me. My cousin Sandy (real name Olga, but nicknamed like my father because of her middle name, Sanderson) was Ned's age, and that summer we spent a lot of time together, really for the first time in our lives. My aunt and uncle were gentle, welcoming hosts, and I quickly fell into the rhythm of their household. Even their big pink-stucco Spanish house on Race Street in Denver was reminiscent of my family's bowdlerized Spanish house on Sedgwick Drive in Syracuse. The Turners embraced me and entertained me, and in return I was helpful and engaged.

This was also the summer I stumbled upon masturbation, quite by accident. More significant, however, was the fact that the trigger for this happy discovery was a boy.

Each of Robert and Barbara Dietz's four children had four children. My mother told me once that her mother-in-law had pointedly expressed her desire for sixteen grandchildren when she was still a new bride. My mother loved my grandmother Dietz, but made it clear to me that she resented the notion that it was somehow her duty to produce four children as her part of the complete set. Pregnancy was not easy for my mother. She had a miscarriage and lost two babies, one stillborn before Jed, and one after, who lived long enough to be named Mary. The successful birth of my sister in 1951 was a significant triumph. Julia and Sandy were both very involved in the local Planned Parenthood in the 1940s and 50s, my father being the first-ever man to act as chairman of that local organization. With my sister's birth in 1951 and mine in 1955 their family was well-spaced and, they felt, complete. But an unanticipated pregnancy had surprised everyone four months after I was born, and Mom ended up gratifying Grandmother's wish for a large, symmetrically-distributed brood of grandchildren.

Olga and Jake Turner, married in 1948, had two boys and two girls. Tim, the eldest, was away that summer. Tom, who like his younger sister Barbara was a redhead, was forced to put up with me sharing his large bedroom over the attached two-car garage. We reached it by going through my cousin Barbara's room. Sandy had a room across the hall from Barbara. She became my constant companion during that time. We prowled the neighborhood, going so far as breaking into a neighbor's house to play with their pet skunk. Sandy was my surrogate sibling that summer, and I know this helped me recover some sense of order.

At fourteen I was clearly not the precocious teenager my little brother had been. I was physically immature and emotionally introspective. Because he was bigger and older and more worldly, I must have imprinted on my eighteen-year-old athlete of a cousin, who was immodest enough to traipse around our shared sleeping quarters in pale blue boxer shorts. Poor unwitting Tom, I suspect, was the origin of my lifelong thing for redheads. I was certainly secretly obsessed with him that summer, although he and my cousin Barbie spent little time with Sandy and me. One warm night, I was prone in my bed, trying to fall asleep, my mind lost in the inchoate, vaguely sexual thoughts common to most adolescent boys. Why, on that night, my body decided to reveal to me the possibilities of self-stimulation, I can't quite say. There is no doubt that the result was rapid and shattering, not to mention humiliating. I had taken another step on my journey to self-awareness, and it left me with decidedly mixed emotions. Alas, my skills at compartmentalization were also developing rapidly, and I locked that experience away like a piece of kryptonite.

My sister went back to Shipley in the fall. My brother graduated from UNC, grew a beard, and started teaching in a public school in Miami. I sailed through ninth grade at Lincoln Junior High at the top of my class, now endowed with the uncomfortable aura of being the brother of the kid who died.

At some point that year I toured prep schools with my mother and father. On our way to New England we stayed with Mary and Bob Arnstein, friends of my parents in Hamden, Connecticut. Dr. Robert Arnstein had been one of dad's roommates at Deerfield Academy in the 1930s. The two strongest recollections I have from this visit are asking for bacon for breakfast in a Jewish household and seeing Yale University.

The first was innocent enough, since I loved bacon and Mary Arnstein had asked what I'd like for breakfast as I went up to bed the evening before. I have no idea how I had any concept of keeping kosher, but I went to my parents' room in a panic before I went to sleep that night, and they assured me that not all Jews, particularly those who were Ethical Culturalists, followed dietary laws.

The second memory is of walking around the Yale campus, where both Bob and Mary Arnstein worked. This would probably determine my future, although I had no clue at the time. I fell in love with Yale's architecture. Not many people have ever found New Haven charming, but somehow, at fourteen, I did.

We visited four schools that fall. Deerfield Academy was where my father and brother had gone, and the headmaster himself made a point of greeting us. At Governor Dummer, which my Uncle Gerry and two cousins had attended, we were welcomed even more warmly. We didn't know anybody at either the Phillips Academy at Andover or the Phillips Exeter Academy, founded by brothers in the eighteenth century. I fell in love with Exeter. I don't know exactly what appealed to me, but I do remember being desperate to go there.

The next couple of years were, oddly enough, among the happiest of my youth. What I didn't understand at the time was that my parents, having already been through an emotional hell, and understanding that it wasn't over yet, decided that *carpe diem* would be the family motto for the time being.

Keeping their three surviving children happy for as long as they could became the game plan. Amazingly, it worked—for a while at least.

There were several trips to New York City in the fall of 1969 and in 1970. I was still deemed too young to be left at home alone, so I went along. Up until that point, I think I'd been to New York City twice: once when I was six or seven and my parents brought Ned and me to see the Bronx Zoo, the Statue of Liberty, and Grant's Tomb; and again when we were a little older and Dad had his secretary, Penny, fly with us down to New York to see the New York Auto Show at the Coliseum on Columbus Circle. Penny Macrides was part of a big Greek community in Syracuse and was my father's executive assistant from my childhood until he retired from the Dietz Company in 1976 at the age of fifty-five. Even as my father took on the directorship of a local foundation, Penny continued to balance his checkbook for him at home until his decline into dementia rendered that unnecessary. She remained a close friend of my mother's until her own death in the early 2000s.

When New York became a part of my parents' life again, because of my sister Edie's ongoing treatment at Sloan Kettering, my great aunt Grace Root gave them the use of her apartment on East 66th Street, since it was convenient to the hospital. It was a drab box of an apartment, but it faced the Park Avenue Armory on one side, while the master bedroom looked into the garden of what was then the China Institute. When Aunt Grace was in residence, we stayed in hotels. I got to know the streets on that part of the Upper East Side during the two years of my sister's illness. I studied the houses, endlessly fascinated by a kind of urban domestic architecture unknown in my upstate childhood. Although my great-grandfather Elihu Root's townhouse, designed by Carrere and Hastings at Park Avenue and 71st Street, had been torn down a few years earlier, the apartment building into which he and Clara had moved in 1910, 998 Fifth Avenue, still stood, and was little changed since its building.

Another landmark of the early 1970s that my father pointed out to me was the Geraldine Rockefeller Dodge house at the corner of Fifth Avenue and 61st Street. Mrs. Dodge was in a coma and had been for years; in the meantime, her mansion in New York and her country house in Madison, New Jersey, were being maintained as if she would awake at any moment. Her beloved dogs were still kept by her staff in the New York house, or so my father told me. I remember not being impressed by the architecture of the five-story brick house on its corner lot, but the idea that her dogs were being cared for appealed to me. I include this story because during my first years as a young curator at the Newark Museum, the chairman of our board turned out to have been Mrs. Dodge's estate lawyer. As she lay in her coma, he had her Cadillac limousine replaced every two years, and made sure the flowers in the house were fresh every week. When Geraldine Dodge finally died, both houses were demolished in short order.

During one of these New York visits, in the spring of 1970, my parents took me to a new exhibition at the Metropolitan Museum. This was long before the massive modern additions had turned the Met into the sprawling behemoth it has since become. *Nineteenth Century America* was an extravaganza mounted to celebrate the museum's centennial anniversary. Period rooms had been created to showcase the dizzying variety of American decorative arts from the first quarter of the nineteenth century to the early years of the twentieth. My interest in old houses was well established by this time, but I had never seen furnishings like those the Met had dragged out of its own storage or borrowed from other museums—including the one where I would eventually spend my career.

The Victorian part of American aesthetic history had been under a cloud since 1900, branded as the embodiment of bad taste by the generations that included my parents and grandparents. You would have been hard pressed to find significant displays of Victorian material in any American museum in 1970 (one exception being the Brooklyn Museum, which had installed two 1850s period rooms in 1953). What I didn't quite grasp as my adolescent eyes popped at all those amazing objects was that this exhibition would be a game-changer for the entire American curatorial world. All I understood at the time was being overwhelmed by ornate carving, bright-colored damask upholstery, and glittering silver, glass and porcelain objects, the likes of which I'd never seen before. It was a transformative moment, a view into a world I hadn't known existed.

What my mother didn't think to mention that day—if indeed she even knew it—was that another great-great-grandfather of mine, Salem Howe Wales, was one of the founding trustees of the Metropolitan Museum in 1870. Publisher of *The Scientific American*, Wales was among that first generation of Met trustees who envisioned a very different museum from the imperial treasure-house created by the likes of J.P. Morgan in the early twentieth century. Wales was prosperous and politically influential, and it was his smart daughter Clara Frances who had won the heart of the rising young lawyer Elihu Root in 1877. Wales's son-in-law would be the first legal counsel to the young Metropolitan Museum, ensuring that they received the six-million-dollar endowment left to them in 1901 by Paterson, New Jersey, locomotive millionaire Jacob Rogers. My great-uncle Elihu Root, Jr. would become the Met's legal counsel after his father. By the time Elihu Jr.'s brother Edward offered his modern art collection to the Metropolitan Museum, however, the institution's board had little interest in modern art. Uncle Edward's collection, offered to and rejected by the Met, would instead go to the Munson Williams Proctor Institute of Art in Utica, not far from the Root compound in Clinton, New York.

More astonishing was the fact that, later that summer, my father took me on a two-week driving tour of English stately homes, using an itinerary I had planned the previous winter by looking through the pages of borrowed copies of *Country Life* magazine. By the age of twelve I had begun to collect books on houses, and had developed a particular interest in floor plans. I knew little of British history and not much more about architecture, but I yearned to see the great mansions that the British aristocracy built and filled with loot from centuries of empire-building.

Because of my father's indulgence of his quirky adolescent son, I turned fifteen in a two-bedroom suite at the Savoy Hotel in London. We were solid upper-middle-class Americans, but places like the Savoy were not routinely part of our travel plans. Looking back, I realize that this was part of my parents' conscious decision to give their surviving children everything they could, even if that included extravagances they otherwise would have avoided.

My father and I arrived in London two days ahead of my mother and sister, who were going on a safari in East Africa. They had first stopped in at Sloan Kettering in New York to check Edie's stats and deal with a low-grade fever. Dad and I and got to the hotel at midnight. I marveled at the soft mattress in my room (in those days, custom-made in the hotel itself). I wondered at the huge bathtub with its lapis-lazuli-blue tiles. I wrote an embarrassing fanboy note to the management with the steel-nibbed pen and bottle of ink on the suite's Louis XVI writing table, thanking the night steward for fixing me sautéed chicken livers at one in the morning (it was on the room service menu, and I seem to recall that every floor in the hotel had its own kitchen).

On my birthday, a day or two into our stay, Dad allowed me two things that seemed impossibly lavish at the time. At dinner in the hotel's Edwardian dining room, known simply as The Restaurant, he let me order caviar off the menu, an indulgence that must have clashed with every Puritan cell in his body. Dad, probably assuming I'd be too shy to go through with it, also told me that we could hire a Rolls Royce and driver to take us around London if I went to the front desk myself and arranged it. I can't imagine what the concierge thought of the scrawny, terrified American teenager with the wrinkled trench coat and the bad haircut; but I persisted and booked a Rolls Royce for the day that Mom and Edie arrived to join us.

Another childhood obsession of mine was cars. I cared nothing of engines; this was all about design. I loved beautiful cars, not racing cars. Other than my Corgi and Dinky toys, the only Rolls Royces I knew about were the car driven by the title character in the television program *Burke's Law;* and the white one driven by one of our neighbors, a man with the unlikely name of Cloud Wampler, the CEO of Carrier Corporation. I knew Mr. Wampler for his huge back yard and the Asian art gallery at the Everson Museum that bore his name; but that white Rolls Royce was unique in Syracuse. My growing collection of toy cars included variations on the Rolls Royce and its sister marque, the Bentley.

The Rolls I hired for us was a dream come true for my fifteen-year-old brain. It was a Phantom V limousine with paintwork in black and dark blue, and a chauffeur named John Broadly who, while himself wonderfully English, had an ancestor who had been a sheriff in the American West. He was also warm and cheerful and put us all at ease. With the four of us settled in the large rear compartment, my sister and I on the jump seats, he took us all over the city, even pulling up right in front of the tourists crowding the sidewalks in front of 10 Downing Street, before post 9/11 security issues made such a thing impossible. With everybody staring at this huge car, we of course made my mother get out and take home-movies of us with the little Kodak Super-8 camera she'd brought to take to Africa. She was mortified, and I'm not sure she ever got over it.

With my mother and sister carefully packed off to tour game parks in East Africa, my father and I set off on our two-week driving tour of stately homes, Dad driving on the left in a hired teal-blue Rover sedan.

I was fairly indiscriminate: I wanted big and fancy, from Victorian Waddesdon Manor to Baroque Blenheim Palace, to Medieval Holyrood House Palace in Scotland and back down south to the faux minarets of the Royal Pavilion at Brighton. Dad and I saw nearly three dozen houses in two weeks. It was all fodder for my fantasy life, and my father was remarkably patient. We had a great time. What never occurred to me as I was putting together a two-week road trip that must have held minimal interest for my father, was that this was being done for me because I was, simply, still alive. My happiness had become paramount to my parents and indulging me in this was their way of giving me the kind of joyful experience they could never again give my little brother.

Remember, also, that my parents had by this time been forewarned about my being gay, although they had never mentioned it to me. While I had begun to grope my way toward that truth, I wouldn't get there for at least another year. I still wonder if they were trying to make my life happier at that moment, anticipating that I might have a rough time ahead of me.

I happily recorded my English adventures in a leather-bound journal stamped with my name in gold, a gift from my great aunt Ethel Nichols. I recorded the number of rooms in each house Dad and I visited, and the colors of those rooms. This was the first travel journal I ever kept, and it is easily the most embarrassing thing I've written. Later in my teen years I went through and crossed out all the exclamation points, as if that would somehow make it less stupid. Nonetheless, I keep this diary by my bedside to this day, as a reminder of how much I was loved, and how fully I took that love for granted as my parents struggled to hold onto their crumbling life. I can only imagine the conversations they had, when alone in their room, about their younger surviving son.

Dad and I arrived back at the Savoy in London just as my mother and sister returned from their safari, sunburned and exhilarated by their own experiences. Edie divulged that she'd developed a crush on the safari leader, a brooding Scandinavian named Sören, and they had seen all the great animal hot spots my parents had visited during their African sojourn in 1966. Edie also found my brother Jed asleep in my parents' bed, announcing this discovery with a scream. On the spur of the moment Jed had gotten a couple of days off from his job as a page at NBC in New York, and decided to surprise our parents with a quick visit for my father's fiftieth birthday on August 6th. He also explained to us that he'd had to get permission to leave the country from his FBI agent—the one assigned to him due to his draft resistance.

Having sent Jed back to the States after a few days with us in London, we concluded the trip with a week in Ireland. Aside from the usual tourist spots—my diary only noting that Dublin was all soot-blackened and thus a little dispiriting—we trekked to the village of Clonmellon, to visit Mom's cousin, Ida Hanbury-Williams, who lived in the Glebe, built as the house of the Anglican rector of the local parish. Ida was the youngest child of Julia and Michael Cantacuzene, her childhood title having been Princess Zenaida Cantacuzene. At thirteen, my mother had been a bridesmaid in Ida's London wedding to Sir John Coldbrook Hanbury-Williams. Widowed in 1965, Lady Hanbury-Williams had exiled herself to Ireland to escape death taxes, and that was where we found her. I was transfixed, not just by the portrait of a Russian Tsarina over her drawing-room chimneypiece, but by her quick wit and her willingness to engage a shy American teenager in what seemed to me at the time to be a clever conversation. The Glebe was not a great house, but it was elegant, rendered more exotic to my provincial eyes by the pair of slender, quivering whippets who hovered politely in the background, awaiting their mistress's commands. Ida had not been at my grandfather's memorial service in 1968 when I met her brother Michael and her mother. This time around I had more questions, although I have no memory of her answers. I noted in my travel diary that Ida reminded me of Aunt Ethel, only livelier.

We quietly celebrated my parents' twenty-fifth anniversary in Dublin, which back then was still black with centuries of coal soot. Two moments toward the end of this trip stick in my mind. One afternoon, as we were all happily driving down some tiny country lane, my father commented on the "typical Irish lass" walking along the side of the road. By complete coincidence, this young woman turned out to be a classmate of Edie's from Shipley. We must have given her lunch and gone our separate ways. At the very end, we had booked our return trip to New York from Shannon Airport. The whole family was upgraded to first class on our BOAC flight—for the only time in my life until I reached my fifties. We were fed foie gras and caviar, and with our champagne we toasted a group of nuns across the aisle, who had been similarly upgraded. First class isn't like that anymore.

CHAPTER SIXTEEN

A SEPARATE PEACE

The idea of boarding school must seem alien to a lot of people. It never seemed that way to me, since it was something people in my family did. I never felt I was being sent away because I was a problem, or to give my mother and father peace and quiet. I loved being with my family, but prep school was simply a part of growing up. My parents gave me every option. I could have stayed in Syracuse and attended Henninger High School (named for the mayor whose widow was our next-door neighbor); I could also have chosen to follow some of my friends to Pebble Hill School out in the suburbs. But I knew what I wanted, and it was Phillips Exeter, founded by John and Elizabeth Phillips in 1781. It was the largest of all the New England prep schools, located in Exeter, New Hampshire, a picturesquely dying mill town on the Squamscott River about an hour north of Boston.

Having grown up as Grant, at Exeter I became Ulysses.

All through my childhood and adolescence thus far, I had always been Grant, or Grant Dietz. In formal moments, when my full name was called for (such as when I signed the guest book at Grant's Tomb, aged eight), I was U. Grant Dietz. Nobody in Syracuse, not even my family, ever called me Ulysses. Somehow Exeter prompted me to redefine myself, to rearrange all those well-crafted compartments in my brain into some better, newer version of who I wanted people to think I was. Ulysses had been a bad name for the 1950s—too weird, too fancy, tainted by the reputation of a historical figure besmirched with seventy years of carefully-wrought misinformation.

I didn't know about that last part yet, and wouldn't for some years to come; but in 1970 the name Ulysses seemed potentially cool. The trauma of not being able to spell it was long past. The 1960s had done their work, and it was no longer quite so dangerous to step away from conformity. Nobody knew me in Exeter, New Hampshire, so I could be who I wanted to be. As a tenth grader (known at Phillips Exeter as a Lower) I began to sign myself Ulysses G. Dietz. I had already affected the use of a fountain pen filled with peacock-blue ink in junior high, imitating my grandfather Grant. He had imitated his own grandfather's distinctive signature, something I've never been able to master due to my left-handedness (and my surname, of course).

It's ironic that it was at this elite Eastern private school that I, for the first time, interacted with Jewish and African American classmates. There were Blacks and Jews in Syracuse, but Jewish kids didn't attend Lincoln Junior High and I wasn't in classes with the Black kids who attended the school. Exeter had lots of Jewish kids from all over the country. It was also famous as one of the first prep schools to offer scholarships to students of color. Of course, I also had Asian and Middle Eastern classmates for the first time as well, including a grandson of the military dictator of Thailand and the son of the Afghani Minister of Education. Exeter was a cosmopolitan school in addition to its conscious effort at racial and economic diversity. Exeter had also just gone co-ed, and in my first year boasted forty girls, though there was quite an imbalance, with some eight hundred boys in the student body. There were no uniforms, but the boys wore jackets and ties to classes, which were held six days a week, with half-days on Wednesdays and Saturdays. There were no exams at Exeter, except in science and math where it was unavoidable. Instead, there were papers. There were no typewriters, and this was a generation before personal computers. We wrote. A lot.

My Lower-year roommate was a white kid from Columbus, Ohio named Rick who had come to Exeter on a scholarship. We shared a spare little room with a boarded-up fireplace on the second floor of Knight House, a Federal clapboard house on the main street that ran through the academy's sprawling tree-filled campus. Rick would be my mainstay through that first year away from home. He had been raised by his grandparents, simple Ohio country people who promptly nicknamed me "General" when we met on the first day of school. This nickname did not stick, and nobody else ever called me General; but Rick's grandparents would use that name for me for the rest of their lives.

Regardless of my ancestry, I was a provincial small-city boy. During that first semester, in a French class taught by an actual Frenchman, I met Tod. He was introduced to the class by his true given name, Wellington, and quickly corrected our teacher with a terse "It's Tod." Tod was tall and lean and aristocratic-looking—he was unlike anyone I had ever met, with his aquiline nose and mop of dirty-blond hair. He was from New York City and he wore an ankle-length Bavarian policeman's cape with a high collar to stave off the autumn chill. But it was his *name* that captured my attention.

I introduced myself to Tod during afternoon sports that first week. Thin and graceless, I was chugging awkwardly around the wooden track in the barrack-like gymnasium building known as the Thompson Cage (now demolished). I saw Tod up ahead of me, gliding along effortlessly like a proper long-distance runner. I huffed and puffed my way alongside him and somehow managed to stammer out a greeting. He responded in kind, and on that modest footing our friendship began. Decades later he would amuse friends and acquaintances by telling his version of the story, how I came panting up behind him like a big-eyed puppy that he was too kind to kick. We were so different, and yet, ultimately, not that different. He knew right away that I was just looking for a friend.

Tod made me promise that I would not tell much about him in my memoir, and I honor that promise by giving him a *nom de plume*. I'll also say that he is still one of the people on this earth dearest to me. He would play a critical role in my life, but that's for another chapter in this book. Suffice it to say that my two new friends at Exeter, Tod and Rick, never really liked each other, and thus my friendships with them were individual rather than communal. This seems to have been a pattern with friends in my life.

Exeter's main job that first year was to give me, and all straight-A-public-school-students, a reality check. Exeter was demanding. It expected the best of you and, surprisingly, often got it. There were jocks at Exeter, and cigarette-smoking bad boys. But all of them—all of us—were smart. Everybody appreciated intelligence, and thus the kids who eventually excelled despite the school's academic rigor were respected, even if grudgingly. This included me.

This matters because, long before it became a public concern, Exeter was not a place for bullies. There were surely unhappy students as well as rule-breakers. Plenty of students were kicked out for various infractions, especially in my second year; but somehow Exeter, at least for me, was a very different kind of place than a public high school would have been. I was smallish and not athletic. I was not the strangest kid in the place, but neither was I favored with any kind of special talent or beauty. As I had been in junior high, I was funny and quick-witted. My skill at deflecting people with humor kept me safe, and my skill at compartmentalizing kept me sane. I liked being a student and I was not homesick, even though my communication with my parents was limited to letters and a weekly call on the single payphone in the dormitory's entrance hall.

My Lower year I was a coxswain for the crew. Having never in my life set foot in a scull, I was small enough, at 108 pounds, to fit the role. The big, strong, lanky oarsmen listened to me shout "stroke, stroke, stroke" rhythmically as we moved up the smelly Squamscott river in the chill autumn afternoons. I did not fall in love with crew, but it is a strangely pleasant memory. Since there were no winter sports I fancied (no sports at all, to be honest), I was assigned to a general afternoon athletics class cleverly known by the students as Spaz, a contraction of the word "spastic," in a not-so-subtle reference to the kind of boys who presumably took classes like this. Nobody ever made fun of any of us for being in this class, as far as I know. We played volleyball, we did calisthenics, we ran laps on the elevated platform between the *two* indoor hockey rinks in the vast, brutalist concrete gymnasium complex that had just opened the fall I arrived. As you can imagine, Spaz was a magnet for the nerds and the closeted gay boys. In later semesters I would take tennis and squash (the gym boasted twenty squash courts), and, disastrously in the fall of my final senior semester, soccer. I also remember a lot of running outside through the acres of woods and fields that the school owned.

The Exeter campus was a mixture of old and new. The centerpiece was the elegant, brick-and-marble neo-Georgian Academy Building, built in the early twentieth century to replace a Victorian building that had burned, which itself had replaced a Federal style building from the early 1800s. The marble staircases and high ceilings made for pleasant classroom spaces, and there was an actual bell closet off the main hall in which a rope hung—a rope actually pulled by paid students to sound the bell in the cupola and thus mark the beginning and end of each class. The back of the Academy Building faced a slope and thus loomed over the lower quadrangle, framed by the science and language buildings, also in brick, and the arcaded brick administration building where we got our mail and visited our guidance counselors.

That first year saw two events that influenced my burgeoning romantic mind. First, the novel *A Separate Peace,* published by John Knowles in 1959, was turned into a Hollywood film, shot on location at Exeter. All of us had to read this novel for English, because Knowles was an alumnus of the academy and it was set entirely on campus. Watching the book transformed into a film (released in 1972) starring academy students and staff people, was one of the most interesting things that had ever happened to me. One of the characters was played by an actor named Parker Stevenson, a pseudonym based on the name Stevenson Parker, who was an actual classmate of mine at Exeter. The re-named Stevenson would go on to wider celebrity in the *Hardy Boys* television series with Shaun Cassidy.

For teenaged me, the real impact of the book, and thus the film based on it, was the emotional relationship between the main characters, Phineas and Gene. I don't think I consciously recognized the homoerotic undertones, but my heart completely understood it. I had desperate crushes on both characters in the book and their real-life counterparts in the film, and I sobbed at the book's tragic denouement. The school's English teachers never discussed this aspect of the story at all, and I certainly never raised it in class; but I knew what it was really about.

The other big event was the completion of the brick and concrete academy library, now known as the Class of 1945 Library. Designed by architect Louis I. Kahn, the monolithic cube of dark red brick had a monumental inner atrium supported by vast cast-concrete circles. The academy students were enlisted to create bucket-brigades to move hundreds of thousands of books from the old Davis Library into the new one, the boxes working their way up the winding corner stairways over many days. Never had I been so physically engaged with a building, nor present at its birth. Even better, Kahn had designed a new dining hall that sat right next to the new library, with square corner towers and tall brick chimneys on each façade. I think eating so many meals in this remarkable space changed my brain, woke it up to modern architecture in a way it had never been. Coincidentally, Louis Kahn's architecture would play an equally important role in my college life. In the wake of my father's and my British adventure that previous summer, the new Louis Kahn buildings at Exeter helped give me a heightened awareness of and love for the built environment that has shaped my view of the world ever since.

Two more subtle incidents marked that first year at Exeter. One was my Ancient History class with Mr. Smith. He was a handsome, mustachioed, Mr. Chips kind of teacher. I adored him, more aware now that his looks were playing a significant role in my admiration. The first book we studied that year was Mary Renault's *The Last of the Wine.* The fact that my first history text in prep school was the story of two Greek boys falling in love two thousand years earlier felt something like fate. I've been a Mary Renault fan ever since, although it would be many years before I understood that she was a lesbian and brought a personal conviction to her historical fiction.

The second occasion took place in the huge open shower room of the academy's gym. Now, I never seemed to have any trouble monitoring myself; I was never afraid of getting hard in the shower or in a locker room. After all, I was all about self-control. Nonetheless, I remember one day being frozen in place at the sight of a senior under the shower. His name now escapes me, but I remember that he had come to Exeter to polish up his transcript for college and to play football. Whatever the case, this guy was breathtaking, in face and physique, and as I stood there, staring dumbly as water poured over him, I'd found another uncomfortable truth to add to my growing collection. I don't think this was anything as crude as lust; this was yearning for something I didn't fully understand. Yet.

CHAPTER SEVENTEEN

BOYS IN THE BAND

T he tenuous normality that my family had cobbled together carried us through my first year at Exeter. The details are terribly muddled in my mind, but my life involved more trips to New York City. Somehow, I managed to disconnect this from my sister's illness, denying the causality that linked one fact to the other. The doctors at Sloan-Kettering had managed to get Edie into remission, healthy enough to be able to plan on attending her freshman year at Stanford University. When we were in the city, I didn't spend any time in the hospital where my sister was, but would do things with whichever parent wasn't with Edie.

In spite of ongoing treatment, Edie had managed to graduate from Shipley and get accepted at Stanford. The drug regimen she was on had caused significant weight gain as they stabilized her cancerous blood cells. As I watched Edie go up to receive her diploma, wearing a sleeveless white cotton eyelet dress, the whole school rose in unison, applauding. She looked abashed, and I knew she understood that it wasn't just because she was well-liked by her classmates and teachers. It was because she was the brave one. She was a fighter. She was marked by a fate that her friends couldn't imagine happening to them.

For Exeter's January 1971 weekend holiday, I flew alone, for the first time ever, from Logan in Boston to LaGuardia Airport in New York, hitching a ride into Manhattan with a classmate in his father's chauffeured Cadillac. As if that wasn't exciting enough, they dropped me off at the Regency Hotel on

Park Avenue long before my parents arrived. I sat for a while in the lobby while our suite was prepared, watching the flow of fancy people in the discreetly luxurious lobby. Once I was allowed into our rooms, I ordered Eggs Benedict from room service and watched cartoons on the color TV in the suite's sitting room. This trip was a chance for me and my parents to have fun in New York City together. My sister Edie was off at college in Palo Alto with her new boyfriend, Wayne.

Another weekend in New York later that winter took us to the Plaza Hotel. Again, there was a suite, and there were limousines to take us out at night. Just as we arrived at the hotel, word came from Syracuse that my grandfather Robert Dietz had died. This was not a surprise; since my grandmother's death he had dwindled, having lost the means to enjoy life without Barbara at his side. My aunt and uncle had funeral preparations in hand, and we carried on with our own plans, knowing that we'd return to Syracuse to another sad family reunion.

Edie spent the day with my mother on this trip, having a wig fitted at Kenneth's—a big-time salon at the time—due to the loss of her long dark-blond hair from the effects of the chemotherapy. She was back to her pretty, slim self, and the short, stylish wig was becoming on her, even though it didn't quite look right to me. We went out to dinner, and to a movie at Radio City Music Hall. This turned out to be an unfortunate choice, as the British film, deceptively titled *The Christmas Tree*, ended with the death of a teenaged boy from leukemia. My parents managed to hold it together, even as my sister assured them she was OK.

To top off the evening, when we returned to the hotel, my mother discovered that all the jewelry she had brought with her, including a pair of Tiffany sapphire clips my father had given her as a wedding gift in 1945, had been stolen. It was a mystery, and of course the hotel simply reminded us that my mother hadn't availed herself of the hotel safe (this was before they offered those convenient little safes in the closet of every room). My father always suspected it was somehow an inside job, tied to our ordering the car for the evening.

That same year, for spring break, came the cruise to the Caribbean on the Nieuw Amsterdam, one of the great transoceanic liners built in the late 1930s and demoted to cruise ship status before it was finally scrapped. All three of us joined Mom and Dad on this adventure. My parents took a wonderful *style moderne* suite on the outside of the ship (meaning it had portholes), while we three kids got windowless inside cabins. Jed and I had bunkbeds in a neatly paneled box with compact plumbing, while our sister got the same type of quarters all to herself.

In the huge art deco dining salon, our family sat at a round table with three older people from Canada, who couldn't have been nicer. Evening clothes had largely disappeared by this time, especially on cruises; but we wore jackets and ties to dinner. I was favoring dark shirts and light ties to conjure a vaguely Mafioso look, along with a particularly unfortunate Norfolk jacket in rusty wool tweed. Double-breasted, with three buttons that came up as high as my sternum, I thought it was the best.

Jed and I made friends with our two Dutch waiters, one tall and dark with a sweet comical face and thinning hair, the other short and blond, whom I remember as particularly cute. Serving out their Dutch military duty in the Merchant Marine, they took my brother and me behind the scenes, letting us see the crew's quarters and other off-limits parts of the ship.

During the days, I wandered around the ship, having glamorous thoughts as I climbed the great staircase. I also shopped and read in the lounge. My siblings both spent hours sunning on the upper decks, far more than I did, lulled into a sense of lazy security by the warm tropical breeze that endlessly caressed the rows of deck chairs. Both of them got so badly sunburned that they developed blisters, my sister worst of all.

That summer, during which I marked my sixteenth birthday, we rented one of the old cottages at The Colony on Skaneateles from another family we knew. These were pretty basic houses, although spacious, with wide porches and lots of bedrooms. Filled with odds and ends as well as painted wicker furniture and sun-bleached chintz curtains, they were widely spaced along a lengthy stretch of the lake's east side, separated by lawns above a shale bluff overlooking the mile-wide lake. I spent a good deal of that summer, when

I wasn't listening to *Tommy* by The Who with my friend Margy, alone in the dormer of my bedroom, wrapped in a lavender satin quilt, reading Tolkien's *Lord of the Rings* trilogy.

In August, my parents and I returned to Sedgwick Drive and started thinking about getting my sister and me back to our respective schools in the fall. There had been a recent trip to Sloan-Kettering for tests in preparation for Edie's return to California. One evening, as we were sitting out on the screened porch off our dining room, I looked up to find my sister slumping to the floor from her chair, a look of surprise and fear on her face. There is another blur here in my memory, but ultimately Edie was taken away in an ambulance, and eventually flown down to Sloan-Kettering. The theory I heard was that a spinal tap had gone awry. Whatever the reason, Edie was now paralyzed from the waist down. She would never leave the hospital, but I didn't know that yet.

My second year at Exeter started well, despite my anxiety over my sister's health. A teenager's self-centeredness can be a blessing, and as I settled into my new dormitory, a big brick affair in which my room boasted a Palladian window that gave me great pleasure, I clung to an innocent belief that the doctors would take care of everything. Aside from my friends Rick and Tod, with whom I ate dinner separately in different dining halls on alternate nights, I'd made some new friends. Through Tod I'd met his friend Michael, who was surely the gayest boy I ever knew at Exeter. Short and dimpled and rich, from Hillsborough, California, Michael was funny and sharp and sometimes cruel. There were also Gordon and Paul and George, three new boys, two of whom were a year younger than I, and one in the eleventh (Upper) class with me. They were all gay, as it turns out, but in the closet just as I was. None of us would come out to each other until years later.

The brightest light in my Upper year at Exeter was Sarah, an adorable redhead from San Francisco who became, in my own compartmentalized brain, the nearest thing to a girlfriend I ever had. I had given Sarah and her parents a tour of the school during my Lower year, and her smarts and enthusiasm had captivated me. As a Lower, she had no classes with me, but I soon began to spend time with her and the other girls at meals and in the common room of one of the two exclusively female dormitories. As had been the case throughout my elementary and junior high years, I made friends far more easily with girls than with boys; and if I wasn't one of the boys who actively tried to date from the small number of female students available, I had plenty of female companionship, which was, in the end, all I really wanted.

Sarah got very involved in theater while we were in school, particularly after a new theater building was finished in the spring of 1972. Later in my Exeter career I would start to write reviews for the school paper, The Exonian, and have vivid memories of ambitious productions of things as varied as Archibald MacLeish's *J.B.*, based on the Book of Job, to a raucous adaptation of Nikolai Gogol's *The Inspector General*, re-titled for some reason as *The Official Investigator*.

Don't think that I imagined that Sarah was really my girlfriend. I was bottled up, not delusional. I know I desperately wanted to *want* a girlfriend, and I genuinely adored Sarah. The two of us had so much in common, including highly romantic imaginations. After all, I was a sixteen-year-old boy who had a poster of King Ludwig of Bavaria's Neuschwanstein Castle on his dorm room wall, alongside (I cringe to remember this) a centerfold of Barbi Benton that I'd carefully torn from a copy of *Playboy* (to which, bizarrely, I subscribed). Sarah and I never once kissed, but we went so far as to organize a student dance held in the Lamont Gallery—what passed then as the school's art gallery, with the art classrooms in the building behind it—that was entirely based on waltz music. I think we even called it The Last Great Waltz, after a popular comic song of the time. On the big night, I wore my one ill-fitting dark suit, but Sarah made her own ball gown, a dark green velvet dress that set off her red hair and her pale, rosy complexion. I won't say that the dance was a triumph exactly, since we were a little inept at choosing classical music set to three-quarter time—not necessarily the kind of waltz one could actually dance to. I do remember that the two of us and our equally corny friends had a lot of fun.

October 21st was my friend Rick's birthday. We were planning to go out for dinner. It was the last period before lunch, and Mr. Weber had just dismissed my English class into the upper corridor of Phillips Hall, the language building where I took English, French and, eventually, Russian. In the midst of the swarm of teenage boys I spotted my brother Jed, weirdly out of place at my prep school in spite of his tweed jacket and dark necktie. He was off to the side of the crowd of boys and girls moving toward the staircases, clearly looking for me. I went over and hugged him, and without questioning why he was suddenly there, rather than in New York City, followed him downstairs and out into the campus.

My sister had died the day before at Sloan-Kettering, still in the coma into which she had slipped some weeks after being flown by air ambulance from Syracuse to New York. The paralysis in August had been the first sign that the heroic treatments, the experimental drugs, had failed. I had known—we all had known—that Edie's days were numbered, and I accepted this news from my brother calmly. I don't remember any tears, or overt feeling of anguish. If anything, I felt a kind of numb resignation, and I remember feeling weird about my own detachment, as if I was watching myself react to the situation rather than experiencing it directly. Inside, on the other hand, another switch clicked. I had lost a second sibling. My world spun further off its axis. The truce with fate that my parents had negotiated for me, and for themselves, evaporated like a mirage. Edie was nineteen, a little over two months shy of her twentieth birthday. At sixteen, I understood that my sister had been everything I was not: beautiful, charming, and beloved by all. I would spend the rest of my adolescence trying to become like her.

Jed took me out to lunch at a cozy local place I recommended. We talked. I had clam chowder. I think what Jed and I really did over that meal was forge our new alliance as the survivors. Jed is seven and a half years my senior, born in January 1948. By the time I was in third grade he was at Deerfield, and by the time I was at Exeter he was already out of college and working, struggling to determine who he wanted to be in a world where Richard Nixon was the president and Vietnam was on everybody's mind. Now Jed, who had always been the least familiar of my siblings, was all I had. During that quiet afternoon, as he drove us to Logan Airport for our flight to Syracuse, he became my rock.

***

As weird as it seems, someone within my circle of friends at Exeter had the original cast album of the stage production of *The Boys in the Band*, which had been released in 1969. Thinking back, I'm sure it belonged to Michael, a year ahead of me, and a good friend of Tod's. Michael tolerated me because Tod liked me, and he was generally nice to me; but I could tell that he thought I was impossibly provincial, and possibly dim-witted. I also suspect he was impatient with us gay boys who hadn't figured it out yet. The point of this is that I vividly remember a small group of us—Tod, Rick, Michael, me, and maybe someone else—sitting in what must have been Michael's dorm room one Saturday afternoon late that fall, absolutely still and silent, listening to Mart Crowley's play performed on stage. Everybody in that room was gay, even if we hadn't acknowledged it yet. Perhaps this was Michael's way of shoving us all a little closer to the closet door. All I know is that listening to *The Boys in the Band*, which was revived on Broadway in 2018 with a cast of gay actors not yet born when I was in high school, represented a moment of insight and personal liberation for me. It tore something loose inside me: it showed me a world where boys like me were adults, with jobs and families. They were bitchy and funny, two things I understood completely. The fact that nearly all the characters in The Boys in the Band were miserable didn't register, or didn't matter. I suppose unhappiness was less worrisome than isolation. For me, it was a glimmer of light at the end of the tunnel of my adolescence.

I would watch the movie version of that play, released in 1970, on public television at home with my parents sometime later that year. The feelings that bubbled up as I listened to the album were reinforced by seeing those men on screen. I identified with them. They were real and alive, however messed-up their lives were. I didn't see the self-loathing, because I myself didn't feel it. I did see their confusion, because I was confused, too. At sixteen, the idea of being gay was not upsetting so much in what it meant about me, as in the implications for my parents and my family.

In the first semester of my second year, I had a roommate, a handsome African American boy named Calvin who had transferred from another prep school that had shut down. We had two rooms that connected. My room was bigger, but Calvin had to walk through it on the way to his room. I was lying in bed one night, staring up at the Palladian window. I might have been praying, or trying to pray. What I was really doing was letting my mind spin with worry about a future I couldn't see or even imagine. I knew I was gay, but I dreaded being an additional burden of sadness or disappointment for my broken and battered mother and father. Two of us were gone, my surviving brother's future was in danger because of his refusal to enlist in the army and go to Vietnam; and now here I was, queer, a sour cherry on top of a dish full of woe.

I have always scoffed at people who claim God speaks to them. Mostly, the idea of God speaking is a delusion used by those who want to justify mistreatment of others or some scheme to aggrandize themselves. I didn't ask God to make me straight. I never did that. I did, however, ask "why?" Why would God do this to my parents? How could God use me to make Mom and Dad even more unhappy? Why?

Maybe that's the reason I was open at that moment to hearing something I'd never heard before and have never heard since: words, as if whispered quietly in my ear, *Be happy. Live a good life.* To my teenage mind this might have been the voice of God. Whatever it was, those six words answered all my questions and soothed all my fears. All I had to do was live a good life and be happy. Easy. From that moment on, God was no longer a problem. I had no idea how I would accomplish those two simple things; but at least I had a goal, and I could take my time.

My heartbeat slowed, my mind quieted, and I fell asleep knowing where my path lay.

At sixteen, I had not yet begun to yearn for sex as some of my peers must have. Maybe I had simply shut it all down, to keep my mental and emotional compartments watertight. I was not a beautiful boy. I was scrawny and awkward, with no interest in or skill at sports. Nobody was going to hit on me or try to coax me out of my carefully decorated closet. I think if someone had tried—one of those handsome, well-built senior jocks I eyed cautiously as they crossed the campus—I would have probably had a nervous breakdown. I was not ready for sex and I think I took shelter in that lack of readiness.

Even with my sister's death, my parents continued to be generous with me. I don't know if they were compensating for their losses by living large, or simply felt that I was old enough to really appreciate the wider world. Jed was mostly unavailable to travel with us, having founded a theater company in North Carolina with a group of classmates from Chapel Hill. He did manage to join us in Hawai'i during spring break in 1972. We spent the bulk of this vacation at the then-undeveloped island of Maui, and specifically on the rainy side, called Hana, where large tracts of land had been preserved. Two significant residents of this island paradise were Samuel Pryor and Charles Lindbergh. Both were deeply involved with the creation of Pan American Airlines. Hana's only hotel was quiet, breezy, and lushly landscaped, filled with barefoot staff people and the scent of plumeria. Guests at the hotel were hosted at a private reception in the Pryors' own house and invited to swim at their private beach. Lindbergh and his wife were not part of this, but we saw their house from a distance through the tropical greenery. Other than watching my parents drink stingers and play backgammon late into the evening, my other memory of this trip is sitting up with Jed in our bungalow, watching Lauren Bacall live on television in *Applause* (a musical adaption of *All About Eve*) at two in the morning.

The summer I turned seventeen marked the last marathon vacation I ever took with my mom and dad, although it was not the last time we'd travel together. My seventeenth birthday was celebrated in Tallinn, Estonia, but that auspicious event, at which I was toasted with sparkling red wine, was near the end of a month-long adventure in Scandinavia and the Soviet Union.

Embracing the notion that Europe was a long way away, and thus one should pack as much as possible into any trip abroad, my parents had conceived a two-part extravaganza. The first was a ten-day round-trip voyage up the Norwegian coast from Bergen to Kirkenes on a mail packet called the Vesterålen. My Aunt Olga and Uncle Jake Turner joined us on the trip with my cousins Olga, Barbie, Tom, and Tim. Although we sailed in and out of endless breathtaking fjords, and went ashore routinely to see the sights, the ship was a working cargo vessel; delivering goods as diverse as washing machines, bicycles, and slabs of frozen reindeer, to cities and towns all up and down that rocky, mountainous coast. Because it was summer, the sun barely set at all, and then only at about two in the morning for an hour or so. Whenever we docked, we'd all drag ourselves out of bed no matter what time it was and go up on deck to see what was going on. An enthusiastic young Norwegian woman named Uni was our group guide, and close enough to us in age to become our compatriot on the trip.

We left the Turners in Bergen in a huge suite at the Hotel Norge that looked like something out of a James Bond movie. My parents and I joined another tour, jumping from Oslo to Stockholm to Copenhagen before we flew to Helsinki, which in those days was the only access point for tourists to the Soviet Union. Russia in 1972 was very different from what people know today. Intourist, the government tourism bureau, controlled every aspect of our stay, from the hotels to the tours we took. One didn't ever wander around unescorted, although you could arrange private taxis to specific approved sites. We stayed at the tall, modern Intourist Hotel in Moscow, just off Red Square, where we ate caviar with every meal and stout, dour women sat at desks on every floor to keep an eye on hotel guests.

My father was convinced our rooms were bugged. The maids left cigarette butts in the toilet.

In Leningrad, we stayed in a new hotel called, unimaginatively, the Leningrad. It had two huge marble foyers, black downstairs and white upstairs, and very comfortable rooms. Even in its Soviet guise of soot and shabbiness, Leningrad was magical for me, with its palaces and Italian baroque architecture. Of course, my big old house fetish was in full sway, as well as my memory of meeting my Great Aunt Julia, the Russian princess, who was ninety-six by this time.

I got frustrated by my inability to read the street signs, and one afternoon I threw a mild tantrum and stayed in my room, sitting with a stack of postcards with bilingual captions, trying to parse out the Cyrillic alphabet. This trip would inspire me to start studying Russian at Exeter in the fall.

The group we traveled with was congenial and surprisingly diverse, though within the subset of Americans who could afford this kind of venture. I was the youngest person on the trip by a quarter century. I enjoyed the attention, since my teen awkwardness was beginning to fade and I had always been comfortable with people older than myself.

After Moscow and Leningrad, we ended the tour in Tallinn, where our bus was t-boned by the only other car in sight in the middle of the day as we rode from the airport to our sleek, Finnish-designed hotel. Our tour guide, a Brit by the name of Powell, was fond of sherry, and was in the midst of telling us something important when the car hit us (I watched it, unbelieving, as it came straight down an empty, tree-lined side street and plowed into us without even slowing). Unbalanced, Mr. Powell toppled down the little stairwell at the front of the bus and got rather banged up, though not hurt badly. None of this prevented him from joining us as I was feted for my birthday that evening. I'm pretty sure I had my first taste of reindeer with my red champagne.

Only with the hindsight of middle age was I first able to look back and realize that it was also during this time of my life that my father's drinking went from social to something a little darker and more desperate. As I've described, cocktails at my grandparents' house were a daily ritual in my family. Now, I was a rule-follower and didn't drink, even college, until I turned eighteen and was legally allowed to (back before the drinking age was raised to twenty-one). My father, on the other hand, was a classic *Mad Men* executive who had martinis at lunch and two more when he got home from a long day at the office. The happy memories associated with these evenings are of my mother, dressed à la Katharine Hepburn in velvet slacks and a silk blouse, sitting in the living room as Vernice cooked dinner, sipping her J&B Scotch while my father read the paper and had his martini. The less happy memories seem to have started after my life at boarding school began, and particularly after my sister's death.

Whichever of my father's inner demons had provoked the family counseling sessions of the mid-1960s, during which Ned and I were studied and tested by the Dietz Company psychiatrist; I think the double whammy of losing two children as he hit his early fifties probably pushed him from being a habitual drinker into what I can now recognize as an alcoholic. Of my parents, my father was the romantic, the emotional one. His gentleness and sensitivity were what appealed to my mother in the first place, and this made their marriage more of a partnership of equals than other marriages I saw growing up in Syracuse. It's easy for me to see how he might use drink to numb the pain of losing both parents and two children in the space of three years.

Understand, of course that never in his lifetime did my father—or my mother, for that matter—acknowledge his alcoholism. Dad was a highly functional drinker, and liquor never affected his work, that I know of. I remember him telling us horror stories in our childhood of his own desperate attempts to save a former Deerfield classmate from drinking himself to death as an adult. But the Dietz family were all drinkers, and I remember waiting with my cousins after the annual company board meetings to see which way the drinking would take the adults that evening: whether they would be sentimental, weeping and hugging; or bellicose, picking fights and arguing. My cousins and I pretended it was funny, but there was an underlying discomfort with alcohol that we couldn't quite hide.

At some point in my Exeter career, in the year or two following my sister's death, I began to come into conflict with my father. I was never the instigator, and it was never over anything I had done. It would always begin with a question, posed randomly by him and without any sort of preamble, something like: "What did you do to help your mother today?" It sounds silly, but moments like these are bad memories for me. My father would ask questions like this, and then, when I couldn't answer adequately (and I never could) he would begin to berate me and criticize my laziness. There aren't many details left in my recollection, but these incidents always ended with me in tears, going up to my room—my late sister's room, which was now my room, her canopied four-poster bed now my bed. If my mother tried to defend me, Dad would just get angry at her as well.

Now, you realize, I was a very easy child, or as easy as any teenager in the 1970s could be. I didn't smoke or drink, I had not yet even kissed another human being other than in a familial way. I didn't break rules, I didn't run up debts, I didn't (yet) cause my parents any anxiety. In addition, I was a great student and would finish both Exeter and Yale with a straight-A average. My overcompensation in reaction to the loss of my siblings was largely complete: I had become, by sheer force of will, charming, outgoing, gregarious—always masking my fears and shyness to appear to be the kind of person that people liked. I had taken on what I saw as the best attributes of my lost siblings, without being able to acquire either their looks or their effortless ease with people.

So where did my father's hateful talk come from? These nasty moments were as confusing as they were wounding. I would in time come to understand that it was the liquor talking, and I have no doubt it was triggered by a mixture of grief and whatever turmoil Dad was battling inside himself.

Honestly, it was only in my forties that my brother talked to me about this, suggesting not only that our father's verbal attacks on me were abusive, but were caused not by anything I did, but by his drinking. By the 1990s, Gary and I had long since learned that visiting my parents always came with the risk that there would be a blow-up from my father. I learned not to take it personally; but I never learned how to make it painless. Never in my life did I doubt that my father loved me and was proud of me. He was always generous with his praise and unstinting in his support of my career. This only made these moments of anger worse, because they made no sense. Always, the next morning, my father would come to breakfast and act as if nothing had happened.

By the end of my senior year, Exeter had become home for me. It might seem odd to say it, but I loved it. I was happy there. I graduated early, in January, high in my class (Exeter didn't publish class rankings, because, as Exonians, we were all seen as exemplary). My parents invited my friend Rick to join us in New York to celebrate, which is largely memorable because of a weird historical coincidence. As Rick and I were watching a replay of Lyndon B. Johnson's recent funeral on television in my parents' suite at the Plaza, a news report came in that President Nixon had rescinded the military draft. Rick and I bounced up and down on our beds in joy as Anita Bryant sang LBJ to his heavenly rest.

Vietnam loomed over all of us back then. My brother Jed had refused the draft back in 1969—which is not the same as dodging the draft. He reported for induction and then stated that he refused to serve in an unjust war. He was assigned an FBI agent, and fully expected, to Mom and Dad's dismay, to go to prison. Jed did not want to flee to Canada (which, by the way, saw one of the largest waves of immigration in its history from the United States because of the Vietnam War). Jed did not want to claim Conscientious Objector status, because he didn't feel his beliefs were religiously based. He, like many other young people at the time, saw this war as unjust and unwinnable (especially after the *Washington Post* revealed how much the government had been lying to us about the pointlessness of the war in 1971). Luckily, my brother's case had been thrown out by the Supreme Court on a technicality, so, by the time I graduated from high school he was finally free of that worry. The Vietnam War had changed my brother from a young Republican to a liberal Democrat. He had friends who'd fled to Canada and others who had gone to prison for their refusal to be drafted.

By the time I graduated from Exeter that January in 1973, college deferments had been eliminated. I knew I was up for the draft lottery that summer when I would be turning eighteen, and I also knew that I would be able to avoid the draft if I "checked the box," declaring that I was homosexual and therefore unfit to serve. As it turned out, my number in the draft that summer was four. Nixon's decision to announce the end the draft the week of Lyndon Johnson's funeral neatly avoided forcing my hand in a decision I wasn't yet ready to make.

After that festive winter weekend in New York, I did something that to this day surprises people: I went back to Exeter after the January break for a post-graduate semester. Tod graduated with me, but had bolted as fast as he could, joining his mother in the South of France. Michael had graduated the year before, but I still had Rick, along with Gordon and Sarah, who were both a year behind me. The attraction to the post-graduate semester that Exeter offered was that you didn't have to take classes on weekends, and all your classes were pass/fail. I continued with Russian and French, and feasted on F. Scott Fitzgerald, which I read on my own, simply writing book reports. My love of Fitzgerald started with *The Great Gatsby*. A book that helped produce my first A paper in English, it fired my imagination. Jay Gatsby's glamour and mystery fascinated me. The pithy quotation under my preppy photograph in the 1973 PEAN (Exeter's yearbook, Phillips Exeter Academy News) was taken from *The Great Gatsby*: "It was testimony to the romantic speculation he inspired that there were whispers about him from people who had found little that it was necessary to whisper about in this world."

I doubt if anyone was really whispering (or even thinking) about me in my senior year at Exeter, but my burgeoning self-awareness made me feel that this quotation was somehow scandalous.

Another major attraction of this post-grad semester was that there was no sports requirement, which was a mercy, since my final attempt at soccer had simply resulted in constant humiliation as ninth graders (Preps) literally ran circles around me. My lack of interest in sport wasn't purely physical (although, I have never enjoyed sweating or any sort of exertion). I am not remotely competitive, and thus the main force that drives most young men forward in these endeavors eluded me. The only thing that motivated me was the enjoyment I took from doing something, and that includes, to this day, both physical and mental effort.

The significant leap I made outside my own box in this final semester was agreeing to act in a melodrama that one of my group of female friends was putting on in the little "black box" theater within the new Fisher theater complex. I continued to cover the main-stage productions for *The Exonian*, but this was a short, comic melodrama called *Love Rides the Rails*. Maybe it was someone's project for a drama class. I suspect the play was written as a spoof, but all I specifically remember about it was my character's name: Simon Darkway (false mustache and all). The very idea that I was willing to take this on suggests that my friend Sarah was very persuasive, and that I had begun to detach myself from my fear of public performance. I couldn't wear my glasses on stage, which left me largely blind, but that actually helped because the audience was blurry and in shadow and thus less intimidating. Hamming it up was no problem, and my aplomb even held up when my scenery-chewing evil minion tripped on the fake railroad tracks and fell through the backdrop, leaving a partial vision of Venice hanging down onto the supposedly rural setting in which *Love Rides the Rails* took place. There was only a single performance, and while it was no artistic triumph, it pushed me forward a little further.

In March of 1973 we all went to our mailboxes to find letters from the colleges to which we had all applied. I had applied to three schools, each for a fairly stupid reason. The first was Williams College, which I'd never seen, because my father had wanted to go there (but didn't get in). The second was Stanford University, because my sister had gone there. I've still never seen it. Finally, I applied to Yale, because I remembered loving the campus architecture when I visited with my parents during my prep school scouting trip.

I got into all three, which made me guilty, because I had friends who didn't get into their top choices. Stanford was too far away from my family, and Williams was barely larger than Exeter. Without too much hesitation, I chose Yale. I knew I'd need a big school in which to reinvent myself yet again. I'd be lying if I wasn't impressed by the idea of going to an Ivy League school. Of my 300 fellow graduates, nearly a third of us attended Harvard, Princeton, or Yale. Thirty of my Exeter classmates would follow me to New Haven. Only my friend Tod, who had decamped for the south of France as soon as we graduated in January, would continue to be a close friend at Yale.

My graduation present from my parents was a Student Eurail Pass and three hundred dollars. This largesse allowed me to spend a month traveling around France by train and to practice my pretty good high-school French with my friend John, who was a year behind me in school. We'd met in French class and become close in my final year at Exeter. It was the first time I'd traveled so far without Mom and Dad, and while the journal I kept of this adventure isn't quite as embarrassing as the one I wrote at fifteen in England, it comes pretty close. By this point, you'll recall, I'd not only affected using fountain pens, but also using peacock-blue ink, mimicking my grandfather Grant. My French journal was all written in peacock blue ink. To this day I use peacock-blue ink and a fountain pen for important signatures.

John's family owned a large electronics manufacturing company that later, like the Dietz Company, disappeared into the maw of corporate mergers in the 1990s. At one point early in our journey around the perimeter of France we stopped in Tours, and checked in with a local affiliate of his family business. There, to our mixed delight and horror, we were treated like visiting dignitaries and given a complete tour of the factory as well as treated to a lavish dinner at a little chateau-restaurant outside the city. The company president's secretary arranged for us to rent *vélo-moteurs* (i.e. bicycles with little motors that could achieve a whopping fifteen miles an hour) so that we could more easily explore the Loire Valley and its châteaux. We did our best to act adult. Although we were only seventeen, our French was honestly passable. However, I confess I cringe at the memory of us, two skinny, over-educated children of privilege, taking all this attention for granted. I didn't tell my parents about the rented motor bikes until I was safely home.

The most remarkable thing about the travel diary I kept for this journey is what I didn't say. For a boy seething with the knowledge of his own unexpressed sexuality, my diary offers nary a hint of it (John, though nerdy like me, was totally straight and we never in all our conversations came anywhere near a discussion of anything related to sex). During our visit to the factory complex in Tours, a young American intern named Alex, who was at Yale, accompanied us. I mention him in my diary, but do not say what I was really thinking during the time he spent with us. He was beautiful, with long light-brown hair, cut in a sort of rock-star shag that was fashionable back then for preppy boys who had good hair. He had blue eyes and a dazzling smile, and I was all but dizzy in his presence the whole time we toured the factory, trying to look fascinated by machinery. It's some indication of how uptight I still was that not a peep about this made it into the turquoise fountain-pen scrawl that filled the pages in that journal.

CHAPTER EIGHTEEN

SEQUINS AT YALE

In 1973 a pseudonymous author calling himself John Reid published a book entitled *The Best Little Boy in the World.* Hilarious and heartbreaking by turns, it tells the story of a young man grappling with his homosexuality while at Yale. It must have appeared in bookstores right around my eighteenth birthday, which I had celebrated at a Michelin two-star restaurant in Biarritz, France with my friend John. Because Yale was the setting for the book, it must have been available in the Yale Co-op, and thus I snatched it up during the first weeks of my freshman year. I kept it under my pillow on the top bunk of room 1888, Silliman College, but that was more to keep it hidden from my roommates than because I needed it that close to me. Ironically, perhaps, the author (who turned out to be the economist and writer Andrew Tobias) went to Harvard, and only used Yale as a setting to throw people off his scent. I read that book cover to cover and held onto it for dear life as I started my college career in New Haven. The title struck home because I, too, was the best little boy in the world.

I had loved my years at Exeter, but I had done well academically as much to make my parents happy as to please myself. I needed to maintain the illusion that I was a perfect child, in spite of what I knew about myself. I needed to excel to make up for the loss of my brother and sister. The greater irony here is that my parents already knew I was not like their other children and had never in any way pressured me to live up to some arbitrary standard of WASP distinction. I should have understood by this time that Julia and Sandy were simply glad that I was alive and only wanted me to be happy.

My exultation at being an Ivy League student lasted all of a moment. Once my three roommates at Yale, Gene, Wayne, Robert, and I settled into our routine, college was college. Thirty of my Exeter classmates had joined me at Yale, and none of us were particularly impressed with each other.

We all had freshman requirements (thank God not calculus, but science, which was do-able) and a whole, new, complex social world to negotiate. In my heart, I had hoped to start college as a blank slate. I had been Ulysses for three years now, and nobody at Yale, other than my friend Tod, had ever known who Grant Dietz was. Of course, I wasn't entirely sure who I was, either. I had no idea what my major would be, or what I wanted to do with my life. The only vague notion rattling around my brain was becoming a French teacher, and with my memories of junior high and the way we treated our French teacher then, it wasn't a wholly appealing prospect. The careerism of today had begun its quiet drumbeat in the wake of the turbulent sixties, but in 1973 we were all still expected to get liberal arts educations, even if we planned on being lawyers or doctors. I signed up for French, Russian and English, with a big freshman survey course in art history, taught by the remarkable Vincent Scully. For my science requirements, I took Psych 101 and an astronomy course (I initially signed up for a geology course, but at the mention of the term "fieldwork" I dropped it like a hot...um...rock). Weirdly, psychology and sociology courses seemed to count as "humanities" for science majors and "science" for humanities students. As it turned out, psych and sociology were not only among my favorite courses but would prove to be useful throughout my subsequent life.

I probably was more in love with the goofball architecture of Yale's urban campus than most students. I was enthralled with its Disneyesque Oxbridge/Colonial New England pretension, which, for all its fraudulence, was beautifully crafted as only old WASP money could make it. The same oil millionaire, Edward S. Harkness, who had endowed Exeter had also dropped a pile at Yale, getting the great gothic campanile in the center of campus named after him. All this collegiate gothic/colonial was mixed with some icons of modern design, like Paul Rudolph's Art and Architecture building, Eero Saarinen's Morse and Stiles colleges, and the marvelous serpentine spine of Saarinen's hockey rink, all from the 1960s. I was less happy with Philip Johnson's dour brown-brick Kline Biology Tower at the top of Hillhouse Avenue. The Kline tower had replaced an important Greek revival mansion called Sachem's Wood that had formerly crowned that storied street, once described by Dickens as the most beautiful street in America. I loved the architecture of New Haven itself—a seventeenth-century Puritan colony layered with successive centuries of architectural patchwork. New Haven was hardly a showplace in the early 1970s, but I arrived there at a happy moment before the slump of the 1980s and the eventual flourishing of the twenty-first century.

Tod was right there, from the start, and I quickly realized that being his friend was more important than fitting in to whatever other collegiate social structure I might have stumbled toward. Yale was then divided into twelve residential undergraduate colleges, each presided over by a professor, whose grand house was incorporated into the structure of the quadrangle dormitory complex. Freshman are housed in the Victorian dormitories on what is known as the Old Campus—except for the freshman of Silliman and Timothy Dwight Colleges. I was in Silliman, and Tod was across the street in Timothy Dwight.

We took astronomy and psychology together, and then shared a comparative religion course the next semester. Because he had to sign into classes with his legal name, Tod was officially Wellington, and with Wellington and Ulysses together on the roster in a freshman lecture, I guess we attracted attention. When we signed into the comparative religion course, taught by a great scholar named Theodor Herzl Gaster, a British Jew who was a practicing Buddhist, we were seated in the last row. Every single student turned to look back at us as the sign-in clipboard moved to the front of the room on the first day of class.

The two of us developed a strange sort of friendship with our bright, diminutive psych professor, Alice, with whom we studied both semesters that year. I think we intrigued her; or puzzled her, more likely. What never occurred to me is that Alice might well have seen me and Tod as a couple (the immediate quip "a couple of what?" jumps to mind). This could possibly have been fueled by the project Tod and I decided to do together in that first semester. To this day I shake my head at it: we cooked up a questionnaire that we distributed to our classmates in Silliman College. I can't quite remember what the precise goal was, but it was supposed to be looking at the identifying traits that college freshmen would use to perceive someone as gay.

I kid you not. We really did this. Why we thought this was a good idea, I can't imagine. Beyond the fact that as eighteen-year-olds we were hardly trained to produce such questionnaires, the idea that two closeted teen-agers would do something that would focus attention on themselves along with this topic seems counterintuitive. Or insane. Or, possibly, wishful.

And that, I think, was the semi-conscious point. Tod and I were doing a dance around each other, each of us knowing who we were, and suspecting who the other was, but having never confessed the truth to each other. This absurd survey project let us talk about it without committing ourselves. It be-came an intellectual exercise, rather than a baring of souls. With totally unprofessional shame I recall a particular freshman in our college, a strapping blond boy with a mane of curly hair, who admitted to posing nude for art clas-ses to earn spending money. I really wanted to know more about him. I suppose I really wanted to know if, to him, I looked gay. The whole thing is utterly crazy in retrospect, but it just seemed like an adventure at the time. I know we got an A on this project, in addition to our friendship with Alice and her hus-band Bruce, who was a fabulous cook. They would invite us to their apartment for long gourmet brunches, filled with laughter and smart Ivy League conver-sation.

Oh, shit, they really did think we were a couple.

My roommates liked Tod, and Tod, in his cool way, liked them enough. He couldn't abide his roommates in Timothy Dwight College and quickly moved to an apartment across the street from Silliman.

Tod didn't like my dowdy prep attire, and he set about making me chic as soon as he could get me into New York City. His mother was in the fashion business, and I was dazzled by Tod's Big City life, as I had been since we first met. This forces me to confess another slightly bizarre behavior that started freshman year, once I decided that I wasn't going to be a boola-boola sort of Yalie. I began to dress more like a 1970s hairdresser than a prep-school trained brainiac. Surely with Tod's influence, I began sporting wide-legged bellbottoms, tightly fitted to my then 29-inch waist. Slim-cut shirts, and gold-rimmed aviator glasses. Sleek little Italian shoes I got at a store in New York called McCreedy & Schreiber were topped off with a swept-back haircut parted in the middle that battled my natural waves and cowlicks. I affected silk scarves knotted at my throat (gayer looking than an ascot). I even bought clogs, those wooden shoes with leather uppers that hit the stores in the early 1970s. Lots of girls wore clogs, but few boys did. Clomping around the Yale campus in those was the kind of indicator that showed up on that psych 101 question-naire Tod and I had cooked up.

The kicker was a shirt that Tod brought me as part of his campaign to give me some style. It was a skin-tight long-sleeved red t-shirt with a scooped neckline. Sewn onto the chest was a large appliqué in the shape of a 1910s open touring car, all done in sequins. I know for a fact that two of my Exeter acquaintances shunned me after they saw me wearing this. I also recall that Wayne, my jock roommate (who went on to be a doctor) told me that he liked that I was true to myself, and that he'd support me.

So, as a freshman, I was apparently out in every way but the actual one.

***

The summer after my freshman year was an accidental life-changer. My family had abandoned Skaneateles Lake. My parents had refurbished and redecorated a little 1930s prefabricated log cabin on a large piece of land on Cazenovia Lake, twenty miles east of Syracuse. The cabin originally came with more than twenty acres of woods and 300 feet of lakefront. Determined not to fill it with crummy leftovers, Dad and I had scoured design stores in Copenhagen during our marathon vacation in 1972. We found everything from spartan Finnish bath towels of striped woven linen to outrageous sofas of laminated plywood lacquered in high-gloss white. We bought folding chairs by Hans Wegner that you could hang on the wall to save space, and stainless-steel Danish flatware that hung in its own little teak case on the wall—again to save space. Heavy Danish glassware and blue and yellow Arabia pottery made sure that this tiny cabin would be bright and stylish and new.

At twenty-three feet square, the cabin was just large enough to have two tiny bedrooms and a bathroom with a stall shower. No closet space at all. A fieldstone "Heatilator" fireplace on one wall and a galley-style kitchen unit that Dad and I found somewhere made it into a functioning house for the summers. Sandy and Julia added a large screened front porch, replacing the tumbledown version that was there already. That became the dining room, furnished with yet another purchase from Denmark, a handmade oak dining table that flipped open to seat six, with a set of modern rope-seated chairs.

At about this time friends of my parents from Syracuse had built a large French style manor-house on a big piece of land farther down the east side of the Cazenovia Lake. They had given it a cute, cottagey name, which rather contrasted with the grandeur of the house itself. Inspired by the naming of that house, in a fit of teenage irony, I commissioned a local potter (whose family had, in fact, built our cabin) to make an elaborate terra cotta plaque that would hang over the entrance to the cottage. I christened our place Versailles and gave the plaque to my parents for their anniversary that summer. Sandy and Julia thought it was hilarious, and it remained in place, long after the house they later built onto the cabin made the joke less amusing.

I was alone with my parents at the lake that summer. One morning, I stood on the shore staring down the lake toward the village of Cazenovia, an adorable confection of old houses and quaint businesses that also served as a community center for the extensive farmland surrounding it. At the eastern end of the lake stood Lorenzo, a grand classical-style mansion of buff-painted brick. I vaguely recalled that it had been built by the founding family of the village in 1807 and had recently been turned over to the state as a museum. Without any forethought beyond my attraction to the house, I drove my new 1974 pee-yellow Chevy Vega hatchback (stick shift, to save gas) over to Lorenzo and parked in the shade of an ancient black locust tree.

Russell Grills was the newly appointed Site Director of Lorenzo. The great house, worthy of any American city in the early 1800s, had been built in the wilderness by John Lincklaen, the Dutch-born upstate agent for the Holland Land Company. Having named the town after his European boss, Theophile de Cazenove, Lincklaen settled in to sell off plots of land on what was then the frontier. The house had remained in the family until the death of the last bachelor resident, George Ledyard, in 1969. The buildings and the land were sold to the State of New York, with the house's full contents given as part of the deal. It was an amazing place, grand and spacious in a very neoclassical way, with 160 years of accumulated stuff crowding every room and closet and attic space. Russell signed me up immediately as a volunteer for the entire summer, and set me to whatever task needed doing, from mopping the tiled front hall to bringing piles of uncatalogued Chinese export porcelain down from the bat-infested attic. Once I knew the history of the house and the family, I started to give tours, and discovered that I had an aptitude for docentry. Russell and his wife Susan became friends and mentors.

Because the house had become the family's summer house by the 1870s, it had never been remodeled in any significant way, retaining all the old bits and pieces of multiple generations. It was a material culture candy store for a kid like me. At one point that summer, as I was cataloguing a first edition set of Voltaire's writings that had belonged to the house's builder, it suddenly dawned on me that *people actually made a living doing what I was having so much fun doing.*

And just like that, I had a career path.

Back at Yale in the fall, my Vega safely stashed in the distant under-graduate garage up on Science Hill, I started taking courses in the history of American decorative arts. Yale was one of the few universities that actually offered such courses, because of the remarkable 1930 gift of Francis P. Garvan, conservative industrialist and Yale alum who was one of the great collectors of Americana in the early twentieth century. He competed with the likes of Delaware's Henry Francis duPont and Boston's Maxim Karolik. A few years before my arrival, the university had hired Charles F. Montgomery to be the curator of this huge collection of furniture, silver and other decorative arts. CFM, as I would come to call him, oversaw the edgy new installation of the Garvan Galleries in the Yale University Art Gallery, designed by Ivan Chermayeff in 1972. Montgomery, and his redoubtable wife Florence, would become my mentors, and the Yale University Art Gallery would become my home over the next four years. Although I had no idea, I had stumbled into the field of American decorative arts at the very moment when Yale was filled with students, graduate and undergraduate, who would help change the face of the field in American museums in the coming generation.

Thus, by sophomore year, I had found an academic direction. I would declare as a French major, because an art history major was unfeasible (that would require German or Italian, and I was overloaded with languages al-ready). I continued with Russian for another two years, but had to drop English, and dig into American art history (taught by the great expert on Martin Johnson Heade, Theodore Stebbins).

I had found my place at Yale. But I still hadn't quite figured out who I was going to be, sequins notwithstanding.

CHAPTER NINETEEN

A Short Story
BORN AGAIN

Ulysses sat at his desk, staring at the book open before him. It was an interesting book, for a course he loved. But the words refused to come into focus; his brain could not shake the image that had been stuck there since he got back from class.

Michael. Feathered dirty-blond hair. Dark eyes. Turned up nose. A suggestion of dark-golden stubble along his jaw line.

Fuck.

Ulysses buried his face in his hands and groaned. He felt he was going crazy.

Freshman and sophomore years had been great. Or, at least, he'd kept himself tightly under control and focused on coursework, which was more or less the same thing. Only one B+ in two years, earning straight A's otherwise. The lack of much social life had been well worth the results. He didn't smoke. He didn't drink. He didn't have sex. He figured social life without those wasn't much different from what he had anyway.

And there had always been Tod—amusing, loyal, cynical Tod—to distract him. Best friends at Exeter. Now roommates at Yale.

Ulysses thought back to his first day at Yale, sitting in the ground-floor living room of the suite he shared with three roommates. Three Jewish roommates, two from Long Island, one from Canada. They had all laughed that the Yale housing people had assumed that the ultra-WASP Ulysses's German surname was Jewish, and had placed him with three Jewish freshmen in order to keep all their minority students safely clustered. Joking aside, Jewish quotas at Yale were not so long in the past in 1973, so maybe his roommates had been right.

Sitting there on the cheesy Salvation Army vinyl couch the four room-mates had purchased together, Ulysses had been staring out the window into the college quad, when suddenly Tod's deeply tanned face had popped into view.

"Hey Grantie," he said, his smile wide and his green eyes flashing beneath a mop of curly sun-bleached hair.

Tod knew that Ulysses hated the diminutive nickname, used only by his Bostonian grandmother when he was a child. Wondering why he'd ever divulged that bit of information to his best friend at prep school, Ulysses beamed back at Tod and gestured for him to come around to the dorm entrance.

As soon as Tod's head disappeared from the window, Gene, one of the Long Island roommates, had looked up from his reading and asked, "Who's the fag?" There was no hostility in the question.

It was in that moment Ulysses had realized that schoolwork was going to be his thing in college. Just as it had in prep school. Although he didn't know that he would keep these roommates for two years, because they essentially got along well and worked at their studies and didn't party over-much, Ulysses had understood in that casual question that his fantasy of a new beginning at university, anonymous and blank-slated, was doomed. If Tod had been tagged so easily, so would he be.

Tod appeared in the doorway, oblivious to the change in climate in the room during the thirty seconds or so since he'd vanished from the window. Tall, aristocratic in both bearing and looks, Tod wore tight bellbottom jeans and a short-sleeved blue gingham shirt that clung to his lean frame. He had fled the snow-packed fields of Exeter in January after they both graduated early, leaving Ulysses to luxuriate in a post-graduate semester, taking his courses pass-fail, sleeping late on Saturdays, and generally learning what he wanted to without the pressure that Exeter used to forge high-achievers. Tod had joined his mother in St. Tropez for the winter, then summered on the Great Lakes with his father. He looked fit and rested. And very gay. That fact hadn't figured into Ulysses' calculations for his new life at Yale.

But he rose from the couch, its cheap faux-leather upholstery squeaking under his sweaty legs, and went to stand by his friend. Turning, he introduced Tod to his roommates.

"Gene, Robert, Wayne; this is Tod, my best friend from high school."

And with that they both turned and walked out into the warm late summer afternoon to catch up on the months they'd been apart.

The odd thing was, while Ulysses was pretty sure Tod was gay—and he had admitted to himself that he was gay back in eleventh grade—neither of them had ever broached the topic with the other. Some things were too intense to discuss, even between best friends. Tod's defection to the leisure worlds of his divorced parents had allowed Ulysses to lull himself into the belief that at college things would be different.

He gave up his vague aspirations to a normal college social life without much regret. He was a born student, and Yale offered plenty of diversions for its underclassmen so that the jocks and the nerds and the artsy crowd all had their comfortable niches. The long list of freshman courses and requirements kept Ulysses' task-driven personality well-shielded from the uncomfortable reality that was pushing ever closer.

He and Tod shared only a few classes, because their interests were divergent enough. Ulysses was majoring in French, Tod in art history. They had managed to take psych 101 and a comparative religion course together. Otherwise, they ate meals together, took long walks together through New Haven's more suburban neighborhoods, and went to movies together. Yale's most welcome perk was the presence of three competing film societies, and there was no night of the week on which one couldn't choose from at least three interesting films, ranging from classics to art films to recent releases that were aimed at cult audiences. They had been unable to sit through the final scene of John Waters's *Pink Flamingos,* and had fled, grossed out and laughing, into the spring evening.

True to form, Tod had chosen to live off campus from the very start, repulsed after a week of sharing cramped quarters with three undergrads who didn't share his standards of cleanliness. Having been packed off to boarding school at the age of ten, Tod had had enough of communal living. Ulysses helped him shop for and arrange his opulent little monk's cell in a rundown old building across the street from Silliman College. It was here, after movies and a late-night snack at the grubby pizza parlor next door that the two friends would retreat and talk about life. Or about as much of life as they dared.

For two years, this arrangement had worked perfectly. Ulysses's roommates were present but not significant. They never again said a word critical of his friend, and even came to appreciate Tod's arch intelligence.

Junior year, Tod had moved back into the college, but only after Ulysses agreed to be his roommate. They had lucked out with a one-bedroom suite in the older part of the dorm, boasting a huge bay window overlooking their favorite pizza parlor and an elaborate Victorian mantelpiece, grain-painted to look like mahogany. The two friends had taken great glee in decorating the room to the hilt—or as much to the hilt as they could on undergraduate budgets.

Given the general level of décor of a college student's room, it wasn't that difficult to upgrade. They painted the walls in the sitting room a high gloss kelly green. Two modern tubular chairs powder-coated in bright orange and lime green sat opposite a white cotton-duck-covered foam sofa. Sleek white plastic storage cubes served as bookshelves and side tables. The scratched oak floor was partly covered with a dark green shag-pile carpet.

In routine college fashion, most of the other guys on their staircase popped in to say hello, took one look at the room, and never came back.

Which was fine with them, really.

But, for Ulysses, things had started going off-kilter from the very beginning of junior year. His hitherto successful campaign of self-suppression and denial had begun to unravel ever since he'd sat down in the lecture hall for the first day of Charles F. Montgomery's overview of American decorative arts, and Michael had casually plopped down next to him, looking adorable and wearing, of all things, a pink Shetland sweater.

Ulysses was obsessed with Michael from the start. He was handsome. He was nice. He had an adorable smile. He wore a pinky ring. He and Ulysses ate lunch together at the Commons after their morning class, sometimes with Tod, but most often without. By junior year Tod and Ulysses' majors had taken them in two different directions, and dinner was the only guaranteed time they spent together outside of their rooms. Even the movie-going had tapered off to a substantial degree, as the amount of reading and writing they needed to do grew.

Michael never seemed uncomfortable with Tod. Ulysses took that as a good sign, but he never quite noticed that Michael's conversation remained neutral and impersonal. The only thing that mattered was being there with him, so that he could look at him.

And throughout all this time, in spite of their closeness as friends, in spite of Ulysses' obvious infatuation with Michael, "topic A" was still never touched on. The fact that neither Ulysses nor Tod had ever remotely approached a female student except in the context of coursework was not raised. The reality that neither of them had ever had—or, apparently, wanted—a girlfriend remained unspoken. They both knew what was going on.

Finally, having turned twenty mid-summer while staying with his parents in upstate New York, Ulysses was having a hard time keeping the lid on his personal truth. He was twenty, gay, and a total virgin. Not so much as a kiss from either gender had ever touched his lips. And it was making him crazy. Michael, whose lips Ulysses would have loved to explore, was driving him crazy. He sat in his crowded bedroom at his chipped and scarred college desk, eyes blind to the unread text before him, and felt sure that he would never live to know what it was to feel another boy's lips on his, to know what body-to-body contact was like. There was an unbridged chasm between self-acceptance and action, and he was paralyzed at the thought of trying to leap that gap.

That it was Tod who pulled Ulysses back from the edge of lunacy came as a surprise to both of them.

They had been to see a Friday-night screening at the Yale Film Society of the newly released cult film *Rocky Horror Picture Show*, which was still so new that it had not yet acquired its audience of costumed interpreters. A few hundred Yale undergrads, many of them stoned (but not Ulysses and Tod: they didn't drink or smoke, because that might allow their control to slip), watched with fascination as Tim Curry, Susan Sarandon, and Barry Bostwick, all impossibly young and adorable, flouted every moral convention with which they'd all been raised, much to Ulysses and Tod's shared delight.

After the film, well past midnight, Ulysses had been scarfing down a liverwurst-and-Swiss sandwich at "their" pizzeria, while Tod worked his way through a large helping of rice pudding. An unusual lull in their normally animated conversation had created an opening. An opening Tod had filled unexpectedly.

"Ulysses, you have to do something about this gay thing."
Ulysses froze, mid-chew, throat clenched, his large hazel eyes wide with shock.

"What?" he managed to mumble through the mouthful.

Tod continued, an oddly grim set to his features. "You know what I mean. This obsession with Michael. He's clueless, you know."

Ulysses just stared at him, unable to speak.

"You know you're gay. You just don't know what to do about it. We've been dancing around this for two years. You have to deal with it." Tod's voice had softened, but there was still a determined look on his face, as if he had an unpleasant task that needed to be taken care of.

"Are you gay?" Ulysses said *sotto voce*, having finally swallowed the lump of macerated sandwich.

Tod just stared at him for a moment, thinking. "I'm not sure I know what I am. I figure if I push you out of the closet, I can see what happens." There was a slight smirk on Tod's lips, but the concern in his eyes hadn't changed.

Ulysses looked down at the uneaten food on his plate, unable to meet his friend's gaze. Tears of relief began to burn his eyes. He could hear the blood pounding in his ears, and he felt slightly giddy. This was all happening so fast. His whole carefully constructed set of defenses was collapsing. He looked up, finally, his whole body having started to tremble.

"I-I'm just so afraid. I don't know what to do."

"There must be some group on campus. You could go to a meeting or something."

Ulysses' expression went wide-eyed with fear. "I couldn't. I wouldn't know what to say. How to behave."

Tod sighed softly in exasperation.

"How about a letter, then? Get someone to come talk to you."

Ulysses started blushing. He lowered his gaze again, feeling the heat rise up his neck, his ears burning.

"I already wrote a letter," he confessed almost inaudibly.

"What?" It was Tod's turn to look surprised.

"To the *Yale Daily News*." He found himself smiling sheepishly. "A couple of weeks ago. Anonymously. Complaining about how hard it is to come out on campus. They didn't publish it."

"Holy shit." Tod's expression took on the look of an indulgent parent. "You are some piece of work, Grantie."

"Fuck you," Ulysses answered, then allowed a soft giggle to escape, which turned into a hiccup.

"I think you need more direct action than that. It's not like they're going to send out a search party when they see that letter. *If* they publish it. Haven't you looked in the student services directory?"

"No."

"Well let's start there and see what we can dig up. You know you're pathetic, right?"

Ulysses could only nod in mute agreement. But as they left the pizzeria for their dormitory that night, Tod put an arm around Ulysses and gave him a sideways hug. Ulysses realized it was the first time in all their years of friendship that they'd ever touched each other.

At dinner the next night, Tod slapped a neon-pink brochure on the table by Ulysses' tray.

"Here you go."

It was a photocopied brochure about the Gay Alliance at Yale, with a phone number and a listing of their weekly meeting time.

"Where'd you find this?"

"In the rack outside the campus post office. Which is where you'd have found it if you'd ever bothered to look instead of just freaking out."

"So, what now?"

"What are you, three? Call them."

"I can't." Ulysses could feel panic welling up inside him.

"Jesus. Then write them a note. Can you do that? What if I give you a crayon so you don't hurt yourself?" he smirked.

Ulysses could see the wicked glint in Tod's eye, but couldn't suppress the overwhelming sense of shame at his own paralysis.

Tod reached over and put a hand on Ulysses' arm. "Look. It's just a note. I know you can write. Say you want someone to come and talk to you. I'll even deliver it for you and risk my reputation over being seen outside their office."

Ulysses couldn't suppress a laugh at that. "I'm really lame, aren't I?"

"That would be a yes."

And the note had been written; short and simple, asking for someone from G.A.Y. to call and make an appointment to talk. And Tod had taken it and delivered it, returning to their room out of breath as if he'd been spying across enemy lines.

Two days later, Ulysses was working on a paper in his room, surrounded by a pile of books, when the phone rang. He bolted into the sitting room and grabbed the receiver before he could think himself into a panic. A perfectly normal male voice on the other end of the line introduced himself as Mark, and offered to meet him on the Silliman quad later that afternoon. Just to talk.

Ulysses agreed to the time and place, and hung up the phone, feeling the weight lift slightly from his shoulders, a weight he hadn't realized had been there.

Mark, it turned out, was a senior. Average-looking, slightly stocky, with a mustache and wire-rimmed glasses. Ulysses figured he couldn't have picked anyone less gay looking if he'd tried. More relevantly, as they sat down on the sun-warmed grass of the Silliman quad, just another couple of Yalies shooting the breeze, Mark's calm self-confidence allowed Ulysses's pulse to slow down to something like normal as they talked.

They must have talked for an hour. Quietly, confidentially, Mark let Ulysses ask questions and encouraged him to express all of the feelings he'd had bottled up since he was sixteen years old and first understood who he was. Ulysses was surprised at the floodgate that opened inside of him, everything that had been dammed up over the years to which he'd never given voice to any other person. As they talked, Ulysses felt the rest of his burden lift off his shoulders, the invisible layers of protection in which he'd wrapped himself more and more tightly over the years evaporating one by one.

By the end of their conversation, he felt…normal. Just two guys talking on a quiet afternoon. Two gay guys. The thought sent a tiny shiver of happiness through him.

"So, do you think you'd be up to coming to a meeting?" Mark asked, his gentle voice reassuring. "Our weekly meetings are pretty free-form," he added. "Someone leads the discussion, if there is one. Otherwise, we just basically chat."

"I guess I can handle that," answered Ulysses, smiling shyly.

"I'm sure you can," Mark replied, holding out his hand for Ulysses to shake. "I'll pick you up by the campus post office at eight, OK?"

Ulysses just shook his hand and nodded, suddenly unable to speak.

***

Dwight Hall, on the Old Campus, was a Gothic Revival building of soft chocolate-colored sandstone that looked sort of like a church, although it had been originally built as the college library. These days it was used for various student organizations, although Ulysses didn't remember ever setting foot inside it before.

Mark led him down a short corridor and paused before an open door, through which the sound of social chatter poured.

"You ready?" he asked, his face encouraging.

A shaky "Sure," was all Ulysses could force out, his heart pounding, his breath shallow. He followed closely in Mark's wake, thinking to make himself less visible.

The room they entered was not terribly large. An empty fireplace centered one of the short walls, and diamond-paned casement windows gave out onto the street. Standing around the room and sitting on a random assortment of folding chairs and cast-off upholstered furniture was a group of men as varied and unexceptional as Mark himself. A quick, anxious survey of the room told Ulysses that the men were of differing ages, some clearly too old to be students, others seemingly his age. And none of them was paying any attention to him.

Mark finger-waved a greeting to someone across the room, and Ulysses turned nervously in the direction of the gesture just in time to find himself facing a very tall young man with a crop of wiry red hair and a bushy mustache over his broad smile.

"Tommy, this is Ulysses."

Ulysses found his hand engulfed by the redhead's strong grip, his arm pumped enthusiastically.

"Welcome. Hey, you're cute!" The camp tone of his voice was at odds with his size and the plaid flannel shirt. Ulysses didn't know what to say, feeling his ears starting to burn.

"Down boy," joked Mark, cuffing the young lumberjack on the arm.

"You'll scare him. He's new."

"New?" Tommy's grip relaxed, although he didn't let go of Ulysses' hand, and his face filled with curiosity and concern.

"Yeah, as in he's just coming out and this is the first time ever meeting a crazy homo like you."

"Oh, shit." Tom dropped Ulysses' hand and placed his own hand gently on Ulysses' shoulder. "I'm sorry. Didn't mean to freak you out. Let me introduce you to people."

Mark let Tom take Ulysses under his burly wing and turned away to greet other friends.

Offering Ulysses a paper cup full of something, which he took gratefully and gulped just to have something to do other than speak, Tom proceeded to introduce him to several of the other men in the room. These included a middle-aged professor who was also Tom's landlord, a handsome bearded graduate student who was one of his housemates, and a slight camo-clad man with a cap and an earring who was apparently an off-campus member of the group and kept them up to speed on political events relating to gay rights.

All this new information whirled around Ulysses's brain, as he tried to concentrate on responding politely and get his voice to function. He shook hands, attempting without much success to absorb what he was hearing, and generally found himself feeling less and less self-conscious as the minutes passed. He was interested to hear that it was unusual for an undergrad to come to one of these meetings, and that his arrival was noteworthy. He pondered that fact, thinking about all the classmates in his position, maybe just as paralyzed by fear as he was, who didn't have a Tod to push them out the closet door, or a Mark to bring them through this one.

The meeting was called to order by someone he didn't see, and Tom pulled Ulysses down next to him on a beat-up old sofa, patting him fraternally on the leg, which nonetheless sent a shiver up Ulysses' spine.

Tom leaned in and whispered in his ear. "Now comes the boring part. Don't worry, it never takes long,"

As everyone took their seats and settled down, all eyes turned expectantly toward the guy who seemed to be in charge of the evening's proceedings, whatever they were going to be. Ulysses hadn't registered him before, sitting cattycorner across the room, slouched in an armchair by the fireplace, looking oddly worried. Slender and wiry, wearing a cocoa-colored print shirt, jeans, and white sneakers, he looked to be one of the younger men in the room. Under a shaggy head of glossy black hair, he had a long straight nose, a pretty mouth, and large bright blue eyes fringed with dark lashes.

He was clutching a copy of the *Yale Daily News.* Ulysses felt his stomach sink.

"Hey, guys," the dark-haired man spoke, his voice low-key, slightly nervous, as if being in charge hadn't been his idea. "Did any of you see today's campus paper?"

A negative murmur went around the room, and he held the paper up, opened to the editorial page.

"There's a long letter here from an anonymous undergrad." Ulysses watched the blue eyes scan the text on the page in front of him. He could feel his ears burning, sure that everyone in the room would notice; then realized that everyone was focused on the speaker. He relaxed just a little.

"Seems like he's having trouble coming out. Doesn't know who to go to or what to do."

"I could suggest a few things," quipped the grad student Ulysses had been introduced to, only to be elbowed in the ribs by the professor sitting next to him.

As a ruffle of laughter went around the room at this aside, Ulysses glanced over at Mark, who was eyeing him with raised eyebrows. Ulysses shot him a look that he hoped was pleading, and apparently got his message through. No one else seemed to notice the exchange.

"Come on, guys," said the dark-haired boy, a slight whine in his voice. "We can't just ignore this."

A few more jokes in the guise of suggestions were thrown out, adding to the general feeling of quiet hilarity in the room. But the joking was mixed in with ideas that were sincere, as this disparate group of men wrestled with the notion of a lonely, frightened student trying to deal with being gay. For all the sexual innuendo and self-conscious campiness, it seemed like these guys all cared. Cared about *him*, even though they had no idea the author of the heartfelt letter was sitting there in their midst.

Through it all, Ulysses kept his eyes on the as-yet unnamed speaker. He noticed the expression on his face, which shifted from exasperation, to concern, to laughter, showing off a disarming smile. He was really...cute.

The discussion wound down after the group formed a spontaneous consensus that the speaker—whose name was finally revealed to be Gary— should write a letter to the *News* in response to this, offering the group's services to the anonymous writer, and, of course, to any Yalies who found themselves feeling isolated and frustrated. Gary rolled his eyes at being assigned the task but accepted it good-naturedly before letting the meeting fall back into the cheerful anarchy that seemed to be its normal mode.

As people began to stand up and mill around, Tom again placed a large hand on Ulysses' thigh and said, "You should come back up to our house." He jumped up off the sofa, grabbing Ulysses' hand, and dragged him over to the graduate student and the professor. "Morris, Arthur, I've invited Ulysses here to come up to the house so he can get to know us better."

Tom turned to Ulysses again. "Arthur owns the house. We rent rooms from him." The suggestion was met with an open delight that made Ulysses a little anxious. He swallowed his anxiety and decided he'd just go along. This is what he was looking for, after all, potential friends. Gay friends.

At that moment, the blue-eyed Gary approached the little group, and Tom pounced on him like an exuberant toddler.

"Gary, this is Ulysses, he's a newbie, and we've invited him over to the house for a pot party."

Ulysses may have gasped at that line. He'd never smoked pot in his life; nor had he drunk so much as a beer during his years at Yale. He was sure that surprise, if not actual panic, showed on his face. But something about Gary's expression allowed him to squelch the fear welling up inside him that he was getting in over his head.

"Tommy, we're not all total potheads like you are. Maybe he'd just like to talk and, you know, get to know us a little when we're *not* stoned?"

"What's the fun in that?" replied the big redhead with false drama, grabbing Ulysses' shoulder and laughing.

"Hi, I'm Gary," said the dark-haired boy, his eyes even more beautiful at this close range. He shook Ulysses' hand and smiled shyly.

"Don't pay attention to any of them. They're all crazy," he added, beaming at the indignant denials that his three housemates offered in response.

As he followed his new maybe-friends out of the meeting room, saying goodbye to people as he followed closely behind Gary, Ulysses caught Mark's eye and mouthed a silent "thank you." Mark gave him a pleased smile and a thumbs-up.

Another gay boy successfully launched.

As the little group made their way back to Arthur's car, Ulysses lingered near Gary, wanting to talk to him more. He noticed that he still clutched the *Yale Daily News* he'd brought to the meeting.

Seeing an opening, he said, "I don't think you'll have to write that letter."

"What letter?" The dark lashes fluttered slightly, making Ulysses tingle.

"To the *News.*"

"Oh, yeah. Why not?"

Ulysses swallowed, his mouth suddenly dry. "Um, 'cause I wrote it."

"What!" Gary's expression lit up with amusement.

"Yeah. A few weeks ago. I figured they'd just thrown it away."

"Good for you." Gary smiled at him as they slowly walked. "You have a way with words."

"Thanks."

They reached Arthur's car, a small, beat-up Volkswagen station wagon. Much joking ensued as to how to fit five grown men into the tiny car, but eventually Morris agreed to sit on Tom's lap, while Arthur drove and Gary rode shotgun. Ulysses squeezed into the back seat next to the giggling Tom.

The overloaded compact wheezed to life and chugged slowly off into the New Haven evening.

Ulysses exchanged shy smiles with Gary, who turned to him from the front seat. He settled back into his own crowded space as he accompanied his newfound friends into the first evening of his new life.

***

Tod was working at his desk when Ulysses slipped in the door well before midnight.

"Well, well. Here you are, a new man."

Ulysses just smiled and walked across the room, plopping down in the orange lounge chair and kicking off his shoes onto the green shag rug. He looked over at his old friend and grinned.

"So?"

"So. I went to the meeting. Met some guys. We went back to their house. Actually, it's not far from here. Just up by Science Hill."

"Aaaaand?" Tod asked, drawing out the word.

"They showed me around the house. One of the guys owns it, and the others rent rooms." Ulysses went silent. Tod just stared at him, brows arched expectantly.

"We all smoked a joint."

"Holy crap. Have you ever done that before?"

"You know I haven't. It didn't actually do anything to me." He shook his head, looking down at his hands clasped in his lap. "I think I pulled it off without letting them know I'd never done it before."

"And so starts your life of wanton debauchery."

Ulysses laughed softly, then looked up.

"I have a date."

"Whoa, that *is* big news. Are you going to tell me who, or do I have to get violent?"

Ulysses studied his friend's eyes. For all the humor in his voice, there was love in those eyes, and understanding, and concern.

"One of the guys in the house, his name is Gary. He asked me out for Friday night."

"You move fast for an imbecile loser." Tod was beaming at him. "Tell me more."

"Well, he just graduated last spring. He's working at the Yale Computer Center."

"I assume he must be attractive, or were you so desperate you didn't look?"

Ulysses giggled softly. "He's very cute. Black hair, huge blue eyes. Seems kinda quiet."

There was a comfortable silence for a few minutes, as the two friends regarded each other, lost in their own thoughts.

"So," Tod ventured after a while. Do you feel better? About all this?"

Ulysses let out a long quiet sigh. "More than better." He looked once more into Tod's eyes. "I feel new. Like I've been born again."

***

Friday at seven there was a knock on their suite door, and Ulysses rushed over to answer it. He had dressed carefully, in his standard khakis-and-polo shirt under a short brown suede jacket. He'd shaved, put on cologne, changed his socks and underwear. Just thinking about the implications of underwear made him anxious.

Gary was there, smiling, dressed in a light blue denim short jacket and faded jeans that brought out the color of his eyes. They shook hands with awkward formality, and then Ulysses pulled him into the living room, where Tod hovered like an anxious parent.

Gary's eyebrows shot up when he saw the room.

"Wow. This is some decorating job." He went over to shake hands with Tod, who introduced himself. Then he surveyed the room again, taking in the framed posters, the shiny deep green walls, the brass floor lamps, the roll-up bamboo blinds in the big bay window.

"And you just came out this week?" he asked, quietly, causing Tod to guffaw in a very ungentlemanly way and Ulysses to blush furiously.

"We figured we'd practice on the room first," Tod answered drily, stifling his laughter.

Gary regarded him. "You, too?"

Tod just gave him a wry smile. "Jury's still out on me. I'm letting Ulysses test the waters before I jump in."

The two young men said goodbye and headed out into the cool October evening. It was a short walk to Woolsey Hall. Gary had gotten them tickets to a jazz concert there.

"I thought we'd go out for pizza after?"

"Sure, that'd be great."

Ulysses only partly heard the concert, his mind awhirl with thoughts of "what next?" Thoughts that both excited and terrified him. They didn't talk much beyond a few exchanged words, but Ulysses noticed that Gary kept looking over at him solicitously and smiling that cute shy smile. It didn't help the nervous pounding of his heart.

Things relaxed after the concert was over and the duo walked over to Broadway Pizza near the Yale Co-op. They made small talk over their food, each of them sharing information about their families, their coming out process, such as it was.

Gary had been out for a little over a year, suddenly finding himself with a boyfriend after breaking up with a girlfriend the summer before his senior year. They had broken up last spring. He hadn't told his parents yet.

Ulysses talked a lot about Tod, about their friendship, about his help in coming out.

As they walked back towards Ulysses' dorm, Gary asked him to come back up to the house, so they could talk some more. Ulysses agreed readily but found himself desperately hoping that talk wouldn't be the end of it. He was twenty and a virgin. He'd had plenty of talk.

The house was at 16 Winchester Avenue, set a couple of blocks behind Yale's famous Saarinen hockey rink, known as "the whale." The place was, blessedly, deserted. It was only about ten-thirty.

"Arthur's out cruising somewhere. Tom and Morris have dates. We've got the place to ourselves."

There was no innuendo in Gary's comment, but Ulysses felt a thrill of anticipation run through him.

They went into the kitchen and sat at the oil-cloth-covered table. Gary got out orange juice and poured them each a glass. They sat, talking, as they sipped their drinks. Finally, Gary locked eyes with Ulysses, and reached over to gently caress his leg, his expression searching, hopeful.

Ulysses felt his heart rate speed up as he placed his own hand over Gary's and squeezed.

"I have to tell you. You're the first guy that's ever touched me."

Gary paused, his eyes suddenly wide.

"Wow. Is this ok?"

"Oh yes. If you stop, I'll scream."

They both laughed, and Gary leaned in and kissed him, gently at first, more urgently as Ulysses figured out what to do.

Seems to come to me pretty naturally.

Ulysses sighed, and Gary broke away from him, his eyes happy, his smile playing across that pretty mouth.

"Let's go to my room. I have something I want to show you."

"By all means." He leaned over and kissed Gary lightly. "I'm a new-born, you'll need to show me lots of things."

Gary stood, and held out his hand to Ulysses in a sweet courtly gesture. Rising from his chair with as much grace as he could muster, Ulysses gripped his new friend's hand, feeling its warmth, feeling the skin and the muscle beneath. They stood there for a moment, hand in hand, simply looking at each other.

Then, as he felt his anxiety sloughing away, his heart filling, not with fear, but with happiness, he allowed this handsome young man with the full dark hair and the beautiful blue eyes to lead him up the stairs and into a future he had so far only imagined.

CHAPTER TWENTY

FOR KEEPS

In the late 1990s, when Gary and I had gotten old enough that there was a generation of gay folks younger than we were, they would look at us in wide-eyed wonder and say things like "Wow, you came out in the 70s? It must have been so hard." Well, it wasn't hard, particularly, and I didn't feel especially courageous for doing so. A scant six years after Stonewall, in a place like New Haven, coming out wasn't difficult so much as emotionally fraught. What's a little heartbreaking is that, for all the openness in our society today, young gay folk coming out face exactly the same fears and anxieties that I faced decades ago. The fear of rejection by family and friends is at the top of the list; the fear of being labeled as an outsider is next. When I came out in 1975 there were virtually no governmental protections of any kind for gay people. There was no "LGBTQ" either. Being gay was still illegal in much of the United States. The very concept of same-sex marriage was too bizarre to have even occurred to most people.

Yet, at Yale in 1975, coming out was the right thing. We understood we were outlaws—sort of. We knew that there was widespread ignorance and prejudice. More important than all that was the fact that there was a community of gay men and women to support me, and once I stepped outside that closet door, I never looked back. When I met new people in those first few months, they were often startled at how comfortable I was in my skin. I guess up until that time I'd been practicing to be gay. By the time I finally left my closet, I must have known what to do.

That fateful October morning, I made my first-ever walk, dressed in my clothes from the night before, back from Gary's house to Silliman college. I was a little giddy and still buzzing from the fact that I had actually, finally, irrevocably slept with another guy. I was a virgin no more. I walked into my dorm room, bursting to tell Tod everything, only to find his very elegant and proper aunt and uncle from Washington, DC sitting in our orange and green chairs and chatting away with their dear nephew. Tod looked as well-groomed and cool as I felt grimy and unshaven; but I settled in and followed his lead, charming them with some inane chatter about a paper I was writing on a seventeenth-century New York silver beaker.

The most important discovery I made in my junior year at Yale was that I could keep my grades up while doing half the work—and having a busy social (and sex) life at the same time. Having shattered all my internal compartments, it was as if my entire self was functioning at full efficiency. I could go out with Gary, smoke a joint, drink and dance till one a.m., and still get my papers done and study for exams.

The second most important discovery I made that year was that romance puts a real strain on friendship. Tod was all gung-ho about the new me but was less enthused with this new part of my life that took me away from our established rituals of movie-going, long chatty walks, and late-night snacks at Naples Pizza. At the time I was aware of this, but, as young people do, I put those thoughts aside in favor of seeking my own long-denied pleasure. My new circle of friends was not entirely Tod's cup of tea, and my rapid immersion in Yale's gay world probably bemused him as much as it exhilarated me. I was not there for him as I had been. I know it hurt him. In time, I tried to make amends, and it mostly worked.

Gary Berger was my first date, my first kiss, my first everything. I did not go out on that date expecting anything more than a night in bed with a boy my age. It was a waterbed, by the way, which seems poignant somehow. I was not looking to fall in love. I was a desperately horny twenty-year-old virgin, and had never even seen any pornography, other than the *Playboy* magazines I laughably gathered in high school (and in which I surely read the articles). My only understanding of homosexuality, other than from *The Best Little Boy in the World* and *The Boys in the Band,* was from clandestine adolescent reading of Havelock Ellis's *The Psychology of Sex* in my parents' library. Published in the late nineteenth century, "Sexual Inversion in Men" comprised the chapters on which I focused breathlessly; although what I mostly remember now is that sexual inversion was somehow related to being able to whistle and one's favorite color. It takes a lot of bottled-up hormones to make that stuff sexy.

My first date with Gary was followed by another one. More proceeded from those first two. We went to concerts, movies, bars. I learned to appreciate the inexpensive, mild-mannered pot of the mid-1970s, smoked in giggling fellowship with the denizens of 16 Winchester Avenue. I was taken to the local gay bar in New Haven, called Partners, just a few blocks from the university art gallery. It was a nondescript two-story place full of smoke, where townies in denim and prepped-out Yalies, male and female, mingled and danced to the songs of Sister Sledge and Vickie Sue Robinson. Further out on the industrial edge of New Haven was a flashy disco-bar called the Neuter Rooster, with throbbing music and lots of silver mylar, orange vinyl, and white plastic. It was overwhelming to me, and we only ventured there a few times, because it required a car and charged a cover fee. Gary was not much of a dancer, and neither of us were heavy drinkers. Partners would become the "Cheers" of the remainder of my undergraduate life. We went there to relax, to have fun, and to surround ourselves with other gay kids.

Gary was a suburban Jewish boy from New Jersey. He had been co-valedictorian at Jonathan Dayton Regional High School in Springfield, where his parents, Morton and Gladys Berger, lived in a 1950s raised ranch. His parents had grown up together in Newark, to which his grandparents had emigrated early in the twentieth century. Gladys's parents had come from the southeastern corner of the Austro-Hungarian empire. Technically they were

Polish but had been listed as Austrian at Ellis Island. Morton Berger, known as Pete (from his childhood nickname PeeWee) was a bartender in a working-class bar in Newark. Gladys was a housewife who couldn't drive. They had spent their honeymoon at Grossinger's in the Catskills in 1946.

Although I'd had Jewish classmates at Exeter, it was only at Yale that I got to know anything about modern American Jews. My freshman and sophomore year roommate Gene, from Long Island, had been gregarious and informative; with a wry sense of humor he delighted in educating this ignorant goy boy from Syracuse. It was, however, Gary who introduced me to a part of American life that was as unknown to me as New Jersey itself. At the age of twenty, the only bagels I'd ever seen (and never eaten) were frozen ones from Lenders that they sold at the New York State Fair. Lox was, for my family, smoked salmon. Chopped liver was paté. In my upstate childhood, Jewish holidays were never mentioned and meant nothing to me. That fact still startles me, because it seems so improbable now, looking back over more than forty-five years with the Jewish family I married into.

When my parents came down to New Haven that fall for Parents' Weekend, just a few weeks after I'd met Gary, he joined us for brunch in Silliman's huge Georgian dining hall. Sandy and Julia were politely puzzled by this handsome, dark-haired boy who was so different from any friends I'd ever had before. It was not as if my parents didn't have Jewish friends, but Gary's family was very much *Goodbye Columbus,* while Bob and Mary Arnstein, my parents' longtime New Haven friends, were quite literally out of Stephen Birmingham's *Our Crowd.* Gary was a computer programmer, not an art historian. My parents couldn't quite figure out what our connection was, and I wasn't quite ready to tell them.

The truth is, Gary had tapped into something within me that went far deeper than a yearning for physical intimacy. He was deeply introspective, tending to overanalyze things (including the weird WASP boy who had blown into his life unexpectedly). My introspection was inclined toward anxiety about the future, rather than puzzling over the present. Neither of us was a natural leader, but we both resented being bossed around, and thus from the start often deferred to each other, each hoping that the other would take charge. Gary was not the kind of friend Tod was, one who dragged me around to experience new things and broaden my horizons. He was shy, diffident, but also smart and curious. He let me suggest our adventures together, but never hesitated to resist if it was something that didn't interest him. Neither of us tried to mold the other into someone we weren't.

I confused my parents even more when, the day after Christmas, 1975, I picked up Gary at the pathetic Syracuse train station, a sad prefabricated structure stranded in an industrial wasteland east of the city. Then we announced to my mildly nonplussed family that Gary and I were driving to Boston for New Year's Eve. Gary's cousin Nancy had gay friends in Concord, Massachusetts, and they had offered us their guest room for the holiday weekend. I can't recall why we thought Boston was the place for us to be. Perhaps it was simply someplace that was away from both of our families, where we could just be together.

We loaded up my yellow Vega and headed east on Interstate 90, unhindered by snow or traffic. The eastern route toward Albany and Boston was familiar to me from my childhood, and now took on a new sheen—me and my boyfriend heading off on what was to become our first long-distance adventure together. At our arrival in Concord, we found ourselves in the middle of an ugly break-up. In fact, Cousin Nancy's friend, after a hasty, somewhat shamefaced greeting, got in his car and drove away, awkwardly leaving his sandy-haired boyfriend behind with these two young strangers. His name has faded from memory, and had no connection to us at all, but dutifully showed us and our bags to the guest room. It was minimally furnished in that grad-student way but had a big made-up mattress on the floor and a friendly Siamese cat who yowled conversationally outside our door.

With this as the backdrop, it seems odd that our romantic mood wasn't derailed. Maybe we should have offered to go to a motel, but I don't think it ever occurred to us. We were easily as embarrassed as our host was, and would have left if we'd been asked to. To his credit, he recalibrated his shaken world and treated us as guests. We decided to nap, not only to rest up for a late night, but to avoid having to talk to our newly-split-up host. Napping was not a euphemism, but it did involve some making out. We held each other, giggling over the absurdity of our circumstances, and at the sounds of the cat outside our closed door, which were weirdly like those of a crying baby.

For whatever reason, this was the moment Gary chose to look deeply into my eyes and say, "I love you" for the first time. His voice was quiet and slightly trembling, as if he was uncertain of my response. I looked back into his amazing blue eyes and answered, "I was just going to say that." I remember smiling so widely it almost hurt. I'd been feeling something serious for Gary for a while but, typically, had been hesitant to speak my mind.

There, in that unfamiliar place, in that awkward situation, we committed ourselves to each other. No fanfare, no witnesses, no family, no laws protecting us. Just we two, together. We had no idea what we had begun. There were no rules for couples like us, and no support either.

That night, what was essentially our Zero Anniversary, we went out to a huge disco in Boston called the 1270 Club on Boylston Street. The only memory I have from that, other than the usual noise and swirling lights of a 1970s disco, was running into Exeter classmate Paul. Paul was a pretty teenager when I knew him at school, and the only gay man of color I knew early in my out life. Paul was also the first of my Exeter classmates to come out to me (hardly avoidable when you're both standing in a gay disco on New Year's Eve, because straight people didn't go to gay clubs in the 1970s).

Later that evening we somehow found ourselves at the Napoleon Club, a celebrated piano bar with a gay clientele. At twenty and twenty-two (legal drinking age, back then, was still eighteen) we were at least twenty years younger than any other patron and we were fêted by the men there; serenaded by the silver-haired guy playing the white grand piano. These were not the sad, angry men of *The Boys in the Band,* or at least they didn't seem that way to us.

There was no one else to celebrate with us, and it felt as if we were being welcomed into a big family.

Of course, family weighed heavily on me during that second semester of my junior year. It was the national Bicentennial and I had been deeply involved as a student flunky in the preparation of a major exhibition at the Yale University Art Gallery, spearheaded by Charles Montgomery, called *American Art 1750-1800: Towards Independence.* The exhibition opened in the early spring of 1976 and traveled from Yale to the Victoria & Albert Museum in London—the first exhibition of its kind to do so. For a budding curator, it was heady stuff, although now it hardly seems revolutionary (no pun intended). It was my first full experience of a large-scale exhibition in the making. This was the beginning of the golden years of decorative arts departments in museums, and Yale was right at the forefront.

So, I had the art gallery and I had Gary; what I didn't have was my family. Still puzzled by Gary's presence in my life, my letters and telephone conversations with my parents had become increasingly defined by what I left out rather than what I said. This was new and uncomfortable for me. My family shares; overshares in fact. My reticence made no sense either to them or to me. Something had to give.

At some point that spring, I typed a long letter to my mother and father, telling them who I was, who Gary was, and hoping that they would accept this new me. I even included a bibliography, if you can believe it. It made perfect sense, really, since both of my parents were voracious readers, and a book would give them a focus as they digested what I assumed to be staggering information for them.

Of course, I did not know about the conversation that the Dietz Company psychiatrist, Robert Cranston, had had with my parents back in the mid-sixties when I was ten years old, forewarning them that I would probably turn out homosexual. I would eventually come to realize that my parents had probably been braced for this news for more than a decade. But that spring, as I made my way from Silliman College to Yale Station on the Old Campus to collect my mail, a constant sense of dread followed me. I was, to be honest, pretty sure I was going to be OK, but the suspense was killing me. Since the death of my brother and sister, nothing had ever felt quite certain.

Both of my parents wrote back to me; my mother on onion-skin paper, tapped out with professional care on her blue-and-white Royal manual typewriter; and my father on yellow legal paper, using a fountain pen, in his distinctive, surprisingly legible scrawl. I have those letters still, tucked away in the archives in my attic. Both Mom and Dad were immediate in their acceptance, showing parental concern for my happiness and worry that my life would possibly be harder than it should be.

My mother's letter was the "official" letter, from both of them, but in my mother's voice. My father went further in his letter, and got more personal, startling me with the news that he, too, had been with men in his youth. Then he went on to irritate me by suggesting that I shouldn't dismiss the possibility of a heterosexual relationship because of my decision. He meant this in the most loving way, but to my ardent, newly-out mind, this was akin to saying it was something I would grow out of as he had. The old "it's a choice" argument never sat well with me. I had spent too long and suffered too much anguish over my orientation to consider the notion that it was a phase. What I didn't think of at the time is that my father was bisexual, a concept that was not well understood (and not necessarily well understood even today). What I didn't understand at the time is that my coming out had stirred up thirty-year-old memories in my father.

My brother had been brought into the loop, as I'd asked my parents to do. His only response was, with characteristic theatricality, to send me a telegram. His message: THANK GOD WE ARE BROTHERS. Still my rock.

Before I went home at the end of my junior year, I forewarned Sandy and Julia that I wouldn't be staying the summer. My plan was to move into a room recently vacated at 16 Winchester Avenue in New Haven. I had a menial job (more or less dusting platforms) at the Yale University Art Gallery for the summer, and I was moving in with my Jewish boyfriend. My rent was seventy dollars a month, and I had to shop and cook for the whole household once a week.

I went home for a month, which gave me plenty of time to talk to my parents and to begin to forge the new normal of our life-without-secrets. While our conversations started out on the stilted side, it got easier. This was the time when I learned things that hadn't been said in those letters. My mother told me, finally, about Dr. Cranston's prophecy; that she and Dad had been surprised, but not shocked, by my news. My father and I made peace about the unequivocal nature of my gayness. He never clarified what his own experience with men had been, but it intrigued me that it was he, raised in a much more socially liberal family, who struggled more with having a gay son. Then again, my mother was the one who had gay friends in the publishing world in the 1930s and was the child who had gently rebelled against her conservative Republican parents in almost every way.

Dad, on the other hand, who had worked on Broadway for years as a young man, had probably always seen his sexual detours with men as something to be hidden, as a youthful phase, and had never expected to have to deal with it once he had locked it neatly away in his past. During my month at home, when I was joining my father for lunch in downtown Syracuse, we met out on the sidewalk of Warren Street. As usual, he hugged and kissed me. We are a family of kissers. Then he pulled back, a startled smile on his face.

"I guess somebody might mistake us for a couple," he said. I saw equal parts amusement and panic on his face.

I'm sure I said something like "Ugh, Daddy, that's gross. You're my *father.*" He just laughed. He never stopped kissing people, I'm glad to say.

Quietly, one day, my mother showed me a Cartier cufflink with the initials of my father and those of another young man engraved on it. He had given it to her, along with the story of a long-ago romance in his youth. Only the one survived, suggesting that the pair had been split as keepsakes when the romance ended. It was enameled silver, the sort of thing that Cartier would have sold to college-age boys in the 1930s. There is more to this story, but it is enough to note that the other boy's initials happen to belong to someone who went on to be quite famous, and very much heterosexual.

Apparently, mom had been slightly blindsided by this revelation of my father's past. In a rather classic bit of intellectual redirection, my mother and I spent some time discussing the genetic possibilities behind what seemed to be a family trait, given that I had two gay cousins. My great-grandfather John E. Dietz (Teddy) became the target of our speculation. His odd, distant marriage with the social-climbing Olga; her solitary travels in Europe with my great-aunt Ethel; the house in Palm Beach which, as far as we knew, Teddy never visited; and Teddy's ultimate death from, according to family lore, over-indulgence in alcohol. It felt like a very apt story of Victorian repression, just as my father's story seemed more suitable to his generation.

After my father's death in 1999, just shy of his eightieth birthday, Mom gave me that single cufflink, and I keep it in my jewelry box. After my father's obituary appeared, that boy, now an old man with grandchildren of his own, wrote Julia a lovely note, reminiscing about his long-ago friendship with my father. It was the first time in sixty years that my family had heard from him.

This might be a good spot to mention a genetic pattern in my family that I find striking. My father and his three siblings produced among them sixteen children (much, you'll recall, to my grandmother Barbara's satisfaction). Three of those families included gay sons; two of those families included multiple redheads. In my generation, redheads appeared in the two families without one, and a gay son appeared in the one family who hadn't had one before. Two generations: gay men and redheads in every branch of the family. There are no apparent gay genetic markers in my mother's family (and, incidentally, no redheads). My gay cousins have been stalwart friends since the 1970s. Our journeys have been different, each with its challenges; but we have never been alone.

My month at home over, I packed up my clothes into the yellow Vega and headed back to New Haven. It didn't quite hit me then that, at twenty-one, I was leaving home for good.

Number 16 Winchester Avenue was a barely-middle-class, two-story house from the early twentieth century. It was adequately maintained, the exterior covered with gray asphalt shingles on the ground floor, and dark green on the second. Arthur, a Yale PhD, and a professor at a nearby community college, rented out four rooms to Yale students, and now I became one of them. I took the small room off the second-floor kitchen (the house had been converted into two apartments at one point, but Arthur had removed the downstairs kitchen to create an extra bedroom). I had no bed, because of course I slept with Gary on his waterbed. His room had two big windows overlooking the back yard. My little room was dark, with a small closet and one window facing the house next door. It became my study/dressing room. My desk and chair (my brother Jed's childhood desk and chair, although I don't remember how I got them into my Vega), and an old chest of drawers that I painted a bright shiny orange, made up my furnishings.

The decorative focus of my room was the wall over the desk, which was covered with two dozen five-by-seven black-and-white photographs, all framed in an identical simple gold molding, but each with a different color mat. Over the course of my first three years at Yale, I'd been taking copies of family pictures to Merwin's Frame Shop on York Street in New Haven. It was a clear sign of my obsession with my dead relatives, and how their distant lives were constantly swirling in my imagination. There was a picture of my sister Edie, but not of my brother Ned. Make of that what you will; but, more importantly, there were images of Grants and Roots, and of course the princess, my great aunt Julia. Eventually my collection would include photographs of my grandfather Dietz and his mother Olga, and an engraving of grandfather's mother-in-law Mary Louise Dun Johnson (known as Mamie). But these would come later, after graduate school shifted my attention to the role that the Dietz family had played in the Gilded Age.

This wall of photographs (some of them still adorn the dressing room I've had for thirty-five years) seems an odd fetish. I think, at not-quite-twenty-one, I still had so little clear sense of who I was, or who I was supposed to be, that I needed these dead people as reminders. The other possibility is that, as a Yalie, I was all too aware of how historically insignificant my *Leave it to Beaver* childhood looked to my own eyes. Maybe these photographs acted as touchstones, helping me legitimize the value of my own existence. For that matter, this entire memoir is possibly just another way for me to tie myself to my antecedents, and thus reassure myself that, through all those who went before, I have worth.

Yikes. Clearly my need for validation was strong, in spite of parents who loved and supported me unconditionally. I had been a top student at a prep school where everybody was smart. Now I was a top student at a university where everybody was also smart. I was pleased, but I really didn't feel all that special. I was still desperately trying to be like my dead brother and sister, to measure up to what my memory had made them. Somehow I felt I was still lacking. Coming out as a gay man was the first time I'd become part of a social community where I felt better than adequate. Outside my few friends—Tod chief among them—I was still awkward with my peers and constantly aware that I was not cool. Being gay was the coolest I'd ever been.

Gary and I drove back to Syracuse, and to my parents' cabin on Cazenovia Lake, for my twenty-first birthday. My friend Tod was there, as was his mother. It was a slightly tense evening, mostly due to Tod's mother, whose veiled antisemitism irritated me. My being gay bothered her more than it bothered my parents, possibly because it raised the issue of her son's orientation, which was a sore subject. I got very drunk, and cut my head open on the toilet seat as I lost my dinner late that evening. I did not have a hangover the next day, but I still have the scar from the toilet seat.

Gary and I crowded into the lower bunkbed in my tiny room, separated from my parents' bed by no more than a wall made of painted two-by-fours. We were oblivious to the structural limitations of the cabin, to my parents' chagrin. Three decades later my mother would confess, to my horror, that we had kept them awake for quite a while.

Senior year was great, mostly. I was in love. I was tied to my family even more closely. I was getting good grades. I loved being at Yale, especially now that I was having fun, too. I had managed to convince Tod to leave campus life and move into a makeshift third-floor apartment in Arthur's house. White foam insulating panels fixed between the roof joists gave the unfinished attic ceiling a sort of faux-Tudor effect. The orange and green chairs, the shag rug, and Tod's great stereo system all moved to Winchester Avenue. He became part of the household, but he was never, I think, fully comfortable there.

Both Tod and I had been invited to join the Elizabethan Club our junior year, sponsored by friends in the art history department. Housed in a charming little Federal house just up the street from Silliman College, the club was quaintly Anglophilic and boasted a remarkable collection of Elizabethan manuscripts and publications in a vault off one of its parlors. This was the best deal on campus. Undergrads paid ten dollars for membership, and that allowed us to drop in every weekday for tea and *free finger sandwiches,* in a comfortable room warmed by a wood fire. Even after we'd both moved off campus to Winchester Avenue, Tod and I would continue to meet and stuff our faces in the afternoons, gulping down Earl Grey and chatting with whomever we knew.

My social life got an interesting academic twist when I was tapped (again, through the good offices of Professor Montgomery) to join Manuscript, a senior society that was adamantly *not* secret; unlike its more celebrated peers, Skull and Bones, Wolf's Head, or Book and Snake, whose mysterious temple-like clubhouses dotted the Yale landscape. Manuscript was housed in a sleek little modernist pavilion, designed by Yale architect King-Lui Wu. I was one of twelve seniors, six men and six women, who, each week, met on Thursdays to cook dinner together, sit in the club's dining room, and talk about whatever came to us—our lives, the world, our studies, hopes, dreams. There were no expectations other than we commit to showing up and being part of the group. On Sundays, dressed up, we collectively hosted a catered dinner for alumni, professors, and various invited guests and honorary members. I have no real memory of what we all talked about all the time; only that I felt welcomed and included in what was (for Yale, back then) an intellectually diverse group of Ivy League students. There was the varsity rower, the harpist, the mathematician, the French major (not me) and an assortment of other young men and women who had little in common beyond our Manuscript membership. This is not a complaint or a criticism, because in retrospect it is rather a wonderful thing to contemplate. For my senior year I had a group of friends whom I would never have had otherwise. We did not have to be or become best friends; we simply had to engage with each other in a way that would (presumably) improve us. They were all great kids. Even though we all went our separate ways and have not really kept in touch, that time in Manuscript remains a bright, warm spot in my college years.

Meanwhile, my parents had begun work on building a real house on the Cazenovia property in 1976, having decided to leave Syracuse finally, accepting that the twenty-mile commute would not destroy their social life and sever all ties with their community in the city. Having rejected a lovely romantic shingle-style design by a talented local architect named Paul Malo, Mom and Dad turned to another local man, Alain Verley, a student of le Corbusier who lived in Cazenovia Village with his glamorous wife, France. My parents were traditionalists who thought they were modernists. They rejected the romantic design of the first architect because it dug up memories of their own grandparents' summer houses (which should have been a good thing). They chose the modernist, and then immediately began to backpedal. It was no help, of course, that they kept asking my advice, since I was, supposedly, "artistic."

More wisely, they dragged my friend Tod into it, and he became their de facto decorator. Convincing WASPs that they need decorators is always an iffy proposition, since there is a weirdly fallacious assumption that good taste automatically implies that one doesn't need a professional's help to decorate a house. Once I had reached the age of gay reason (which was about the same time I got to Exeter, I think), I had become increasingly unhappy with the way my parents' house looked. The core conflict between traditionalism and modernism was the problem. By contrast, Tod has always had not just great taste, but a professional's eye. He has never lived anywhere ugly. In 1976, I had only seen his mother's apartment in New York and her country house in Shelter Island, but they were both gorgeous, glamorous places. My parents loved Tod, and they trusted his ability to bridge the gap between Corbusier and Colonial Williamsburg.

Strangely enough, on what was our first anniversary as a couple, I left Gary in New Haven after Christmas with my family in Cazenovia and joined Tod and his mother on a New Year's week in Mustique in the Caribbean. Even more bizarrely, Tod's mother, by some quirk of fate, was dating a friend of my parents, and he had a dreamily theatrical little villa called Blue Water on this tiny island. Mustique is a private island of barely more than two square miles. Close to St. Vincent in the Lesser Antilles, it was developed as a resort by Colin Tennant, who later became Lord Glenconner. He hired British stage de-signer Oliver Messel to create a scattered community of romantic stucco villas. My parents' friend John (a casket manufacturer whose factory was next to the Dietz factory in Syracuse) had bought Blue Water on a lark, and it only seemed logical that Tod and I would accompany them. I have no memory of Gary's reaction to my defection, but he knew that Tod was no threat. Tod's glamour drew me away from Winchester Avenue. After all, Princess Margaret had a house in Mustique, and that was as far from *Leave it to Beaver* as could be. Tod and I had a wonderful week together, and any number of moments that thrilled me with a sense of being part of a rarified, jet-setty world. It would be the last time, however.

The only dramatic failure of my senior year was not getting accepted into the Winterthur Program, a remarkable two-year master's course offered by Henry Francis DuPont's Winterthur Museum outside of Wilmington, Del-aware. A fellowship to this program included full tuition at the University of Delaware, and a modest annual stipend. The application process included a carefully scripted weekend visit, several interviews, socializing with the other candidates, and a formal dinner at a trustee's estate that (in my day) went so far as to separate the men from the women after the meal for cigars and brandy in the library. I knew how to play the social game well enough, but the final interview killed me because I forgot one of the golden rules of the museum world in the 1970s: never speak well of dealers. Dealers might sell you masterpieces for your collection, indeed they might be indispensable; but they were never *friends*. They were tainted by commerce, whereas curators (and by extension rich collectors) were scholars, above considerations of money. In 1977 I still believed this nonsense, but I was also naïve to the point of idiocy. I had not managed to have a final interview with Charles Montgomery before I left New Haven. He would have made sure I didn't stick my foot in it. News of my rejection, which I received at my parents' house in Syracuse over spring break, crushed me. It also gave me and Gary the opportunity to do some adulting together.

I graduated with my parents and Gary by my side. Summa Cum Laude, Phi Beta Kappa. It feels stupid to write that, but after all, I had focused on being a student. Those Latin and Greek words were the equivalent of sports trophies or gold medals for me. I had carefully choreographed my undergraduate years to avoid things in which I knew I'd do poorly. My major specialty in seventeenth-century French satire was fun but meaningless. My art history and decorative arts studies were what mattered. With an inadvertent gap year ahead of me, Gary and I moved into a snug little apartment on Broadway just down the street from the Yale Co-op. We were in a quirky little brick building that looked Olde England, our flat on top of the Y Barber Shop. Our landlady, an ancient little woman named Mrs. Kligerman, lived upstairs. Our bedroom overlooked a bus stop (fumes and street noise) while our knotty-pine living/dining room overlooked the alley behind a rock saloon called Toad's Place (vomit and drunken carousing). It was our slice of heaven, two blocks from the Yale University Art Gallery, only a few more blocks to Partner's, our local gay bar. I got permission to park my car in the student garage up Science Hill, but we only used the car for trips west to Syracuse or south to Manhattan.

At some point in senior year, I had been to New Jersey to meet Gary's parents, Gladys and Pete. They put each of us in one of the little twin-bedded rooms in which Gary and his older brother Alan had spent their teen years. Gary would sneak into my room once his parents were asleep. It was during this otherwise unmemorable visit that Gary took me to the Newark Museum. There was a big loan exhibition on Chinese export porcelain, and I got to see the partly restored Ballantine House, an 1885 beer-baron's mansion that still housed the museum's executive offices on its upper floors. I had never visited either Newark or this museum, and of course had no idea what a part it would play in my life.

Coming out is a never-ending process, as any gay person will tell you. That year, we got to deal with Gary's family. Gladys and Pete threatened to come visit us in New Haven, and suddenly our one-bedroom apartment loomed large (or small, as it were) in that scenario. Gary handled it much more succinctly than I had with my parents: he came out to them in a short, carefully-considered phone message. The only reaction was an equally short phone message, with Gladys sighing loudly and telling her son that "it's all right." They came to visit us for the day from New Jersey, and the topic of his being gay and my being his boyfriend was never raised again. I mean that literally, until the day they died, decades later. Gradually I would work my way into Gary's extended New Jersey family, but that would come later.

Gladys Berger's little brother Phil came to visit us while we were in the Broadway flat. Then in his early fifties, Philip Lehner was the youngest of Gertie and Kalman Lehner's surviving children, growing up in Newark's heavily Jewish south end and attending high school with Ed Koch, who would grow up to be the mayor of New York City. Phil had accompanied his sisters Beatrice and Ruth to California in 1943. At the end of their stay, as his sisters were about to get on the train, Phil announced that he was staying in Los Angeles. He had seventy dollars in his pocket. He was nineteen years old and gay. He figured Los Angeles was a long way from Newark and his large female family. It seemed like a good move.

Phil worked in Hollywood for a while, accumulating a collection of rather well-done pencil portraits of studio stars he met that he had drawn himself while working for one of the studios in some low-level capacity. He lived in both Silver Lake and West Hollywood, finding his way in the dating world of gay LA in the 1940s. He told us that once he got pulled off the street late at night by the LAPD, who were on edge because of the Black Dahlia murder in 1947. Eventually, Phil parlayed his artistic talent into a design position for the Broadway department store chain. In the early 1950s Phil met Fritz Steinbach, an ex-marine turned interior designer. In the early sixties they moved south to the newly developed sprawl of Huntington Beach in Orange County. By the time Phil came to visit us in New Haven, Fritz had long ago stopped coming east over some political set-to with Gary's Aunt Ruth.

Clearly, Phil was excited to see his nephew and to meet what appeared to be said nephew's boyfriend. Phil spent a night sleeping on the floor in our little apartment, but we could never get him to talk directly about the elephant in the room—that we were a couple. Nevertheless, he became "our" uncle that visit. Over the years he would relax and talk more openly about his life as a young gay man in Los Angeles in the 1940s and 50s. Leaving Newark, apparently, had been a good choice.

It was a year of firsts for Gary and me as a couple. We went to Europe for three weeks in the summer, and then went to California to visit Phil and Fritz later that year. Mostly, however, we learned how to be together. Without guidelines from the greater society around us, we had to negotiate our own pathways into a shared future. It was, amazingly, pretty easy.

On our European trip—a week each in London, Paris, and Amsterdam—we began to really see ourselves as a couple in the context of the larger world. We met up with an Exeter and Yale friend, Martha, who was getting her masters at the Warburg Institute and working as a cataloguer in the woodwork department of the Victoria and Albert Museum. Martha was enormous fun, and with her we visited Kew Gardens and had a giddy picnic on the lawn at Osterley Park with food Gary and I had bought at Harrod's. She gave us a behind-the-scenes tour at Osterley, where part of the V&A's woodwork collection was squirreled away in the upper bedrooms that weren't part of the public tours. Martha would go on to become a lawyer with a focus on art law.

While we were in London, we stayed with my mother's cousin John Root, son of Edward Root, my grandmother's younger brother, and his wife Grace. John's wife was a flamboyant and warm-hearted Athenian named Nanda. My mother and John had grown up close friends in Clinton, but until this point I only knew him vaguely as the tall, debonair oil executive who had lived in exotic places like Tripoli and Beirut. John had grown up on the Hamilton College campus, where his father, my grandmother's brother, taught art history and collected modern art. His mother Grace, whom I knew well as a child, was an old-school bluestocking from Albany. Grace was a serious gardener, and to this day her gardens are part of Hamilton College, and the place where we've scattered my family's ashes.

Nanda was exotic to me as a boy, European in her chic fashion sense and daring in her not-entirely-natural blond hair. She always joked about her odd place in her husband's stuffy and slightly eccentric Wasp family, but always seemed to take joy in the contrast between her fiery self and her cool, courtly spouse. Nanda was also seriously involved in theater and named their only child after the Greek actress Melina Mercouri, who was also her godmother.

With no reason other than his lifelong affection for my mother, John invited us to stay at their sprawling Victorian flat near Westminster Cathedral in London. Throughout our stay there, John, Nanda, and teenaged daughter Melina treated us like family, embracing Gary as my partner with no hesitation. Nanda assigned us a private room and bath at the end of a long corridor and made us breakfast every morning in her enormous kitchen. Although Melina was still in her mid-teens at this point, she was a more cosmopolitan adolescent than I'd ever been. That week in London imprinted in us a special fondness for the Roots that never faded away. Melina would go to Yale, study costume design, and win Emmy Awards for her work on television shows such as *Third Rock from the Sun* and *That Seventies Show.*

The California trip that summer introduced me to my new uncle Fritz. Phil and Fritz were our first experience of a gay couple of our parents' generation. They had moved to Huntington Beach when it was still a distant outpost of Los Angeles, and bought a three-bedroom California ranch, in which they would live for the rest of their lives. Fritz had embraced Orange County political views and would become increasingly conservative as he got older. He was a fan of Ronald Reagan, both as governor and eventually as president. I suspect it was his politics rather than his orientation that was the reason he had stopped going east on family visits with Phil. Until he was no longer physically able, Phil would make periodic trips to visit various relatives in the Lehner family, leaving Fritz at home to care for their pets.

When we visited them in 1977, a kind of happy chaos reigned. As the house of a decorator, the ranch on Potomac Lane was in constant flux, with bits and pieces of Fritz's various jobs finding their way into the décor. Then there were the animals. When we walked in the door we were greeted by two affectionate Irish wolfhounds, a little Maltese-like dust-mop of a dog who trailed around among their legs, several cats, and an African gray parrot named Dudley who walked around the house calling out "I love you" with random enthusiasm. A detail we missed until very early the next morning was the aviary in the back yard filled with a hundred or so canaries, who all burst into song outside our bedroom window when a light set on a timer switched on in the pre-dawn darkness.

On their twenty-fifth anniversary I bought a Victorian silver presentation mug and sent it to Huntington Beach. Fritz told me over the phone that it made him cry.

CHAPTER TWENTY-ONE

Speculation #6
THE BARGAIN

Teddy worked his way up the lawn toward the house. The sun was warmer than he had expected, despite the breeze off the water, and his white linen suit felt damp and confining. He had forgotten his hat, and felt his head burning. He wasn't quite huffing and puffing, but he was, perhaps, more conscious of his breathing than a man just reaching forty should have been. As he approached the looming brownstone bulk of the house, he could just see a white smudge among the cooler shadows of the deep porch.

Olga lazed indulgently against the soft linen cushions of the rattan armchair. The muslin gown clung to her uncomfortably, and the brightness of the sunshine on the rolling lawn hurt her eyes. A glass pitcher of lemonade and a half-finished tumbler of it sat abandoned on a table at her side. A copy of Edith Wharton's recent book on decorating lay open in her lap. Through half-closed eyes, she watched as her husband neared, spoiling her seclusion. "Where are the children?" she asked, without moving, as Teddy came up the steps and across the stone floor.

"Still playing down by the water with Nanny," he answered, pouring himself a glass of lemonade and lowering himself with a grateful sigh into the chair next to his wife's. "Their energy is boundless, and I confess the heat has rather gotten the better of me. I figured I'd let them tire themselves out." He took a deep swallow of his drink and sighed again.

Olga turned her head, her eyes hooded, and studied her husband.

Teddy was still a good-looking man, she thought, as he had been when they first met in Chicago over a decade earlier. Well-groomed and well dressed, he was a bit stouter now than he should be, and a telltale network of fine capillaries on his tanned cheeks told of his fondness for alcohol. Olga wondered if perhaps that should worry her more than it did.

"I'm glad you're here," she said softly. Her voice was deep for a woman, melodious. "I've something I need to discuss with you."

Teddy took another swig of his lemonade, his expression suddenly alert. He turned and looked squarely at his wife.

"Yes?"

"I'm planning to travel abroad soon. I've booked passage on the Bretagne to le Havre for next month. I'll spend a week or so in Paris, then take *le train bleu* to Nice. I've taken a villa in Saint Jean Cap Ferrat for two months." Teddy looked slightly stunned by this news. "And when were you planning to tell me this?" he asked.

Olga laughed softly. "I'm telling you now, dear."

Teddy stared hard at his wife for a moment. A low tremor of fear began to work its way through his bones. "I presume you're planning on traveling alone?"

Olga's large, dark eyes were no longer sleepy. She fixed their full force on her husband. "Of course not. I'll be accompanied by my maid." She paused, then continued. "And I'm taking Ethel with me."

"Olga, she's barely eleven years old!"

"Yes, and it's time she began to learn to comport herself in company." Olga spoke with apparent patience. "She's spent far too much time with no companion other than her brother. I wish to introduce her into adult society. I want people to know her. She's a bright child. She will charm them, and they will remember her."

"Remember her? Whatever for?" Teddy looked genuinely puzzled.

Olga sighed, as if trying to communicate with a dim-witted child. "Teddy, Ethel is an heiress. She and Robert are the only children in their generation. Eventually, she must marry."

"I repeat, she's only just eleven. And in any case, why can't she marry a young man from here?"

Olga's smile was smug. "That's all well and good for you, perhaps. But it is not what I have in mind for my daughter."

"Our daughter," said Teddy softly, his wife's plan gradually taking shape in his imagination. Then, as if rousing himself, he focused upon Olga once again. "What about Robert and me? What shall we do?"

"Whatever you like, dear. You can have a happy bachelor time together here. Or you can close up this house and take him to Hempstead to stay with his grandmother and your sister."

Olga couldn't abide her mother-in-law, Anna, widow of the family patriarch, dead two years since. She told herself it was Anna's tiresome Anglo-Irish priggishness that irritated her; but Olga was less inclined to admit the uncomfortable truth that Anna's less-than-exalted origins echoed too closely her own. She had no regrets about catching the eye of the handsome son of a New York industrialist; but she would make very sure that her daughter didn't marry beneath her.

"This is all rather expensive, you know," Teddy started. "I'm not sure I'm willing to support such self-indulgent…"

"That's just what I wanted to talk to you about, Teddy," Olga interrupted, her voice still pitched low, but somehow sharper.

He stopped, flustered. "What?" He looked at his wife, the tingle of fear noticeably stronger.

"I think it's time that I had an income of my own." She made sure he was paying attention. "I'd like you to arrange with your lawyer to have a monthly stipend paid to my personal account."

"You what?"

"That way, I can arrange for wire transfers as I travel. I shan't need to trouble you at all."

"Why on earth do you think I'd do this?" Teddy asked. "Haven't I always been generous with your expenses?"

Olga sat up, straightening her back, and turned her whole body toward her husband. A coldness in her expression belied the gentle sonority of her tone.

"I think you will do it, Teddy."

She paused, giving full weight to the next words she spoke. "You see, if you don't do as I wish, I'm afraid I'll be forced to ask for a divorce."

Teddy looked stunned. "On what possible grounds?"

Again, Olga fixed her eyes on her husband's. Teddy visibly shrank from her stare.

"I had you followed in the city, Teddy. I had a man follow you over a period of several weeks."

His eyes went wide. "What?"

Her small smile was sad. "You are discreet, Teddy, I grant you that, and no doubt should thank you for it. There has been no gossip. But my man was very careful. He watched you enter that saloon on the Bowery, and he saw you leave a while later. He made careful note of the man with whom you left."

Teddy said nothing. His body sagged as he let himself fall back against the cushions, his high forehead shining with perspiration. He closed his eyes and let escape a low moan.

"I am fond of you, Teddy." The coldness was gone from Olga's voice, replaced with a sweetness that, if perhaps not entirely convincing, was not wholly insincere.

"We have been married for a long time. I have been a good wife. I have given you two beautiful children, one of them a son. They will inherit the company. They will be the future of this family, Teddy. They will give you grandchildren and great-grandchildren."

Teddy looked dully at her. Whatever fear he had felt had changed to a simple sense of defeat.

"I don't see at all why I, who have done my duty to you faithfully, should suffer because you do not—cannot—do yours. It is simply not fair."

Olga's expression had brightened. There was an odd sort of enthusiasm in her voice now, as if she were describing a marvelous scheme and expected her husband's full endorsement.

"I do not judge you. You are who you are, as God made you. All I ask is that you let me live with some independence. To go where I like, when I like. Of course, I shan't be always traveling. I will come back here. I will come to New York. I will continue to be your wife, the mistress of your household, the mother of your children."

She reached out and grasped the forgotten glass of lemonade, drinking with relish. Setting the empty glass down again, she finished her proposal.

"Give me what I want, and I will be no trouble at all."

They sat there for a while in silence, eyeing each other; her eyes bright and predatory, his dull and filled with resignation.

Suddenly, Teddy sat up and, leaning forward, grasped the silver bell on the lemonade tray. He rang it vigorously a few times and set it down. When a maid appeared from the dim recesses of the house, he looked up at her, his face again composed and showing a cheerfulness he surely didn't feel.

"Bring me the bottle of gin from the butler's pantry. I think I'd like something a bit stronger to invigorate this lovely lemonade you've brought us."

The maid gave a small bob and disappeared back into the house. Teddy slumped back into the cushions and closed his eyes. His hands gripped the armrests of the chair.

"I will do as you wish, my dear," he said.

In the distance, the animated squeals of Robert and his big sister Ethel could be heard, as they returned from their adventure down by the water with Nanny.

CHAPTER TWENTY-TWO

FINIAL LAND

Winterthur is a city near Zurich in Switzerland. It is pronounced with the W as a V and the TH as a T, and with all the vowels spoken in their European inflection. The DuPont estate outside of Wilmington, Delaware, called Winterthur, is pronounced as an American hybrid, ending up sounding like "winter-tour." I'm just giving the facts, not explaining them. The original house at Winterthur was built in the 1830s, a stylish neoclassical box with a small Doric portico at the front door. In the 1880s, when Henry Francis DuPont and his sister Louise were kids, the house was enlarged by adding a high, vaguely Renaissance-style hipped roof with elaborate dormers and more rooms under its terra cotta tiles. In 1906, Harry and Louise's father, Henry Algernon DuPont, expanded the house again, turning it into a sort of sprawling French Renaissance hunting lodge with still more tiled roofs and the sort of eclectic interiors that exemplified the Euro-centric opulence of the late Gilded Age. Colonel DuPont served in the U.S. Senate at this time, where he surely knew my great-grandfather Elihu Root, who was also a Republican senator with strong ties to corporate America.

When the colonel died in 1926, Henry Francis, known as Harry and by now married to Senator Root's niece Ruth Wales, inherited the rambling pile. Harry, who had done a lot of the original decorating for his father in the early 1900s, began a three-decade reimagining and expansion of the house into a fantasy of American colonial revivalism, filling its scores of rooms and subsidiary spaces with paneling and furnishings gathered from all over the original thirteen colonies. By the time I was finally accepted into Winterthur's graduate program in the spring of 1978, the place was a vast, T-shaped structure that cascaded down a hillside on 1200 acres outside of Wilmington.

In the 1950s, an education wing and visitors' entrance had been created out of Winterthur's original servants' quarters, and in the 1960s Harry had built a conservation center and research library named after his sister, Louise Crowninshield, onto that. When I arrived there as a student, the house had nine stories, and a gaggle of small Otis elevators to facilitate tours, each one lined with Georgian-style walnut paneling. It was a labyrinth of period rooms, hallways, staircases, all dimly lit with little electric candles in period fixtures. Carefully-trained docents—all women—gave tours in hushed tones using flashlights. It was a treasure-trove of Americana and a pilgrimage site for people interested in antiques. It was the Vatican of American-style Good Taste. Harry DuPont had been called on to help Mrs. Kennedy restore the White House (which, given that he was a Republican, must have been a double-edged honor). For would-be decorative arts curators, it was Yale Law School or Harvard Business School or Johns Hopkins Medical School. For me it was a dream come true. My classmates and I would come to refer to it fondly as Finial Land, because of the museum's logo then: the name Winterthur centered on a spiral-turned furniture finial.

There were nine other students in my year, ten being the maximum in any Winterthur class. I had only met my new classmates once, during the second interview weekend. One of my Yale classmates, Ned Cooke, had made it in the first time around, and thus there was at least one familiar face during the arcane proceedings of the interview weekend. This time I did not screw up my interview; even when one of the trustees, who was Harry and Ruth DuPont's older daughter, and thus my second cousin once removed, asked me if I would attend the program even if I did not receive the financial support that normally accompanied the fellowship. I was slightly floored by the question, since I knew that she knew my parents, and would probably also have met my grand-parents, Ulysses and Edith Grant, when they visited Winterthur as houseguests in the 1940s. Apparently, I answered that question correctly. I really wanted to be part of Winterthur.

Gary quit his job at the Yale Computer Center and readily found another in an office park near Route 95 outside of Newark, Delaware, where the university was located. He went to work for a firm called Autotote, a tech company that produced computer hardware and software for the management of betting at horse-racing tracks around the world. I hope I understood at the time what his willingness to simply leave a secure job at an Ivy League university meant. I needed to move to Delaware, and Gary never questioned the fact that he needed to come with me. It was easy for smart computer code-writers to find jobs back then; but I still look back and am awed by what Gary did for me—and would do more than once.

Having found a surprisingly large 1960s garden apartment on the south side of Newark (pronounced, by the way, New-Ark, and in fact named after the Newark in which I would eventually spend my career), Gary and I settled into the second phase of our life as a couple. Among my graduate class-mates, Gary and I had scored big in terms of domestic amenities. All that sculpted avocado wall-to-wall carpeting; the two full bathrooms (one yellow, one blue); the garbage disposal and dishwasher in the kitchen. It was all very deluxe (for $300 a month) by graduate student standards. My Winterthur stipend of $3600 a year covered our rent.

Naturally, I took Gary to the first communal gathering of the staff and students, held on a warm August evening in the garden of one of the Winterthur guides. Along with the new fellows, there was a new class of guides being trained that summer. These women, many of whom were tied somehow to the DuPont company through their husbands, would become my allies over the next two years. I introduced Gary around, being typically vague, as one was in those days, as to our relationship. I blush to think that I might have used the term "roommate." It was 1978, and the idea of introducing Gary as my boyfriend was unimaginable in this context. This was standard procedure for gay couples back then; let everyone meet him and then draw their own conclusions. That gave people a chance to ignore what they didn't want to deal with. It was a surprisingly effective strategy that had served gay couples for a long time.

The party was well underway, plenty of drink and food and conversation on a lovely summer evening, when one of my new classmates, Susan, came up behind me and actually bit me on the shoulder. Clearly, she was feeling no pain, and in her South Boston accent said something both sweet and snarky about having figured us out. I probably didn't even have the good grace to feel grateful that coming out in my new world was going to be this easy. Looking back forty-odd years, I realize that Gary and I were probably the first openly gay couple ever to be part of the Winterthur program. I had other gay classmates in my two years there, but either they weren't out yet or they weren't part of a pair. Without any intention of doing so, Gary and I had become trailblazers. I wish I could say it was because we were brave and we had a plan, but really it was just the two of us bumbling forward without paying much attention. The obliviousness that had served me so well in my middle- and high-school years continued to provide a strangely effective shield.

Our graduate education began with Guide Training and what was called the Summer Institute. The former was only for new fellows and new guides; the latter was open to interested members of the public for a fee. Basically, it prepared me to begin my academic year, like a three-week orientation program. I got to know both the museum and my nine new classmates, as well as the group of women who had decided to join that rarified crew who took visitors through the labyrinth of Winterthur's two hundred rooms and 70,000 objects.

Although all the fellows (as we were called) were required to give tours at least once a week, I really took to it. We all got paid, and the extra income was welcome, but I found that, as I had at Lorenzo in Cazenovia, I loved the face-to-face contact with the public. I loved talking about things. I guided several times a week, in between classes and study time. I'd sit with a book in the guides' waiting room, either reading or chatting with this group of smart women who reminded me of my mother and her friends.

Tours at Winterthur in the late 1970s were carefully choreographed. Each one lasted an hour and a half, the day being divided into morning and afternoon sessions. One needed to take more than one tour to see everything, and a full day was a considerable time commitment. Tour groups consisted of no more than five people and a guide, given the small spaces and tiny elevators that abounded in the museum complex. Each guide was given a slip of paper with her route laid out in precise sequence. Each route covered everything in the rooms one passed through, unless someone requested and paid for a Special Subject Tour (silver, rugs, glass, Chippendale furniture, etc.). It was up to the guides to keep out of each other's way, so that every tour felt personal and intimate. It was a remarkable way to interpret such a huge collection, and for the kind of people who flocked to Winterthur in those days, a memorable experience.

What an extraordinary place it was to be trained. With the possible exception of a statistics course that was required (supposedly to assist in our research skills), most of the coursework was about what I already loved. Connoisseurship was important in those days; understanding how to evaluate all kinds of domestic objects by material and design and construction, and being able to place them in context within the world for which they were made. Part of our training was learning to understand the social and economic strata of material culture—which objects were at the top of the pyramid, and where all the others fell below them. The secondary purpose was to understand them culturally, where their design roots were, and how different parts of Colonial and Federal America produced objects that were both part of their historical moment and distinctively of their geographical place.

Winterthur's collections were huge, but limited by Mr. DuPont's taste and prejudices. Like many children of the late Victorian era, he hated most things Victorian, and shunned the Gilded Age aesthetic that his father had embraced. Fortunately, Winterthur's amazing research library was not so limited, and included remarkable holdings covering a great deal of the nineteenth century from trade catalogues to household inventories. The true gaps in Winterthur's comprehensive holdings were things made in the American South, the formerly Spanish and French-held parts of the country, and things by anyone who wasn't white. The understanding and study of Southern decorative arts was still young, and it was through visits to places like the Museum of Early Southern Decorative Arts (MESDA) in Winston-Salem, North Carolina, and Colonial Williamsburg, that we got to see and understand the larger story of American domestic goods.

While Yale had been all about objects displayed as art, Winterthur was all about context. There were heavily Anglophilic rooms from all of the major colonial centers; but also German-American interiors from Pennsylvania and Dutch American interiors from upstate New York. As mentioned, there were no Spanish-American objects or interiors, since those areas were Spanish-held and not part of the original thirteen colonies. Not that there wasn't enough for us all to learn just inside the colonies. Museum curators were still a generation away from grappling with the reality of enslaved labor in the trades in Colonial and Federal America.

***

My degree required three courses at the University of Delaware that were outside the object-related coursework at the museum, and I was lucky enough to have three fantastic professors for those classes. Richard Bushman taught a semester's course on Jacksonian history and politics, waking my mind up to the joy of history in a way I wouldn't have thought possible. Wayne Craven taught us American landscape painting, giving a deeper focus to what I'd learned from Ted Stebbins at Yale. Most wonderfully, Edward Rosenberry taught me and a few of my classmates about nineteenth-century American fiction, from Poe and Melville to Hawthorne. This course rekindled my love of reading and sparked an interest in Victorian literature that would open a new world to me. I began to understand nineteenth-century novels as time-travel devices, allowing me to see the world through the eyes of people who had lived in the past.

Gary and I had no trouble shifting our New Haven life to our new Delaware locale. We had begun to march in the New York Gay Pride Marches (not parades, *marches*) in 1976, along with other college groups. The Gay Alliance at Yale was a small but loud clutch of men back in the days when the participants far outnumbered the spectators. This was, remember, only seven years after Stonewall, and New York's annual march, which we traveled to the city to take part in, was timed to mark the anniversary of the Stonewall rebellion. The last Sunday in June was our Independence Day, and as young gay men we took it to heart. There were few if any political faces present at the marches back then, and absolutely no mainstream commercial sponsors as there are today. The police lining the parade route were civil but not friendly, and there were plenty of anti-gay protestors and catcalls from the sidelines. If you had told us that, three decades later, our children would go to the Pride March with their friends *for fun,* we would have laughed at you (not to mention the idea of being parents). After the parade ended in Greenwich Village, we'd pile into the Riviera Café and eat mediocre food as we watched the hubbub out on the street. It was great fun.

Greenwich Village became our getaway place, our gay Disneyland where we could hold hands and kiss publicly and go to restaurants openly as a couple. Being there amidst "our people" was exhilarating for twinks like us. Gary and I were neither party boys nor club kids, but we were comfortable in our skin, especially in terms of our generation, when the closet was a constant presence in the lives of many gay men. Being circumspect in the rest of the world was automatic. None of this seemed awkward or strange, it's just the way things were. David's Pot Belly restaurant on Christopher Street became a favorite weekend brunch place, and we visited whatever bar was nearby or suited our mood. Greenwich Village was a very gay place.

Leaving our Yale friends in New Haven meant that we had to make new gay friends and a gay life in Delaware. We had chosen our apartment, as far as could be from where the rest of the Winterthur fellows rented, presuming that we would have little to do with my classmates socially. To be honest, I doubt Gary thought much about it; this was really about me and my assumptions. The fact is that I immediately liked all my classmates—in both years—and we all got along famously. That I was part of a male couple seems to have made no difference at all. As would happen repeatedly over the next decade, I anticipated homophobia where none appeared. The joy of Winterthur and its fellows was that we were all "object oriented," the only orientation that mattered.

That said, Gary and I did want some sort of a gay social life in Delaware. We were a long way from thinking in phrases like "dominant culture" and such socio-demographic buzzwords, but even though we both wanted to be part of the "regular" world, we also wanted people like us around us. Gay identity includes having kindred spirits affirming who you are and commiserating when necessary. However well-accepted we were, nobody straight was going to encourage us to divulge anything remotely personal or talk about our lives.

Soon enough, we met David and Dennis, a couple in their early forties who lived in a ranch house on the outskirts of the university not far from our apartment. Through them we met Tom and Asa, a couple who lived in our apartment complex. There was a gay alliance at the University of Delaware, and we were peripherally involved with them, marching with them in the first gay pride march on Washington in 1979 (again, it was not called LGBT then, it was just Gay Pride). The march coincided with the fourth anniversary of the day Gary and I met, and we actually got tear-gassed next to the new East Wing of the National Gallery (honestly, we don't know who threw the tear gas canister, and it was likely not the police but some anti-gay crank). Oddly, I don't think we ever were afraid during these marches. Harvey Milk had been assassinated in 1978, but that was specific and political. Terrorism had not yet reshaped the American psyche, and the anti-gay right wing (including Anita Bryant in 1977) was vociferous rather than violent. This was long before gay pride events had become ubiquitous across the country. San Francisco and New York offered the only celebrations of any size. The observance in Washington was new.

By a bizarre coincidence, a Newark, Delaware mother and her gay son decided to open a gay bar in a strip-mall on Route 896 (aka College Avenue). It was right next to the Howard Johnson's, and across the street from Welsh Tract Road, where our apartment complex was located. Once again, we had a bar we could walk to from home, and a place to go for a late-night snack after the bar closed at 1:00 a.m. The all-night HoJo's (Howard Johnson's) was often full of workers from the nearby Chrysler plant, taking their wives to dinner after the night shift as those of us from the bar had an early breakfast. All those places are gone now, and it startles me how readily we took them for granted.

***

The very term still gives me shivers: *touching privileges*. This was the magic power that Winterthur fellows received along with their tuition and their stipend. During office hours (in addition to public hours), we all had free access to the scores of galleries and period rooms. Armed with white gloves and notebooks, the fellows could roam at will, handling objects, opening drawers. Learning to know objects means looking at and touching them. This kind of free access to collections is one of the greatest privileges of being a curator. It was an experience I will never forget.

Despite Winterthur's emphasis on "early" Americana, my own interests were tipping more and more to the nineteenth century, especially under the fervent mentorship of Kenneth Ames, one of the professors based at Winterthur. Ken was charged with teaching us about the aesthetic and cultural complexities of the Victorian era. During the opening lecture of our orientation training, the entire Victorian period was covered in a single slide: a shot of the reception room of the 1885 Ballantine House at the Newark Museum. For Harry DuPont and all those imbued with the Winterthur ethos, the years after 1840 at best elicited a mild shudder of distaste, and at worst outright disparagement or dismissal as "bad taste." There were Victorian objects in Winterthur's collections, but they were either accidental, or expressive of Mr. DuPont's personal decorating taste. For example, he loved transfer-printed English earthenware, and had hundreds of pieces in every possibly color. True, some of this, the "Historic Blue" of the 1820s counts as "early American," but the bulk of it is 1830s, 40s and 50s, and is about as industrial as any product of any factory ever was. Generally, however, Winterthur focused on pre-industrial goods made in or imported to America's original thirteen colonies.

Ken Ames opened a magic door for me and would set the tone for the rest of my career. Having started as a volunteer in an 1807 house with multiple generations of nineteenth-century accumulation, I was already sympathetic. With a burgeoning awareness of my own political ancestry, one that exemplified the Victorian narrative in America, I might have been primed for Ken's passionate love for and profound understanding of all things Victorian. (By the way, Ken also taught me to hate the term Victorian, which lumped the incredible social and aesthetic complexities of the 1830-1900 period together.)

At some point in my Winterthur career, I remembered stumbling across an incredible 1860 lighting catalogue in the archives of my family's factory in Syracuse. Large in format—fourteen by twenty inches—the Dietz & Company product catalogue included beautiful color-printed woodcut pages, many of them embellished with metallic gold ink. The objects featured ranged from ornate cased-and-cut glass parlor lamps to flat-wick kerosene burners— the device that gave the Dietz brothers their technological edge in the late 1850s. There was also a page of figural candle holders of a type unique to American production, known in the period as girandoles. These were all from the 1840s and early 1850s, representing the company's older production. The catalogue was a showpiece of American trade catalogue printing and remains to this day a unique survivor of its kind.

During the post-Civil-War expansion, the Dietz Company had evolved into a manufacturer of lighting related to construction and the automotive industry. Kerosene-fueled tubular lanterns were the last link to the nineteenth-century product line, and by 1960 those were all produced in the company's new Hong Kong factory. In its two Syracuse factories, Dietz made the injection-molded plastic domes for police car lights, as well as the red and amber reflectors for Winnebago recreational vehicles and mail delivery trucks. I had known nothing of the company's early products, and thus the discovery that my family had once produced *decorative arts,* from the whale-oil lamps of the 1840s to the kerosene fixtures of the 1860s, was a jolt and an inspiration. I decided to do my thesis on the early lighting of Dietz & Company. Thenceforth, thanks to my classmate Jeanne (who would go on to a long and distinguished career at Christie's auction house in New York), my thesis was referred to as Dietz by Dietz by Dietz (which I guess meant the Ulysses Dietz thesis on the Dietz lamps made by the Dietz family).

CHAPTER TWENTY-THREE

THE ANTI-AMERICAN WING

During our last six months in Delaware, we bought a golden cocker spaniel puppy at a pet store in the Christiana Mall near Newark. There was a no-pet rule at the Villa Belmont Apartments, but the ladies at the front desk knew us as "the boys with the antiques," and figured they could trust us. Named Gilda (probably inspired by Gilda Radner, but also by her silky golden coat), she was adorable, although as she got older she would demonstrate in full why one should never buy puppies from pet shops in malls. Gilda would be the first of a line of beloved house pets that has continued for over forty years.

When you live through the span of two years, it seems like a lot of time. Looking back, especially from decades later, it's like nothing, a blink. In the spring of 1980, with my thesis heading toward completion, I started my job hunt. I don't think Winterthur offered anything much in the way of job placement (not like the good old days, when Mr. DuPont could pick up the phone and get a favored fellow a position). I must have looked in places for job listings but can recall nothing specific. In the end, I had four job interviews. Of course, in my romantic imagination my dream job was in the American Wing at the Metropolitan Museum. I may have known one person at the Met by this point in my life, and the American Wing had in fact been closed for expansion during my entire education, and I had not seen it since my visit in 1970 when I was fifteen.

A curatorial position at the Rosenbach Museum and Library in Philadelphia was posted in a local newspaper, but the agency to which I went for my interview looked suspiciously like the kind of seedy place that found entry-level positions in low-end retail establishments: plastic chairs, ugly stained carpet, the whole deal. I knew something of the Rosenbach, having explored it on my own on a different weekend with Gary. It was a cool place, housed in an old mansion and full of interesting stories, not to mention the original manuscript of *Dracula* by Bram Stoker. On a mantelpiece in a Victorian parlor was a pair of gilt brass girandoles I attributed to Dietz & Company and illustrated in my thesis. I was, however, never interviewed at the museum nor did I speak to any staff there. In retrospect, there must have been an inside hire in the works, and this was some sort of compliance posting for which they never expected a Winterthur graduate to apply. It was an inauspicious start, but a start.

The next prospect was at Raynham Hall in Oyster Bay, New York. This was an on-site interview, and I arrived in almost total ignorance of the site (because, after all, there was no Internet). I remember being charmed by the house, a colonial building with many generations of additions, followed by some severe re-interpretation back to its colonial roots in the years after World War II. I never heard back from this interview either, and in retrospect understood that it wouldn't have been ideal for me.

My third attempt was at the Brooklyn Museum, where the august Diane Pilgrim, then curator of decorative arts, interviewed me alone. Of course, Brooklyn and its decorative arts collection is astonishing, not to mention having some of the earliest period rooms in any American art museum, and the very first installation of Victorian interiors in any art museum. Brooklyn was not a chic place to live in the late 1970s, but that didn't matter to me. This was the kind of job I wanted.

I didn't get that job either, but I have always taken solace in the fact that Kevin Stayton, a good friend from Yale, got the job instead. He was there for thirty-eight years.

Meanwhile, I had heard second-hand through one of my teachers at Winterthur that Philip Curtis was leaving his job at the Newark Museum, to take the position vacated by Arlene Palmer, Winterthur's ceramics and glass curator, when she married. Philip knew that my thesis was on nineteenth-century lighting and recommended I apply for the position, figuring that I might be a good fit for Newark.

Was I anxious about any of these interviews? I don't think so. I trust that this was obliviousness rather than arrogance. It was a different world from today. Winterthur still packed a lot of clout in the decorative arts world, and its influence was felt in museums across the country. I had visited Newark, with Gary, while I was working at Winterthur, during a visit to New Jersey to stay with his parents for Rosh Hashanah or Thanksgiving or something. We toured a loan exhibition of Chinese export porcelain, augmented with pieces from the museum collection. I saw the 1885 Ballantine House, its first floor restored for the national Bicentennial in 1976. We looked at Tibetan art, ancient glass, African art, and a show about animals represented in American art. The Museum was (and is) deceptive, since the vast majority of its collections are always in storage. This was even more extreme when I first saw the museum in the late 1970s. I had no idea of the extent of the decorative arts collection other than the quick tour that the curator gave me as part of my interview.

Looking back, it is clear to me that I was not really experienced enough to take over a curatorial department in a museum. Newark, however, had recently let go its last Assistant Curator for Decorative Arts, and they were not in a financial position to hire more than one curator for this collection. Then again, Newark was not the Met, and it was a quiet moment in the marketplace for nascent curators. Apparently, I seemed bright, I was certainly well-educated, and I (significantly) was more than happy to take the lowest salary offered in the range for this position. I was hired on my second interview, and taken to lunch at Newark's Essex Club, founded in 1876 by the city's leading white Protestant citizens (men, of course). I had poached salmon with a dill mayonnaise. The director, Samuel C. Miller, had a martini. I had a glass of sherry.

My starting salary was $14,500 annually, plus healthcare and twenty-three vacation days each year. On the strength of that I got an American Express card. Truth be told, the job had twofold appeal for me. There was a great historic mansion to play with, and a huge, wildly diverse decorative arts collection to care for. Even better, Newark was ten miles from Manhattan, and was surrounded by old, green suburbs.

No, Newark was not the Met and my department was not the American Wing, which was still somewhere in the back of my mind as an ultimate goal, the Emerald City before which Newark was just a stop along the Yellow Brick Road. What I would not understand for some years was that Newark's American art and decorative arts collections were a kind of anti-American Wing, created from similar materials but with a very different intention. Newark was not focused on the accumulation of masterworks for the pleasure of collectors and scholars. It was a museum all about the audience, an institution designed to please and educate the people. This was something I didn't fully grasp at the start of my career.

What I would come to appreciate, long after the museum's registrar left me in my strange, cramped little office on June 30, 1980, is that Newark was an untapped treasure trove. Lacking the institutional complexity or wealth of places like the Metropolitan Museum, the Newark Museum would offer me a kind of curatorial autonomy I could have found nowhere else. It would be a place where I would never stop needing to learn. Most of its collections were overlooked and under-researched, simply because the curatorial staff was enormously outnumbered by objects. Every storeroom was a window into something about which I was ignorant, but not *totally* ignorant. In the end, I would grasp that there were over 40,000 objects in my department alone:

furniture, metalwork, glass, ceramics, textiles, costumes, accessories, dolls, toys, and jewelry. Some of these objects I would not come to know for years. Some of them would become old friends right away.

And it was all mine, with full touching privileges. My learning curve would last thirty-seven years.

Strangely, other than a basic institutional overview, I was given no guidance or instruction at my new job. I was a department head, without ever having been an assistant. My office was the lower floor of a two-level storage vault from the 1920s (used then for toys and dolls), complete with a little iron staircase in the corner. I remember sitting at my desk and pondering my Beatrix Potter desk calendar. What was I supposed to do? A curator cared for a collection. What did that mean? I was left to figure it out on my own. It was brilliant.

In 1980 there were six curators at the Newark Museum. Four of us were full-time: Fern Thurlow in Painting and Sculpture; Valrae Reynolds in Oriental Art; Anne Spencer in Ethnology (Africa, the Americas, and the Pacific as it would come to be known); and me in the Decorative Arts. There were also two part-time curators who worked three days a week (with full benefits): Susan Auth in the Classical Collection (Egypt, Greece, and Rome) and Dorothy Bartle in Numismatics. The curators and the two registrars shared space at the back of the museum's second floor in the 1926 building funded by department store millionaire Louis Bamberger. The curators shared a secretary, Lois, a pretty, friendly redhead who typed all our correspondence and fielded our phones.

In 1980 we used carbon paper, and I brought in my Smith-Corona electric typewriter, since I would not be assigned one by the museum. There was no photocopier in our building. The one copying machine in the museum was next to the museum's telephone operator, Gladys, whose station was upstairs on "the other side." This referred to the administration offices, housed on the second floor of the Ballantine House, which was located at the front of what was called "the addition." The addition was a three-story brick office building added to the back of the Ballantine house by an insurance company between 1922 and 1926. It had been purchased by the museum in 1937, and its big open spaces subdivided into classrooms, storage, and the museum library. The museum had originally intended to tear down the 1885 Ballantine house, but was stymied by the outbreak of World War II. By the late 1960s, a second plan to tear down the house and expand the museum was put in place by the board, headed by precious metal mogul Charles Engelhard. A then unknown young architect named Michael Graves was brought up from Princeton to design something edgy and modern to replace the "ugly" Ballantine House. It never occurred to anyone on the board that the largely intact mansion of Newark's most famous beer baron might be worth saving. The sixties were a bad time for old houses, especially Victorian ones. Until the Met's benediction of the nineteenth century in 1970, Victorian and Bad Taste would remain synonymous in the mind of cultured Americans.

It was the Newark uprising in 1967 that killed the plans to demolish the last surviving house on Washington Park, which had been a residential enclave of Newark's Protestant elite since the 1790s. Thus, two calamities in two different decades held back the wrecking ball. It was at this point that Sam Miller, who had come to Newark as Associate Director from the Albright-Knox Museum in Buffalo, suggested that maybe it would be better to save the old house as a Bicentennial project. Thus, when I arrived four years after the national birthday celebrations, the ground floor of the house had been restored and interpreted in a way that was cutting edge for the late 1970s. The linoleum, light fixtures and layout upstairs were exactly as the insurance company had left them in 1937.

My first real task as Curator of the Decorative Arts Collection was to dismantle a 1979 exhibition marking the seventieth anniversary of the museum's founding in 1909. The focus of this exhibition was the founding director, John Cotton Dana, who had been a celebrated librarian and the head of Newark's Free Public Library. I learned in that process that Mr. Dana had created this museum as a sort of material counterpart to the great public library that was its first home. If people learned from books, Mr. Dana reasoned, they could learn different things from objects. Objects of everyday life, the art of everyday life, offered a pathway to understanding the cultures of the world across geography and time. Things taught you how to look.

Winterthur had taught me to understand pre-industrial, Euro-American objects profoundly, and also to be able to place them in their specific cultural context. Newark gave me a far wider context in which to place an enormously more complex variety of objects. Newark was not, as Winterthur had been, a hushed treasure trove, devoted to the hagiography of Americana, to the lives of fine old families and their beautiful possessions. I didn't fully get this at first, of course. It would take me years to grasp the depth and breadth of Newark's collection, mixed up as it was with discarded relics of old Newark families and things purchased at department stores in the first fifty years of the twentieth century. There was a huge story in Newark's decorative arts collection, and it would take time for me to learn it.

What my long career gradually taught me is that, while Newark's museum seems like a normal museum, it really isn't. When it was founded, it was with a radical concept for the time, a museum whose primary mission was to bring visual literacy to ordinary people. Newark was not, as its founder emphasized, "a temple in a park." To drive this point home, in 1909, Newark had two great parks, both designed by the Olmstead Brothers: Branch Brook on the north, Weequahic Park on the south. Either of these had plenty of space for a museum; but Mr. Dana's first museum building was built just down the street from the city's public library where it was born, right on the trolley lines and near both train stations. It was designed to be accessible to the city's men and women who worked in factories and office buildings. It was open seven days a week and free to all (and continued to be so until well into my own career there, when city budget cuts and staff limits forced the imposition of entrance fees and closure to the public two days a week). The Newark Museum was consciously founded to be an antidote to the Metropolitan Museum, at a time when, you must realize, only the Metropolitan and Brooklyn Museums existed as art museums in New York City.

Newark was never intended to be a quasi-public club where rich people stored their treasures to delight each other and to edify the unwashed when it so pleased them. Mr. Dana was suspicious of the concept of "fine art," and proclaimed tirelessly the art-ness of the applied arts. And Dana meant the *global* applied arts, which included non-white cultures. The museum's founding collection was several thousand Japanese objects of the Edo and Meiji periods assembled by a Newark pharmacist named George T. Rockwell. This sprawling collection incorporated every craft and medium. The city gave the newborn museum $10,000 in 1909, and the board used that money to purchase Rockwell's collection. Mr. Dana loved the lack of divisions between fine and applied arts in Asian cultures. He was also suspicious of the concept of "masterpiece," because he felt it was inevitably used as a tool by rich people to intimidate ordinary people. A masterpiece was something presented as being above the experience of average citizens, something which, if they made the effort, they could aspire to understand. Mr. Dana felt strongly that the monetary or inherent value of a rare old object should not automatically make it worthier of study and consideration than a more ordinary object. The design and making of a piece of modern pottery, for example, was just as important to explore as the production of a rare piece of Meissen porcelain from the early 1700s. This was a radical idea in 1909, especially in an art museum.

Even when it came to paintings and sculpture, which Mr. Dana reluctantly agreed to make part of his museum's collecting mission under pressure from his trustees, he felt it should be American art, not European art, and modern art, not old art. The American museum fetish for the old and European really bothered Mr. Dana, because it went hand in hand with rich people's fetish for the rare and the costly. A Yankee and a Dartmouth graduate, Mr. Dana was a frugal middle-class Vermonter with old colonial bloodlines that passed for blue in this country. The founding librarian of the Denver Public Library, Dana was very smart, a true visionary; but he had strong prejudices, and never hesitated to make them known to the people upon whom he depended for financial support.

It eventually dawned on me that the chronic financial insecurity that the Newark Museum has known since the day I walked in the door is probably due to the fact that Mr. Dana would never compromise his philosophy to get money. He spent his career irritating the very people in Newark who had the wherewithal to make his museum a wealthy institution. Some of those people, in particular Louis Bamberger and his sister Caroline Fuld (widow of her brother's business partner Felix Fuld), remained loyal and generous. Mr. Bamberger paid for the new museum building of 1926 out of his own pocket; and Mrs. Fuld funded the most important modern art acquisitions of the 1920s and 30s. However, in the year before he died, Mr. Dana could not raise an endowment of one million dollars, in a city as rich as Newark was then. To me, this suggests not that Newark couldn't do it, but that Mr. Dana had, somehow, disinclined Newark's rich from giving the kind of money his museum needed. Even Louis Bamberger and Caroline Fuld, in the end, turned most of their millions toward the Institute for Advanced Study in Princeton, some sixty miles south of Newark.

John Cotton Dana to this day is a legend in the library world, seen as the creator of the modern public library. In museology circles (i.e. the study of the history of museums), Dana is held up as the visionary behind the modern American museum. But he was not a diplomat. His right-hand-man, a formidable maiden lady named Beatrice Winser, was a pioneer in her own right, and would follow Mr. Dana as the director of his rule-breaking institution. Miss Winser would likely have been better at coaxing money out of Newark's movers and shakers without bruising their feelings. However, Miss Winser was a lady, and in America in the late 1920s, a lady didn't talk about money.

CHAPTER TWENTY-FOUR

LEAVE IT TO BEAVER REPRISE

With a job in a gritty urban enclave, a scant ten miles from the center of the East Coast post-Stonewall gay world, why on earth did my boyfriend and I move immediately to suburbia? Being young, tolerably cute, and gay, we should have been drawn to a still-affordable Greenwich Village and its supportive community. There is a deeper truth here, one that had not yet begun to divide the gay community into factions, politically and socially. Gary and I both realized right away that we really didn't want to live in New York City. Since college days, New York had been a place to which we escaped for fun. If we tended to end up in Greenwich Village, it was to be in a place where we didn't feel alone as a couple of twinks who wanted to walk down the street holding hands. However, we were not party boys. We were not into bars and pick-ups and late, boozy nights. Nor were we attracted by the idea of cramped, roach-infested walk-ups (which was way more commonplace in the late 1970s than today). New York had not yet revived itself into the glittering global center it became in the 2000s, full of billionaires and million-dollar one-bedroom apartments. It was dirty and dangerous in parts; the subways were graffiti-laden and unpleasant to ride in the early 1980s. There was nothing fashionable about Harlem or the Lower East Side back then. Living in New York the way my family had once lived there was not possible for Gary and me. At twenty-four I had a vision in my head, and Gary, bless his heart, went along with me.

The Newark Museum is fifteen miles from the Metropolitan Museum, just ten miles from the Holland Tunnel into Manhattan. Immediately to the west of Newark is a suburban greenbelt of old towns, all of them part of the original Newark plantation as established in 1666 and granted a royal charter by Queen Anne in 1713. Developed between the 1850s and the 1930s, these suburban towns had drained much of Newark's wealth as the city ceased to expand outside of its nineteenth-century boundaries. By World War I, New Jersey's unique obsession with political autonomy had turned Essex County into a balkanized patchwork of independent communities, all of which were established, it seems, to avoid paying taxes to Newark. Even in its most prosperous days, the suburbs had seen the city as something of a nemesis, a place to shop and make money, but a place to keep at arm's length, too. The very first planned suburb in America, and its first gated community, was Llewellyn Park in Orange (now West Orange), a bit more than four miles from the Newark border. By the 1850s affluent Americans had realized that the cities whence they drew their wealth were also places where poor people worked and lived. Poor people, they realized, were often immigrants (Irish and German in those days) and the wealthy associated them with unpleasant things such as crime and disease. The factories that made people rich also produced clouds of toxic coal soot and spilled unimaginable waste into the city's river and canals. By 1880 the mortality rate for infants under a year of age in Newark was one in four. The solution was obvious, then as now: move away. The story of the American suburb is the story of Americans abandoning their cities to the poor and the marginalized.

Of course, Newark had (and has) a substantial population, but its most affluent neighborhoods were confined to Forest Hill at the north end and Weequahic on the south side. The wealth of these two neighborhoods couldn't compete with the burgeoning affluence of the growing suburbs, especially after the Second World War. By the time of the civil disturbances of 1967, Newark had become a city of workers and absentee business owners. The biggest business and factory owners had long since moved to suburban Essex County, taking their tax dollars with them as well as their active presence in the residential life of the city.

Gary and I knew nothing of this, nor did we fully understand the complicated role of race in every aspect of New Jersey's development since the Great Migration of the 1920s, 30s and 40s. Gary's parents, the children of Jewish immigrants, had grown up on the same street in Newark, and had moved first to Belleville, then to Verona, and, since the mid-1960s, had lived in Springfield. Springfield is a colonial town in northern Union County that was developed with minimal aesthetic consideration, in the years after World War II, for middle-class white house-hunters. It is only ten minutes south of Maplewood, with which it had strong ties in the eighteenth and nineteenth centuries.

Gary and I agreed that we wanted an older town, one with trees and greenery and old houses. At least, I think we agreed. Gary might well have gone along with me because it mattered to me. He was ready to give up yet another good job and follow me to New Jersey, but he had no *Leave it to Beaver* delusions; that was my territory. We stayed with Gary's parents while we house-hunted, and found an outrageous realtor, a youngish woman with big hair, prone to wearing huge sunglasses and Candies, (a hot brand of backless high heels). I'm sure she would have liked to sell us a house in Springfield or Short Hills (the fancy part of Millburn Township that abutted Maplewood). I saw no charm in Springfield and we couldn't afford Short Hills, so Maplewood-South Orange became our target. We looked at a half-dozen houses before settling on a 1929 "English colonial," whatever that meant.

What we saw was a cute, substantial little house, its street-facing gable front centered with a chimney. It had eccentric tan-and-brown tapestry brick on the ground floor, brown shingles on the second floor, and a slate roof. Typical of the majority of houses built as many New Jersey suburbs were developed in the 1920s, the house on Ball Place had three bedrooms, one bathroom with a separate shower and a tub set into an arched niche (lushly tiled in lavender and green) and boasted both a little sunroom off the living room and a glassed-in porch off the dining room. The living room had a brick fireplace with a wide mantel shelf and an arched opening. The master bedroom was really large. We were sold.

Our realtor made sure to let us know that the town was "mixed," by which she meant that Black people lived in the community. In the lingo of realtors in 1980, this was less alarming than the word "changing." Remember, gentrification had not really begun to transform places like Park Slope in Brooklyn, while elsewhere in the borough was a no-go zone. Brooklyn wasn't cool yet. The positive concept of a transitional neighborhood had not yet captured the minds of realtors, nor had the power of gay pioneers in architecturally rich urban outposts yet become widely appreciated.

On the other hand, awareness of race was probably the single most powerful driver of New Jersey's real estate market in 1980, and we, in our own naïve way, understood this. We shrugged and signed on the dotted line. Our house cost us $77,000 with a 30-year-fixed mortgage of 13%. I was twenty-five and Gary was twenty-seven. For the first time in our five years together, we were legally bound to each other. A mortgage (joint owners with rights of survivorship) was as close to being married as a gay couple could then get in the United States.

Maplewood's identity as a town was affirmed in 1922 when it formally split from South Orange, although both the name and some early residential areas had existed by the 1910s. Most of Maplewood was still taken up with apple and peach orchards in 1920, and the names of the farms would appear on the streets: Ball, Pierson, Lewis, Tower, Durand, Roosevelt. An uncle of Teddy Roosevelt's had owned a large part of Maplewood's west side, an estate called The Hickories. The great American landscape painter Asher Durand had grown up in Maplewood when it was a farm community known as Jefferson Village. By 1840 the train stop after South Orange was known as Maplewood Station, and the town evolved from there. I would commute from that train station to Newark for thirty-eight years.

In 1980 Maplewood was virtually unchanged from its post-war identity. It was still heavily Republican, mostly Christian, and ninety percent white. The Village (on the west side of the train tracks) boasted a five-and-dime, a hardware store, two pharmacies, a pizza parlor and one "good" restaurant called the Winolear, which had lousy food and a full-service bar. Men's and women's clothing stores, two supermarkets (both small), a dry-cleaner run by Al Gottlieb, and a video rental place rounded off Maplewood Village's retail establishments. Memorial Park (east of the train tracks) was a sprawling green space with athletic facilities, the town hall, police department and fire station. When you pulled into Maplewood on the train (originally the Erie-Lackawanna, but by 1980 New Jersey Transit, in spite of the rattling 1920s Edison electric trains), you saw a sea of old trees, quaint houses, and a stately columned town hall across the park. What you didn't see was Springfield Avenue, a colonial era coach road and the main traffic artery between Newark and Springfield. This much-less-loved thoroughfare was the center of the less affluent side of Maplewood. The honest truth is that Maplewood was simply a subdivision of 25,000 people cheek-by-jowl with Irvington on the east, South Orange and Newark on the north, and Union and Millburn on the south. Because of the Village flanking the train station, it was easy enough to pretend that it was a little country town, far away from the drama of Newark or the towns that were "changing."

Well, Maplewood *was* changing, and Gary and I would be part of that change. Little did we know it, though. Our largest fear as we faced homeownership was that we would be shunned or treated even worse as an openly gay couple. Since 1975 we had gotten very used to being out. We really had no concept of what strong anti-gay prejudice might look like, but we expected that we would have to face it.

Apparently not. Not only did our worst nightmares never materialize, but our mildest concerns didn't either. Eleven years after Stonewall, tolerance had already spread at least as far as suburban New Jersey. Tolerance was fine by us. Acceptance would come later, but like most twenty-somethings, we were very much concerned about the present.

The night we signed the contract on the Ball Place house, we joined Gary's family for dinner at a restaurant in Madison called Widow Brown's. The gathering included most of what would come to be my Jewish family for the next two decades: Gladys and Pete Berger; Gladys' older sisters Beatrice (Beaty) and her husband Seymour Marder; and Ruth, with her husband Harry Hillard. Beaty and Seymour lived in Springfield, while Ruth and Harry lived in Brick Township. Guests of honor were Kalman and Gertrude Lehner, Gladys' parents, whom I had first met on their sixty-fifth wedding anniversary in 1977. Gertie and Kalman had come from the same town in the eastern Austrian empire (aka Galicia in Poland). They had married in Newark in 1912. At this point Gertie and Kalman still lived in a tidy flat in a squalid senior-citizen high-rise in Newark on the edge of Weequahic Park, the same neighborhood author Philip Roth would celebrate in many of his novels. Soon after we moved to Maplewood, the Lehner sisters would find their parents a place in a newly developed assisted-living building on a short dead-end street in Springfield called Independence Way.

For the first six weeks of my career at the Newark Museum, I stayed with Gladys and Pete in their raised ranch in Springfield, occupying Gary's childhood twin bed. At the end of each day, I'd catch the bus in front of the museum on Broad Street and be dropped off by the Evergreen Deli on South Springfield Avenue, just a few blocks from the Bergers' house. I usually got back to 25 Christy Lane by 5:30, where dinner was always on the table in the little dining room, Pete and Gladys awaiting my return.

Gary would drive up from Delaware for the weekends in his beige Volkswagen Rabbit. By this time, my yellow Chevy Vega had been done in by a drunk man in a pick-up truck, late one night as I was bringing my Winterthur classmate Nancy back from a party at our English professor's house. He blew through a stoplight and t-boned my car, whose steering wheel I fortunately turned just enough so that he didn't score a direct hit on my door. The poor little car was demolished, but all I ended up with was some mild aches and salad on my shoes (Nancy had been holding the remains of the salad Gary had made for me to take to the party). My mother, in typical Julia Dietz fashion, "sold" me her old, brown Volkswagen Dasher wagon (meaning that, after a year, she told me to stop sending her checks for it).

First job, first house, first boyfriend: I was all set. But, as a last hurrah for his career in racetrack computer systems, Gary was sent to Denmark and Finland for a month in November and December to install systems in several racetracks. We as yet had no friends in New Jersey, and I muddled through on my own as best I could. I vaguely remember sipping my way through whatever minimal liquor supply we had in the house.

Soon after Gary returned to the States, he found a fantastic job with a family-run firm called Dubner Computer Systems, which had just moved from Manhattan to Fort Lee, New Jersey. Involved in real-time computer graphics for television broadcasting, Dubner was literally a mom-and-pop operation. Harvey Dubner and three of his children (Doug, Bobby and Emily) all worked at the firm, while Mrs. Dubner, Harriet, mothered everyone. Although Harvey would sell the firm and his family would fade from our lives, the company itself, in one form or another, would be Gary's workplace for the rest of his career.

We still had friends in New York City, one of whom dubbed our new place of residence "Leave it to Beaver Land." It dawned on me over time that the distance from Maplewood to Manhattan was much shorter than the reverse. Suburbanites (i.e. bridge and tunnel crowd) flocked into Manhattan when one of its many attractions lured them onto the train or even onto the highways (two major high-speed arteries, Route 280 and Route 78 were both completed after we moved to New Jersey). We would discover that luring our New York friends out to deepest suburbia was more difficult.

Once Gary was settled in permanently in Maplewood, we started what would become a long-standing tradition: consulting with our decorator friends for help in making our dream house. Here again, I think Gary was more indulgent than enthusiastic, but he always enjoyed the results. My best friend from Exeter, Rick, had established himself in Columbus, Ohio, as a hot young decorator. He helped us acquire some good, custom-made upholstered furniture covered in dark green whipcord. He also provided us with elegantly simple heavy cotton draperies for the three big windows in the living room, off-white with widely spaced thin stripes of dark green and ochre.

My oldest friend, Tod, who has the best taste of any person I've ever known, gave us a new color scheme. Although devotees of woodwork and brick were and would still be horrified, we painted all of the downstairs chestnut woodwork and the brick mantelpiece a glossy white, and the typical 1920s rough stucco walls a bright, egg-yolk yellow. Even on the darkest days, the house was warm and cozy. Our bedroom scheme, also provided by Tod, was a deep Kelly green with dark green carpeting peppered with little white spots. The centerpiece of the master bedroom was a massive Victorian bed in the neo-Grec style of the late 1860s, all burled walnut, pediments, and incised gilt details. I had bought it from my Winterthur professor and mentor, Ken Ames, who sold it because he couldn't fit it up the staircase of his new house. Gary had a horror of sleeping in a four-poster with curtains, and the ornate headboard on our new bed was the ideal compromise. It didn't shut Gary in, and gave me the opulence I seemed to crave.

Into the large guest room we stuffed two 1890s mahogany beds that came from the blue guest room in my great-grandfather's house in Clinton, New York, along with the matching faux-Chippendale lady's desk from that same room. Amazingly, in the world before personal computers, this was my desk, and I kept it tidy. The third and smallest bedroom became Gary's study and our library, thanks to a modern office desk and a bunch of assemble-yourself rosewood-veneer-on-chipboard bookcases from Norsk, a modern design store in New York. Back then, our library was heavily weighted by my growing collection of decorative arts and architecture books, but still included college textbooks and whatever random volumes we'd accumulated in our first five years together.

Driving into New York wasn't as fraught with anxiety in the 1980s as it is for us now, but we still tended to opt for the train on our routine trips into the city. We got to know the Hoboken terminal and the PATH (Port Authority Trans-Hudson) trains well, since we could hop off the train right on Christopher Street in Greenwich Village. Our infrequent forays into bars all happened in the Village. Soon enough we discovered the Oscar Wilde Memorial Bookshop and its hands-on owner, Craig Rodwell. One of the most important independent bookstores in the country, it had moved to the corner of Christopher and Gay Streets in 1973 and became a regular stop on our visits to New York. The early 1980s was a boom time for gay writers, and our gay library grew by leaps and bounds. I was a regular enough customer, and thanks to my name, got to the point of being recognized as "Ulysses from Jersey" when I dropped in to pick up books for my collection.

There wasn't all that much for us to do in suburbia, socially speaking. While we were welcomed by all our neighbors, we never became part of their social lives. I was a lot younger than my co-curators at the museum, although we always got on very well. My one gay friend from the museum early on was in the exhibitions department. David must have heard rumors about me and sought me out in my little office under the stairs. We remained fast friends until the end of his career.

I always marvel at the idea that we found anything before the Internet. Somehow, in our second year in New Jersey, we found O.G.A. The Organization for Gay Awareness was, to be honest, a cozy little group that was as benignly anarchistic as any gay organization ever founded. It met in the parish lounge of St. George's Episcopal Church in Maplewood and had been established in the late 1970s when a New Jersey legislator stirred up efforts to recriminalize homosexual behavior. Once that crisis had been resolved in 1978, the group settled in as just one of the various gay groups (still not yet called LGBT) in New Jersey. O.G.A. was the smallest group. The Gay Activists Alliance of Morris County was a big group, whose events we participated in regularly. Even larger was the Gay Activist Alliance of Bergen County. A statewide group called the New Jersey Gay Coalition would also draw us in, as it evolved into the New Jersey Lesbian and Gay Coalition. Gary even served as president at one point, and we both served as presidents of O.G.A. over the years we were active.

The stalwarts of O.G.A. were Joe, an Irish boy from Jersey City, who was, among other things, a film buff. Joe had endless energy and managed to convince surprisingly important people from the New York gay world to trek out to Maplewood and speak to us—people like Arthur Bell, a major figure in gay journalism; and Vito Russo whose book *The Celluloid Closet* was a landmark in documenting gay history in film. Barry, another steadfast member, was a social worker in Newark. He wore his gray hair long, with a generous mustache. Barry was not averse to painting his nails lavender now and then. He was gentle, poetic, and wise. Rick, a middle-aged middle school teacher, was a proud nerd and a talker, as I was. Jim, living on disability because of his cerebral palsy, was our conscience. After O.G.A. faded away, he would go on to be a volunteer at the Newark Museum, where he carried on his tireless crusade on behalf of people with disabilities.

There were quite a few other people who came and went over the years, some regularly, some passing through on the way to some bigger group. Two, Ron and Greg, would become longtime friends of Gary's and mine. Ron was still in high school when he first ventured to O.G.A., living with his Italian family in Linden and dreaming of becoming an interior designer. Greg was a shy, quiet guy who obsessed about celebrities and had an amazing storehouse of minutiae in his brain.

Our first close friends in New Jersey, however, were Bill and Michael. We met them at a big gay bar in East Orange called Charlie's West. The event was some sort of consciousness-raising effort on a crowded weekend evening, when the place was packed with gay men from all over the suburbs and disco was pumping out full tilt. Different organizations had spaces at tables to promote their groups and let the assembled revelers know that there was support for them if they needed it.

Michael, who then worked for NBC in Rockefeller Center, was a darkly handsome Italian man from Bergen County. He was the same age as my brother Jed. His partner Bill (we just used the word "lover" back then, boyfriend being reserved for the earliest part of any relationship), was a lawyer and a deputy attorney general for the state of New Jersey. Bill, an Irish-German man who had grown up in East Orange, was another seven years' Michael's senior. As it turned out, they had lived in Maplewood too, since 1973, not far from our house on Ball Place. Both were members of Dignity, a support group for gay Catholics. Dignity, coincidentally, also met at St. George's Episcopal Church (needless to say, the local Catholic churches wouldn't allow Dignity into their sacred spaces).

The four of us clicked instantly, and I clearly recall the exhilaration of this new friendship, comparing it in my own mind to the feeling of falling in love. What I didn't quite understand at the time was that the four of us would inadvertently become the gay vanguard for Maplewood, two openly-gay male couples who would begin to challenge the status quo in this placid suburb, drawing attention from outside the community to us and to the place we had chosen to build our nests. We, of course, were not the only gay people in Maplewood-South Orange. We were, however, among the first who didn't just quietly assimilate and disappear.

In 1981, Rabbi Harold Kushner published *When Bad Things Happen to Good People*. Just as Andrew Tobias's *The Best Little Boy in the World* became a beacon for me at eighteen, Kushner's slim inspirational volume would do the same for me at twenty-six. Faced with the appalling death of his son Aaron from progeria, a disease that results in rapid aging and early death, Rabbi Kushner wrote about his faith and his understanding of God, as a Jew and a grieving father. A dozen years after the death of my brother and sister, this book helped me put to rest the confusion and pain at the idea of a deity that would let children die, ostensibly as part of some bigger plan that was beyond lowly human understanding. God, the rabbi reasoned, was supposed to be All Knowing, All Powerful, and All Loving. Given not just the death of his son, but the deaths of countless millions of people through war, famine, disease, and other tragedies, how could one reconcile belief in any god, much less the Judeo-Christian version with which both the rabbi and I had been raised? The answer (as I remember it, forty years later) was shockingly simple: for innocent people to die, God can be all-knowing and all-loving, but not all-powerful. God didn't make bad things happen, but he couldn't prevent bad things from happening, either. God couldn't protect us, but only console us. God couldn't change events, but he could change the way we responded to events.

Another switch was flicked in my heart and my mind. I was at last able to let go of the idiotic notion that somehow Ned had "deserved" his untimely death, while Edie hadn't. My sister's fate had pushed my mother away from church entirely, while it had pushed my father more deeply into church involvement, as he desperately looked for answers to questions for which there were none. I, of course, had other reasons for drifting away from active participation in the Episcopal church. Curiously, accepting a God who was not all-powerful didn't diminish the idea of divine presence. With no humor intended, I began to embrace a notion of God as more akin to the Force from George's Lucas's *Star Wars* than to anything like the paternalistic, chastising deity of my childhood. I had no way then of foreseeing the ultimate result of this revelation.

By the mid-1980s, we had accumulated a nice group of gay friends in Leave it to Beaver Land. There was enough critical mass that we were able to make some socio-political waves in Maplewood. Gary and I tried to join the Maplewood town pool and discovered that we could only join as two individuals, which cost twice as much as the cost of a family membership. Our friends Sue and Faith, recently moved to town from Hoboken, had the same experience, as had Bill and Michael. Rather than just pay up, we challenged the rule that allowed only married (hence, straight couples) to style themselves as families. Sue and Faith let the Maplewood town council know that the local ACLU would be *very* interested in a case like this. The town council promptly changed the rules, allowing us all to join the pool with family memberships. Eventually, of course, we would not only have children, but get married; but none of this was even a fantasy for us in those early years.

On a warm day in 1985, the summer I turned thirty, Gary and I were walking down Christopher Street in New York's Greenwich Village. I don't remember if this was calculated or spontaneous, but we stopped into a little hole-in-the-wall jewelry store. We ended up buying simple fourteen-karat gold wedding bands to mark our tenth anniversary together. The span of time seemed momentous, and the symbolism of those gold rings felt both comforting and subversive. We would wear those rings until they had to be cut off our middle-aged fingers fifteen years later. But that's another story. The real punchline of this jewelry store visit was that the owners were an older gay couple who happened to live a few blocks from us in Maplewood. This did not turn into a great friendship, but it was the sort of coincidence that affirmed our decision to settle in suburbia, a world away from the rainbow shadows of Stonewall.

CHAPTER TWENTY-FIVE

Speculation #7
GERTIE GOES AWAY

Gertie walked with a steady pace toward the Jasło train station. Her little suitcase was heavier than it looked. She wanted to get to the train, the train that would take her to Krakow, and eventually far beyond that. On the other hand, she didn't want to call attention to herself. *Don't walk too fast, or too slowly*, she told herself. Her thoughts were focused on her destination, and on the flat, carefully wrapped packet hidden in her undergarments.

As she passed through the looming shadow of the Great Synagogue, Gertie thought of its lofty, ornate sanctuary, quiet now after the long Shabbat services of the previous day. She had been there at its dedication on Rosh Hashanah just two years before, with her mother and her sisters, in the gallery with the women. How proud they all were of this grand symbol of Jewish achievement. The Jews of Jasło had done well. Too well, some people thought.

The Geltzeilers didn't live among the rich Jews who built the synagogue. They spoke Yiddish at home, rather than Polish. They had their own neighborhood. The Polish-speaking Jews of Jasło dressed like everyone else. They ran successful businesses, were involved with the refinery over in Gorlice, whose influence had spread to Jasło in the decades before. They had fine homes on the wider streets of the town. Everyone met at the Great Synagogue, but outside its walls, they tended to live separate lives. Gertie didn't mind. She liked her little house and her big family.

She was pulled out of her reverie at the sound of her name from across the street.

"Gittel! Gittel Geltzeiler, where are you off to in such a rush?" It was her friend Nettie. Exactly the person she didn't want to see right now.

Choking back a sigh, Gertie nodded to Nettie, who had hurried across the unpaved street.

"Good day, Nettie." She forced herself to sound friendly.

"So, where are you going?" At Gertie's innocent look, she huffed.

"The suitcase, Gittel. I'm not blind."

"Ah," Gertie answered, falling back on plan B, since her plan A of meeting nobody had failed. "I'm going to visit my friend in Krajowice. Just a short stay."

"What friend do you have up there?"

Gertie tried not to roll her eyes. "You don't know her. An acquaintance of my brother Isidore."

"Your brother Isidore. The one who left?"

"Yes, Nettie, my brother Isidore, who's in America now."

"Have you heard from him recently, then?"

Really, Gertie thought, *she is just too irritating.* But all she said was, "A few weeks ago. A nice long letter. He's settled himself in a place called Newark, near to New York City."

"They have Jews there?"

Failing to quite stifle a small derisive snort, Gertie answered, "Plenty of Jews. German Jews. Russian Jews. And Jews from Galicia, even from Jasło. There's another boy from our neighborhood there, named Kalman Lehner."

"Lehner, eh? That's a big family. Old Abraham married his dead wife's sister. I think this Kalman is the eldest. From the dead wife. Maybe nineteen?"

"You seem to know him better than I do, Nettie. I've never met him."
She added, "But my brother knows him," she added stupidly, mentally kicking
herself for dragging on this pointless conversation.

"Well, I could never leave Jasło," Nettie intoned, waving her arm at
an attempt at drama, then adjusting her kerchief. "Why would anyone leave?"
Gertie felt herself flush and prayed that it wouldn't be visible.

"There are plenty of reasons to leave. One hears about the opportuni-
ties in America." What Gertie didn't mention were the pogroms in other parts
of the empire, and the anti-Jewish incidents that, while infrequent, suggested
something disturbing below the surface. She assumed that Nettie would just
dismiss such things as paranoia.

"So, this friend in Krajowice…" Hettie paused, clearly trying to glean
some gossip from Gertie.

"She's getting married. She wanted me to visit, to talk with her about
her trousseau."

"And you're staying for how long?"

"Just for the night. I'll be back tomorrow evening." Gertie hesitated,
then decided that gilding the lily was better than vagueness. "My mother needs
me at home. You know how lazy my sister is."

As if giving up her fishing expedition as a bad job, Nettie shrugged.
"Well, I'll let you go on your way. I'll be sure to ask you all about it when you
get home."

Gertie plastered a bright smile on her face. "You can come to our
house. I'll make you tea and we can have cake." Nettie had no idea that there
would be no such get-together.

This seemed to satisfy and cheer Nettie, who waved a goodbye as she
retraced her steps back across the road and headed in the opposite direction.
Gertie took a deep breath, and resumed her trek to the station, shifting the
small-but-heavy valise to her other hand.

She knew why some of the young men of Jasło had left, despite its
outward prosperity, and the success of the Jewish community—especially the

Polish-speaking Jews, who also knew Austrian German and made great effort to fit in with the other Poles. The Great Synagogue was a grand building, for sure. But it was only a building. Emperor Franz Josef was a good and just emperor, and his laws had made life for the Jews in his empire easier. Gertie knew that as well as anyone.

But still, Isidore had left for America. He and the Lehner boy had plans. They saw that the future was not here, buried in the eastern part of an ancient empire, surrounded by another ancient empire that was not known to be good to its Jews. Gertie had heard her brother talking, especially after the Kishinev pogrom back in 1903. Moldava was not Galicia, but it was just next door. The Russian empire was seething below the surface.

She shook her head, a slight shudder perhaps, as she continued toward the station. Her foolish sister was like Nettie. She had her papers to emigrate just as Isidore had done. But she had gotten cold feet. The idea of leaving her cozy neighborhood in this prosperous town where the Jews were doing so well scared her. The lure of a future in America was less appealing than the comfort of a well-known life here.

So be it, Gertie thought to herself. Right now, at home, her parents and her siblings were doing housework, studying, gossiping about local things. None of them knew that Gertie was going away at all, much less for some imaginary overnight with a made-up friend in Krajowice. Her mother thought she was off doing an errand that would require some time. Gertie was skilled at being unclear about details. Her sister had no idea that her passport and emigration documents were carefully wrapped up and tucked in between some of the fine cotton underthings that Gertie herself had embroidered with her sister's initials. They wore the same size, and nobody would notice the identity switch until Gertie was long gone.

Isidore was in America, in the city of Newark in the province called New Jersey. That Lehner boy was in Newark, too. She would have to find her brother, once she got to the Ellis Island on whatever ship she could book herself a berth. A shiver of fear—or excitement—ran down Gertie's spine. In the distance she heard the whistle of the train, just a few miles from the Jasło station. Gertie scanned the street ahead. There was nobody ahead to waylay her again and ask stupid questions. She would get on that train. She would go to Newark. She would find her brother, or this Kalman Lehner. Adjusting her grip on the valise, Gertie quickened her pace, every step bringing her closer to her future.

CHAPTER TWENTY-SIX

COME TO JESUS

W hy would any gay person of my generation *join* a mainstream church in the mid-1980s? In the post-Stonewall years the lines had been clearly drawn, and there were precious few congregations—and no mainstream denominations—that acknowledged gay and lesbian people as other than damaged goods. Troy Perry had created the Metropolitan Community Church in Los Angeles in 1968 in response to the overwhelming hostility of all organized American religion to its non-straight children.

There was no dramatic schism on my part. I had simply drifted away from my childhood Episcopal church, after years of Sunday school, children's choir, and acolyte training. I remember my confirmation at thirteen, the Easter before my brother died, and I still have the gold cufflinks my parents gave me to commemorate that event. I recall vividly that sense of privilege I felt when I was, finally, allowed to go up to receive communion on the one Sunday a month when Episcopalians celebrated the Eucharist at the main morning service. I would sometimes get up early on Sundays to attend the weekly eight o'clock service, which was shorter, without music, but which always offered communion. I fully embraced the idea of myself as a young Christian and had not, yet, questioned what I had been taught. We were not, oddly enough, a religious family, nor did we seem, to me, to be devout in any overt way. Neither did I question the idea of going to church, or the beliefs that had been presented to me as a child and adolescent.

I have no memory of any sort of negative reference to sex or sexuality in all of my childhood religious learning, much less the sort of Bible-thumping condemnations drawn from Leviticus or Romans that I would come to know as the drumbeat of right-wing Evangelicals later in my life. Yet, somehow, I knew, as the years went on, that the church was no longer for *me*. After my siblings died and I left home for boarding school and college, my churchgoing became perfunctory rather than purposeful. Aware of who I was sexually, at least in theory, religion began to seem more and more alien.

Once, early in our Yale years, my friend Tod convinced me to attend a Sunday service of the Episcopal Church at Yale, then housed in the nave-like main hall of the former Dwight Library on Old Campus (the same building where I would later meet Gary). By the mid-1970s the Episcopal church was going through its earthy phase, complete with whole-wheat loaves and bear hugs during the passing of the peace. It was not the careful, polite church I remembered from Syracuse, where the peace had consisted of a smile and, if you were close friends, maybe a handshake with the person next to you. By the end of the service Tod and I were so unnerved that we barely kept ourselves from bolting. We laughed nervously with each other all the way back to our college rooms. I never experimented with religion after that, other than the annual Christmas Eves with my parents. In retrospect, I'm sorry about that. I suspect that I would have found spiritual support at Yale even that early on. I just wasn't ready for all that hugging. I had to sort myself out before I could deal with wider issues of religion and belief.

My resistance held firm right up to 1986, by which time two signifi-cant changes in our suburban life altered my trajectory and drew me more deeply into a kind of gay lifestyle never imagined by fundamentalists, whose power had begun its insidious rise under the smiling rhetoric of Ronald Reagan and neo-conservatism. By this time AIDS had emerged and begun its horrific devastation of the gay community—Gary's and my community. Larry Kramer had co-founded GMHC (Gay Men's Health Crisis) in 1982. GMHC had published the first safer sex guidelines in 1984, once the medical vectors of the disease were more clearly understood. Rock Hudson had publicly admitted that he had AIDS in 1985, bringing the plague into mainstream America's consciousness. That same year gay men were forbidden to donate blood for fear of contamination, adding to the stigma of contagion that surrounded all of us. Gary and I, through the New Jersey Lesbian and Gay Coalition as well as our ongoing activity in OGA, were involved in the increasingly angry activism fueled by the indifference of Washington as the body count rose.

I suppose it is no surprise that our decision to go to Maplewood rather than to Manhattan might ultimately have shielded us from the worst devastation of AIDS. The mysterious complex of diseases that began affecting gay men appeared first in large cities—cities with large gay communities. It took longer for the full impact of the virus to make its way out of the large urban areas and into the rest of America. But suburbia was no magic castle, and eventually the plague engulfed all of us in its shadow.

The fact that my return to organized religion coincided with our increasing anxiety over matters of health and the growing threat from AIDS is probably not coincidental. It never dawned on me at the time, but looking back it seems obvious.

Although the big boom in suburban New Jersey real estate would not come until 1996, when Midtown Direct trains began running straight into Manhattan's Penn Station, our faux-rural enclave began to be noticed by the mid-1980s as a place where urban diversity met suburban tranquility. Gay and lesbian couples had begun to follow us to Maplewood/South Orange, along with interracial couples and more families of color. This was a time of anxiety in our town, with fears of white flight and the quality of the schools being placed in counterpoint with the outward movement of young families from Manhattan as real estate prices there pushed middle-class families west across the Hudson River. Brooklyn's phenomenal upswing was just beginning, and (hard as it is to believe) nobody we knew would have considered *going* to a place like

Williamsburg or Bedford-Stuyvesant, much less living there. The next decade would be one of transformation, but meanwhile, I was getting restless.

We went to Europe in the summer of 1985 with our friends Bill and Michael, flying into Frankfurt and renting a silver BMW sedan for the drive to Munich, south through the Alps via Innsbruck, Austria, and into Italy via Turin. We listened to trashy Euro-disco as we barreled down the autobahn, visited gay clubs and historic sites, and generally got used to the ins and outs of traveling with friends. Bill and Michael were disconcerted with the way Gary and I bickered as we navigated unfamiliar streets in foreign cities; but we all enjoyed eating our way through local cuisines and seeing the countryside from inside a car. Bill had brought his new video camera, the latest in high-tech gear. The video recorder was the size of a substantial home-movie camera, and the battery pack weighed thirty pounds. We took turns carrying this massive thing on our backs as we trooped from Heidelberg to Venice. We ended up with eight hours of video, which we all sat and watched (just once) in the years after the trip.

Gary and I started looking for a new house all over Maplewood and South Orange that fall. I don't think Gary had any specific ideas of what he wanted, but I did. I wanted built-in bookcases, a front hall with a nice staircase, and more than one bathroom on the second floor. Fortunately, I wasn't entirely delusional, and we avoided a huge Victorian in South Orange's Montrose section in spite of a grand staircase, complete with a stained-glass window on the landing. Even I understood that it was more than we could handle, with a tumble-down barn at the back of its one-acre lot rather than a working garage. There was too much shag carpeting and bad 1960s plumbing. Another house in a lovely location bit the dust when we found an ancient apple tree in the back yard (Maplewood had once been covered with orchards); the grass covered with hundreds of pounds of rotting apples in which our food-obsessed dog took great interest. Eventually we zeroed in on two houses on a dead-end street in the northwest corner of town. Woodhill Drive rises steeply up into the South Mountain Reservation, right on the Maplewood/South Orange border. Our first choice was a colonial with an in-ground pool and a fantastic family room with a stone fireplace and barn-siding on the walls. In second place was its Tudor counterpart, but with no pool and only a modest 1961 family room with vertical Weldwood paneling. That family room, however, had two walls of built-in bookshelves. Both houses had nice entrance halls and open staircases to the second floor. We lost out on our first choice to a couple who would be our neighbors for years, and the Tudor became ours—with a forty-five percent down payment and help from both of our families.

We put the Ball Place house on the market in the late fall of 1985, and sold it within twenty-four hours for more than our asking price, and double what we'd paid five years earlier. The new house was built in 1937 on a steeply terraced lot due to the hill, It had a two-car garage under the dining room, and there were four bedrooms and three bathrooms on two upper floors. It had a wrought-iron stair rail with a brass handgrip (real wrought iron, not the bad 1960s stuff). It was not the mansion of my dreams, but it was close enough to my Sedgwick Farm memories to satisfy that yearning. We did not need a house this big. I needed this house, and Gary let me have it.

We moved into the Woodhill Drive house on February 14, 1986, in a torrential downpour. Both the basement of our old house and the basement of the new house flooded.

It was my dream house, for now.

In the spring of 1986, Bill and Michael asked me to accompany them to Palm Sunday services at the church where the Organization for Gay Awareness, and the Dignity chapter to which they belonged both met: Saint George's Episcopal. Saint George's was different. Not only did they offer shelter to two gay groups, the first Episcopal parish in the Diocese of Newark to do so, but had been longtime supporters of a large AA group. The parish rector, a warm and charming man named Craig Burlington, had come to speak to OGA one Tuesday evening, and made it clear that any of us would be welcome in his congregation. He had also sent a note to Bill and Michael, inviting them personally, as a couple, after a long telephone conversation with Bill about the

way the Catholic Church treated gay people. The idea that a mainstream cler-
gyman from an old-guard WASP church would make an invitation like this
was amazing to us.

Bill and Michael were curious, but as lifelong Catholics were anxious
about attending a non-Catholic church (something they had been explicitly and
repeatedly warned against as children). Thus, with me as their—what? spiritual
bodyguard?—in case someone tried to force them to become Protestants, we
all showed up on Palm Sunday.

Something about that service tapped into my childhood experience at
Saint Paul's in Syracuse. There was a warmth, a welcoming community, that
drew me in. There were no sermons about hellfire for sinners or condemnations
of people like us, and by that they meant gay men and women; but also and
explicitly same-sex couples. The idea that a church would take our couple-
hood seriously, as if we were married, was something we had never imagined.
Gary had no interest in becoming a Christian, but he was fascinated by this
place that didn't shy away from him as a Jewish partner to a gay man.

St. George's is a beautiful, if slightly stodgy, 1920s riff on a medieval
English country parish. Massive, rough-textured stone walls, tall gothic windows narrating the life of Christ, and a high beamed nave. Having been
founded in the early twentieth century as a small outlier to South Orange's
wealthy Victorian parish of Holy Communion, it had grown and prospered.
Stymied by the Depression just three years after its completion in 1926, the
new church completed its extensive suite of stained-glass windows only in the
1950s, to designs prepared in the late 1920s by the Charles J. Connick Studio
of Boston. In the 1960s St. George's was referred to as the country club parish,
and was peopled with the expected enclave of professionals, nearly all of
whom were white. It had been conceived as a shrine to Anglo-Saxon American
Protestantism of the most genteel kind. Ultimately, though, St. George's would
become a beacon of hope to marginalized people yearning for a spiritual home
and notorious as the gayest parish in the most liberal diocese on the East Coast.

After more than three decades as a parishioner, I have turned from the chatty gay boy with the Jewish boyfriend to one of the graying elders at St. George's. I was on the parish vestry (board) for eleven years, six of them as Warden. For two decades I've been managing (badly) the Altar Guild, that onetime bastion of hatted-and-gloved parish women who see to the flowers and the linens for Sunday services. I not only wrote the Altar Guild Prayer but coined our tagline: "We set the table. We do the dishes. We're the Altar Guild."

Although the Cleavers didn't apparently attend any church wherever it was they lived in the early 1960s, I still smile at how *Leave it to Beaver* it all is.

As a background for my re-entry into church, you need to know that the Bishop of Newark in the 1980s was a man named John Shelby Spong. A prolific writer and outspoken liberal theologian, Jack Spong had been raised as an evangelical Christian in the South and attended a conservative seminary. Ironically, he was no friend to the closeted gay priests in the Diocese of Newark when he arrived there in the late 1970s (they were all closeted by necessity); but by the time I walked into St. George's, Bishop Spong had experienced his conversion on the road to Damascus. He was loved by as many people as hated him, and feelings about him always ran high. Even his strongest supporters blanched at some of his more outlandish proposals; but I loved him and his theology like a dying man offered water in the middle of a desert. The Christian Right had taken Jesus away from me because I was gay and because I loved a Jew. Jack Spong, through Saint George's, gave Jesus back to me. For a young man who had seen the Bible used as a weapon against him and his kind, the Diocese of Newark showed me how to use the Bible as a shield.

I understood pretty much from the start that I was, and would remain, a contingent Christian. I saw that the Episcopal Church nationally, the Diocese of Newark regionally, and St. George's locally had all become something other than the uptight church I knew as a child. Even as the Presbyterians, Lutherans and Methodists struggled over the status of gay and lesbian people within their denominations, Episcopalians, the "Frozen Chosen," had made a clear change. There was plenty of dissent on the national level, with bishops who saw Jack Spong and his diocese as their worst nightmare. I was tickled to be part of that nightmare. I also knew that I could walk away, and that I would remain committed to the church only so long as the church remained committed to me as a gay man.

***

One of my joys of being a curator was spending time puttering in the museum storerooms, learning the collection, and conjuring up exhibition ideas. One random afternoon in 1989 I was called to the phone in the basement of the Newark Museum, where I'd been working in the silver vault. It was Bishop Spong, calling from Cathedral House on Rector Street, the offices of the Diocese of Newark, whose lovely Federal period cathedral, Trinity and St. Philips, was just a few blocks away from the museum.

The bishop had called to tell me about the creation of The Oasis, a new mission of the Diocese of Newark, that would minister to lesbian and gay Episcopalians (again, this is before LGBT was the norm), who still felt marginalized by the church. Jack Spong had a young ordinand named Robert Williams in mind for founding director of The Oasis. Williams was a day older than I (he and I both turned thirty-four in July of that year). As an openly gay priest—meaning that it was publicly acknowledged before the ordination took place—Williams would be hard-pressed to find a job in a parish church, and the bishop felt that this was a perfect solution to that dilemma.

The Oasis was needed because, even in the relatively liberal Diocese of Newark, gay folk didn't necessarily feel the kind of welcome and comfort I enjoyed at St. George's. Church was still not a safe space for most gay men and women, and Robert Williams' ministry would offer weekly eucharists at different parishes around the diocese. The ministry's very existence would force the wider diocese to acknowledge the presence of queer sheep in its flock—sheep who were not being cared for fully. You must keep in mind that the Episcopal church still took the official position on a national level that sex outside of heterosexual marriage was inappropriate for Christians.

Bishop Spong asked me to be on the founding board of directors of The Oasis. Why did my name pop up? Easy. My dear friend Michael had by then left his job at NBC news to become the diocesan administrator for the Bishop of Newark, and would remain so under three bishops. Bishop Spong was clearly trolling for likely gay Episcopalians who would be willing to step into the spotlight for the inevitable blow-back over the Oasis and its soon-to-be-ordained leader. Robert Williams was in a same-sex relationship, and so was I.

I said yes. It was very hard to say no to Jack Spong.

Jack would wrangle a founding board of directors for The Oasis made up of gay men and women, augmented by some strong straight allies. It was an astonishing group to be part of and placed me for a time in the midst of church politics. Robert Williams, whom I liked a great deal, would ultimately be hoisted by his own radical attitudes on issues of monogamy and clerical celibacy (he didn't feel either one was necessary to be a good Christian). Forced to resign from The Oasis, Williams was succeeded by David Norgard, another gay priest with a partner. David and Joseph would become familiar faces at St. George's, their warmth and comfort with who they were easing the way. The Oasis itself would help change the course of Episcopalian history in our diocese, eventually evolving into a diocesan commission as more and more parishes became explicitly welcoming, eliminating the need for separate services.

Soon after the founding of The Oasis, my quiet suburban parish became the focus of a notorious heresy trial (yes, you read that correctly) in the early 1990s when the Right Reverend Walter Righter, at Bishop Spong's request, ordained an openly gay man living with a same-sex partner to the Episcopal diaconate. Righter was the retired bishop of Iowa and was spending time in Newark assisting Bishop Spong. He got tagged to ordain the smart and charismatic Barry Stopfel because Bishop Spong knew that the ecclesiastical shit would hit the fan if he did it himself. I've always felt Walter Righter was a damned good sport for taking this on and that Jack Spong was wise to choose him. Spong ordained Barry Stopfel to the priesthood, but the die was cast.

Not long after he was ordained, Barry would become the rector of St. George's, thus unwittingly sparking another aspect of this clerical tempest in a teapot. Gay priests were not such a huge novelty, but Barry's call to St. George's was historical because there was no prevaricating. I was on the parish search committee, as a gay voice. We knew what we were doing. We knew the circumstances of Barry's ordination. We knew his partner Will, also an ordained minister. We understood that we were taking a big step.

We did not, however, anticipate national attention or accusations of heresy flung at a retired bishop by the Episcopal Church's right wing, incensed at Bishop Spong's liberal agenda. For weeks we had news teams waiting outside St. George's at Sunday services, expecting to see something happen. We never did figure out what they expected to see. Both Barry's call to our parish and the hubbub surrounding the trial did scare away some parishioners and made the rest of us feel somewhat put upon.

Mostly, however, we were all fascinated and bemused at the ruckus. The national church ruled against the heresy accusation a few weeks later at the trial venue in Wilmington, Delaware, and our parish went back to normal. Needless to say, with all that attention in a town already appealing to gay people, St. George's got a little gayer. There are a lot of LGBTQ folk looking for spiritual shelter and we were there waiting.

Barry Stopfel left us after seven years, and we went and hired *another* gay priest. Bernie Poppe, a cradle Episcopalian, was a very different sort of priest. His arrival in Maplewood cause no stir whatsoever. I'd been on the search committee that called Barry, but this time around I was just on the vestry, and only interviewed Reverend Poppe at the end of the process. The most startling thing about him was that his being gay was barely a blip on the parish radar. Gay was nothing for us; we were more concerned with his preaching ability and his management style.

By the time Bernie left St. George's eighteen years later, he had become a remarkably compelling and interesting preacher. He was never the sharpest administrator, but he was a gentle man and nurtured his flock with all his heart. As I watched the national church veer toward schism and breaking with the Anglican Communion over the ordination of an openly gay bishop (Gene Robinson), I kept my contingency plan handy. If the American church ever backtracked, ever reneged on the promises it had made to me and my LGBT kindred, I would simply leave. Lord knows pledging to St. George's cost me enough. The savings alone, I figured, would justify a departure if anything went sideways.

St. George's is still a mostly straight and mostly white congregation; but such a description does it an injustice. It's also comprised of people of color; LGBT families; mixed-race families; and families like mine with non-Christian spouses and non-white adopted children. These days it seems like half of the congregation used to live in Hoboken or Brooklyn, and probably as many of them were raised Catholic—or some other orthodox denomination that made them feel unwelcome. I'm sure that the only reason I've never been to therapy is that St. George's has always been a place of utter goodness, a shelter and a spot of serenity amid my turbulent weeks. I have never loved the building itself, in spite of its 1920s Anglophile pretensions; but when the people are there, then I feel it: the goodness of the people who make the parish what it is. Most of the elders who first knew me as a chatty thirty-year-old are dead, but the younger people, gay and straight, Black and white, far removed from the country club crowd who created St. George's, embody the crazy bubble of liberalism that Maplewood/South Orange has become. In my decades as a parishioner, a surprising number of gay kids have emerged from among the families at St. George's. I know their path was made smoother by the existence of a church community so far removed from what I knew as a child.

As the religious right continues its unconstitutional attempts to take over the government and interfere in all our lives, I worry more about what might happen to my country than I do about my own faith community. St. George's is solid.

CHAPTER TWENTY-SEVEN

MOUTHS OF BABES

arly in my relationship with Gary, at some quiet moment during a family visit, my mother told me that she didn't expect to have any grandchildren. Although there was a wistfulness to her words, I didn't sense she was trying to put any guilt on me. WASP guilt is real, but my mother had no part in it. My brother and his wife, married in 1974 at dusk in an outdoor amphitheater in Chapel Hill, North Carolina, had apparently expressed the "I'm not bringing children into this horrible world" mindset. It didn't even occur to my mother—or to me—that two gay men would ever become parents.

Strangely enough, Gary and I had never discussed children. I suppose we tacitly accepted the fact that gay couples were childless, unless one or the other had been married and had children from that heterosexual part of their life. Surely in the first decade of our relationship we were too young to even ponder the possibilities, our careers evolving and our life moving forward. Our involvement with children would be through other people's kids. For the first twenty years of our relationship, that was the simple truth.

Jed and Julia would break their own resolution in 1978 with the birth of my niece Edith, named for my late sister (and my mother's sister, and my grandmother Grant). This newest Edith brought the Dietz redhead gene into my branch of the family, not to mention joy and laughter. My parents were beside themselves. Julia, who was at this point in her pediatric residency at Upstate Medical Center in Syracuse, had clearly rethought her stand on children. Two other babies, our nephew Robert, and our nephew Elihu, would follow their big sister at well-spaced intervals.

A vivid image from that era is of me sitting in the dining room at Jed and Julia's house in Syracuse and talking with my sister-in-law, while Edith and Robert dragged the infant Elihu around and around the dining table in a wicker laundry basket. I remember her amusement and her patience with her kids' antics. I marveled at her dedication to her career on top of being a fantastic mother. I don't think I was remotely envious.

Christmas visits to Syracuse and Cazenovia would become happily child-centric, and Gary and I reveled in being the gay uncles who could indulge the kids and then leave them in the care of their parents. Jed and Julia had settled into a big architect-designed 1950s house on three acres in a part of Syracuse called Solvay, named for the builder of the huge chemical plant that had polluted Onondaga Lake for decades. I have particularly happy memories of helping my niece put together a Barbie Dreamhouse (or maybe it was just a Barbie dream kitchen). The near-painful anticipatory excitement I had always felt at the approaching gift orgy of Christmas could be transferred to my brother's children. It would also cement into place the tradition that Gary and I would never have Christmas in our own house, and that I would never attend Christmas celebrations at my own church in New Jersey, even when I had taken charge of the annual holiday decoration of my parish. It would take until the global pandemic in 2020 before Gary and I spent Christmas in our own house for the first time, after forty years in New Jersey.

In the 1980s, Gary and I had other things on our minds than speculating about children of our own. We both had new jobs and our first house to settle into. We had a dog and two cats. We were young men in our mid-twenties at the start of the decade and had no idea what was waiting for us and our community over the next twenty years. By the time we moved into our second house and I had joined St. George's church in 1986, a new wave of demonization of gay men and their "lifestyle" had swung into play because of AIDS. President Reagan, patron saint of the new right's rise, first mentioned AIDS in 1985, the same year the FDA approved the first test for HIV. The New Jersey Lesbian and Gay Coalition, of which Gary was an officer, was struggling to understand how to act, what to do, amidst the fear and confusion surrounding the plague. The annual death toll would rise exponentially over the course of the decade. Within our gay social and political circles in New Jersey, AIDS and its impact on our world had become all-consuming.

So, you ask, what has this to do with children?

Imagine my surprise, on Valentine's Day in 1989, when Gary told me over dinner that he'd been tested and was HIV negative. My response was to go up to St. Michael's Hospital in Newark, a block up the hill from the museum, and have my blood tested anonymously. Everybody got tested anonymously, because of the repercussions of having HIV at the time. There was no job protection for people with HIV. You also had to wait two weeks for the results, meaning two weeks passed by in gut-twisting apprehension.

Fortunately, I was negative, too. It was as if something dark and heavy had lifted from our shoulders. Now all we had to worry about was every other disaster and disease that could eventually kill us. At the time it seemed like a Get Out of Jail Free card.

An unanticipated outcome of our negative HIV status was that dear friends of ours, a lesbian couple we'd known for years, asked us to be sperm donors, and with Gary ultimately taking that honor, we helped add another child to our world in a way we'd never imagined. Like my brother's children, and Gary's nephew Mark, this child has played an important role in our lives.

You'd think all these children of others would be enough, wouldn't you? Well, we thought so, too, until early in 1992. At a Super Bowl party across the street, our wonderful next-door neighbor Alyson came up to us, beaming as if with a private joke. She reported to us that her older child, then about five, had told her that Gary and I ought to have a baby, because we were a family, and families had babies. We all laughed at the very idea. Then Gary and I left to see the hot new film at the Maplewood theater, *Grand Canyon.*

As we walked down the hill to our house, our brief conversation went something like this:

"You don't want children, do you?"

"I never said I didn't want children. I like children."

"Why haven't we ever talked about it in sixteen years?"

Why hadn't we ever talked about it? Partly, we just had never imagined that it was possible. Other than the friends we'd helped, we knew no other gay couple with kids that hadn't come from previous marriages. Deeper than that for me was a fear that stemmed from the deaths of my brother and sister. Losing a child was a parent's ultimate nightmare, and I'd seen my own mother and father, who were strong people, all but crushed by it. They carried on with their lives, but they never got over it.

Not having children meant you didn't have to worry about them, in theory at least. Gary and I, however, had come to realize that we worried about Jed and Julia's children, and we also worried about our friends' child—because, after all, we had helped. We were not quite narcissistic enough to worry only about our immediate concerns. There was more than enough worry to spare for everyone in the world that mattered to us, including children.

Add to this the fact that one of the main subplots in the film *Grand Canyon,* the movie we saw that Super Bowl Sunday, concerns a housewife, bereft over her youngest child going off to summer camp, who goes out for a jog and finds a baby abandoned by the side of the road in Beverly Hills.

I'm pretty sure that by the end of that day Gary and I were desperate to be parents. Between our neighbor's throw-away comment at a Super Bowl party, and the random plot arc of a Hollywood movie, all our buttons had been well and truly pushed.

Thus began an odyssey that would, in the end, take four years. The first two years seem to have been taken up with choosing a path and discovering possibilities. I remember a trip to Vermont, and realizing that I somehow had never been to Vermont, although I'd been to every state surrounding it multiple times. The purpose of that trip was to attend a group session at an adoption agency, sitting with an assortment of young straight couples and talking about our reasons for wanting to adopt a baby. This was the moment when we realized that our quest was different. We knew we could produce babies if we wanted to. It had never dawned on us—even though I'd grown up with adopted friends, in a world where adoption was acknowledged but seldom talked about—that adoption was rarely the first choice for a couple. Infertility was not something we'd confronted before, and this was something important for us to grasp.

We understood that, in the end, adoption is a selfish, not a selfless action. All the rhetoric about rescuing unwanted children, blah blah blah, never resonated with us, any more than the notion that parents were expected to sacrifice everything for their children. We understood from the get-go that adopting a baby, raising a child, was something we were doing for ourselves. Oh, we wanted to be good parents, and like all those other childless couples in the room that day, we believed we were up to the task; but we also understood that no child asks to be born or adopted. We knew that we had more than enough love for a child in our lives, but we also knew that we were in this for our own hopes and dreams.

It's important to point out that our experience in Vermont was almost entirely positive. Not one of the couples we met that day voiced any discomfort at the idea of two men adopting a baby. This probably had to do with the agency we chose, for sure, but it reminded us that we were not surrounded by enemies (of course, we were in Vermont, not Alabama, and that no doubt made a difference). The only negative note in the long weekend was that our genteel dowager hostess at the elegant bed-and-breakfast where we stayed all but accused Gary of stealing one of her silver teaspoons when we checked out. What made this more unsettling is that she knew he was Jewish, whereas I was a WASP (and a museum curator), which somehow rendered me above suspicion. I may have written a terse, polite little note to the lady after we got back to

New Jersey, assuring her of Mr. Berger's integrity. I do remember that she ultimately found the spoon and wrote her own note, apologizing to us.

We looked into two options in 1992, both restricted by whatever prejudices and legal limitations we faced as a gay male couple linked only by a thirty-year mortgage. There were open adoptions, which meant that you literally advertised for a young pregnant woman looking to place her baby with a loving couple. You never said "give up" her baby. Ours was not to judge, but to support. We were made to understand from the start how difficult the idea of placing a baby for adoption was for the birth mother. Open adoption was facilitated by various kinds of licensed agencies, who looked out for the rights and the health of the birth mother, while encouraging the would-be parents to be supportive without interfering in the birth mother's life. The greatest appeal of open adoption was that you knew who the birth mother was, and sometimes the birth father, too. Adoption was something historically shrouded in mystery and tainted with shame. These modern adoptions put aside all of that. Everyone came to an agreement about whether regular contact would be maintained going forward, but there was no secrecy.

The other adoption option we looked into was international (not *foreign*), what would now be called transnational adoption. This was not only more complicated and more expensive, but it pretty much guaranteed that the adoptive parents would know little or nothing about the birthparents of their child. At the time we started our adoption search, the international adoption world was burgeoning. We had no idea that we were at the beginning of a tremendous wave that would make headlines across the country and the world as the next decade unfolded.

We read books and talked with each other and decided to pursue the domestic adoption route. This involved creating a family profile for ourselves and printing a photograph that was an advertisement for this obviously desirable family-to-be. We posed in our front yard, in front of our little Japanese maple, its leaves ruby-red with the fall, our big brown poodle, Penny, between us. There was a brief elevator pitch printed on the back, with our phone number. I think we actually sent these out like Christmas cards that year, the fall of 1992. The idea with domestic adoption is that you never knew where you might find your baby. Far from keeping it a secret, you were supposed to tell everyone.

The other strategy was to literally advertise. We crafted a precisely worded ad that we placed in local supermarket papers such as *The Pennysaver*. It was an even shorter elevator pitch that, in as few words as possible, was meant to appeal to the lonely, possibly confused pregnant women, searching for a solution to her dilemma. We had to sound wholesome and prosperous, without being obnoxious or too desperate.

Although we had been warned, the process was no slam-dunk. We got calls, for sure. Sometimes they were frightened unmarried women who had just learned they were pregnant and didn't know what to do next. Sometimes they were chatty and curious, seemingly checking out their options just as we were. But there were also the fakers, who would call more than once, engaging us in long positive-seeming conversations over the course of several weeks, only to ghost us when they'd satisfied whatever it was they'd been looking for. These women, we were told, were probably not even pregnant.

It was clear from the start: seeking a baby was not like shopping for a car. It was not point-and-click. We really had no idea what we were in for.

By the end of 1993 we had struck gold, or so we thought. A young married couple in Ogden, Utah answered our ad in the *Village Voice* (we had graduated from *The Pennysaver*). We had a long, intense conversation over the phone, and then arranged to fly to Salt Lake City, where we rented a car and drove to Ogden.

They were both blond and blue-eyed. They were good-looking, about twenty-one, and poor—too poor, they thought, to be able to care for a child. In the heart of the gay-hating Mormon world, they were native non-Mormons and found our unconventional family profile especially appealing. They loved the idea of helping us as a couple to become a family.

It was a brief, emotionally charged and happy rendezvous. I remember sitting in the Salt Lake City airport, looking at the magnificent mountain ranges that provided its backdrop, full of a sense that our dream was going to come true. It had been a year and a half since that fateful Super Bowl game. Everything was falling into place. Having arrived in Utah with the baby names Alice and Adam in our minds, we left with Alice and Alexander for our potential child, incorporating the couple's first names as middle names. If these young people were going to be part of our lives through their baby, we were going to embrace it.

I started writing a journal in January 1994, to document what I knew was going to be a big year. I'd been writing journals when I traveled abroad since I was fifteen and my great aunt Ethel gave me that little leather-bound blank book with my name in gold on the cover for the England trip with my father. I'd never even tried to keep a long-term diary of any sort, but it now felt like a good time to try. As a curator, what I saw in the twelve months before me was the final massive push to restore, reinterpret and open the museum's 1885 Ballantine House, something that would be a crowning achievement of my fourteen-year career. In the middle of all that, Gary and I would become fathers. I would take parental leave, because my job paid half of what Gary's salary did, and I worked close to home, while Gary's office was up in Bergen County and he had a twenty-five-mile commute on the Garden State Parkway twice a day. The anxiety over picturing how to balance these two parts of my soon-to-be life were largely pleasurable.

My diary was purposely detailed. I wanted to record the world as it was in 1994, and our lives in that world before we became parents. The result, looking back a quarter of a century, is interesting. The just-beginning adoption saga is the least of it; the sense of time-travel to a world pre-9/11, when I was still young, is startling.

Fairly soon in my diary I reported that the young woman had determined that she was carrying a girl, and so the name Alice became my mantra as we considered what to do with the bedroom that was my study and would ultimately become the nursery.

Our agency would act as facilitator. Gary and I would step back and communicate only through them. I remember that even the word "facilitator" made the agency uncomfortable, since it smacked of a transactional relationship (which to be honest, it was). They wanted us to think of them as good people helping other good people become a happy family. There was, frankly, something slightly cult-ish about joining the world of would-be adoptive parents. You had to buy into it; you had to *believe.* I suggest no criticism here, because those folks understood exactly how emotionally and legally complicated this whole process was. This was not the old-fashioned, clinical world of adoption that had prevailed when I was a child. This brave new adoption industry (because that's what it was), was trying very hard to be compassionate, humanistic, and helping. They took their role in creating new families very seriously. Ultimately, our trust in the various agencies we used over the next two years was not misplaced. We were just naïve when we started.

The very first notes of concern appeared in my journal by the end of January, when our birth parents missed a weekly call to the agency. At first we shrugged it off—being young and pregnant had its own complications. As the month unfurled, however, it became increasingly hard to ignore the fact that our Ogden friends had ghosted us. We should have seen it coming, and even at the time we said this to each other. They were poor and under-educated, but they were not alone. They had large families surrounding them on both sides. What we didn't ask them about, and chose not to dwell on, was the truth that this baby would be the first grandchild in either family. They were not teenagers, they were not addicts or homeless or alienated from their parents. In retrospect, we were, all four of us, naive to think it would turn out any other way.

Eventually, after we had already moved on, we did get a letter, telling us of the birth of their little girl. She was blond and blue-eyed like her parents. Both Gary and I felt that this is the way it should have been, and we wrote a letter to them assuring them of our love and support in their choice. Our hearts were broken, but we knew what was right.

I forged ahead with my diary. We shifted gears, deciding that perhaps the personal aspects that had made domestic adoption so appealing were maybe not as attractive as we'd thought. International adoption guaranteed anonymity, and (we thought) guaranteed delivery of a child. We applied to another agency, which was in fact two agencies. There was the agency that dealt directly with the source countries, and the agency that dealt with the adoptive parents in the USA. Although they also paid lip-service to compassion and being helpful, these international agencies were very conscious of laws. As adoptive parents we had to be studied and studied and studied for suitability. I have no argument with that, since the horror stories when things went wrong would become national news in the next two decades. Starting down the path to international adoption was, however, the most intrusive experience of our lives.

Straight couples the world over have no rules for having babies. They do it entirely under their own guidance and at their own whim. I must acknowledge couples for whom infertility looms as a barrier. Straight couples don't have to be able to afford a baby. They don't have to be healthy or employed or of good habits. Moral character is irrelevant, as are faith systems and community standards. Not so for any couple adopting, and especially for a same-sex couple. As two not-yet-middle-aged men linked only by a house in the suburbs and our wills, we were at the very bottom of the list of desirable adoptive parents in the international market (yeah, market is cynical, but it is not inaccurate).

At first the most appealing route was Eastern Europe. The former Soviet bloc had lots of orphanages with lots of children ready to be placed in the waiting arms of appropriately affluent Americans. Of course, for this to happen, one had to negotiate the bureaucracy at every level of whatever country one chose. What we didn't understand is that every level of any country's bureaucracy had the power to halt any adoption based entirely on personal bias.

That, of course, was something we would learn the hard way, and more than once.

At home, we were vetted and studied and interviewed. I hasten to say that the home-study process, while invasive, was never ugly or negative. We were treated with great kindness and even affection by the agency that took us on as clients. They liked our spacious house, our nice furnishings, our friendly poodle (and absurd cats). They liked us as two respectable, Ivy-League-educated, affluent white men. They were impressed that we had already been together for eighteen years. We were more stable than a lot of heterosexual couples who sought to adopt. The fact that we were not treated differently as a gay couple was something we understood and appreciated.

There was, however, one kink in the wire. We could not present ourselves as a couple to a foreign country for an international adoption. One of us had to apply as a single man wishing to adopt a child. The other one had to essentially become invisible. Since Gary's income was the one that made this costly adoption process possible, I was the one who had to become "the nice man who rented the room on the third floor." I am not joking. The home-study people laughed with us over the ruse, but it was deadly serious. I suspect it also might have skirted close to the edge of some laws here and there. But those were foreign laws, and we didn't respect those laws, driven as they were by bias and ignorance. As long as we played the game (and paid the bills) we would get our baby.

There were for us, amazingly, four failed adoptions in Eastern Europe that year, each one getting just so far before fate and bureaucratic prejudice stepped in and crushed our dream. The briefest disappointment was over a little baby girl named Olga. Olga had red hair and blue eyes. Maybe she was Rumanian; that detail escapes me now. We were very taken with her prettiness, and her name (my aunt and my great-grandmother were both named Olga) as well as her red hair. We were so ready to leap at this chance because of coincidences that we wanted to see as momentous. Olga never got beyond the stage of a video clip. Our initial interest went nowhere, stopped before it started by the implacable reality that what we wanted was important to nobody but us.

Maxim was another, greater letdown. He was adorable, blond and blue-eyed. He was in a Russian orphanage, and while there was no indication of alcohol during his mother's pregnancy, there was a disturbing comment in his medical record about a "hole" in his heart. We consulted with the man who eventually would become our pediatrician. We questioned the documents and pushed our agency for clarification. We went so far as to consult with the father of a friend of ours, a celebrated endocrinologist who worked in the team called in after the Chernobyl meltdown near Kyiv. A line from my journal stands out:

Maybe we have to act more on faith than on fact, which seems stupid when you're paying a small fortune. But maybe that's the point. You're not "buying" anything. You're having a baby. And that means taking chances.

In the end, we didn't care; we submitted our application for adoption. That is to say, Gary submitted his application as a single father, and I sat back and held my breath. The paperwork and the fees made their way into the wheels of Russian bureaucracy. It went on for a while, until one day it was summarily rejected. Too many single men trying to adopt all of a sudden, and the door was slammed shut.

Something I should note: by this point we were no longer telling people much about our adoption activities. Only our closest friends and people we had to tell for practical reasons were in on our week-to-week progress, or lack of it. We referred to Maxim as our "secret baby." The problem was that we had early on told everybody about our wish to adopt, and so everybody constantly asked for updates, unaware of the specifics of each disaster.

After Maxim came the first Sasha, a sixteen-month-old in a Rumanian orphanage. To be honest, until I reread my diary, I'd forgotten him entirely, which horrifies me. That adoption process didn't get as far as Maxim's, but it got far enough to break our hearts yet again. There was ongoing concern about any mention of my existence in any of the paperwork, thinking that maybe this had triggered a red flag for the Rumanian bureaucracy. To their credit, our agency got us right back on the horse, and delved back into Russia. We just gritted our teeth and got on with our lives.

Through this entire year I was deeply involved in the evolving Oasis ministry in the Diocese of Newark, not to mention a good deal of travel for the museum. The Ballantine House project had become a $4.5 million juggernaut, and I was juggling lots of different aspects of the project while working on other incoming exhibitions and looking forward to future exhibitions. It was, as young people say now, a lot.

At the same time, my father was beginning a descent into dementia, which none of us completely recognized. Part of that process was his increasingly unregulated drinking, which I was seeing as a cause rather than a symptom. On top of that, my parents had decided to sell the house on the lake in Cazenovia, and to move into a townhouse-condominium in suburban Fayetteville, New York. I was distressed about it at the time but realized that it was my mother looking to her own future as she approached eighty and my father deteriorated.

We had begun to compartmentalize our life, keeping all things adoption-related neatly set aside, to be thought about only when we had to. Of course, we were always subject to other people's babies, whom we found irresistible. Everything we did that summer—visiting my parents, going to Newport and Provincetown—was colored by our unrealized dream of being parents. We rarely talked about it, but it was always there in our minds.

As we said our final farewells to the couple from Utah—with their newborn baby girl—we began to focus more on the second Sasha, a Russian baby approaching twenty months of age, living in an orphanage in Petrozavodsk, a city well north of Saint Petersburg and the capital of the Republic of Karelia. This Sasha, we were told, was half Roma. He was very fair-skinned, with round cheeks, curly dark hair, and bright dark eyes. The Roma are a much-maligned minority in Russia, and we wondered if this might not have been part of the reason he was legally orphaned. There were no medical issues beyond a slightly worrying note that his head was rather small. That turned out to be a clerical error.

By the start of September, we were planning Gary's trip to Russia to meet his (our) baby, and we had named him: Alexander Ulysses Berger, although we called him Sasha. The gay Macedonian hero of the ancient world, and the great military hero of the American Civil War. I had become very aware of the fact that I was the only Ulysses in my generation of descendants from the general/president. We had dropped the idea of Adam as a first name, and not only was Sasha a Russian nickname for Alexander, but Gary's Russian paternal grandfather had been named Alexander—although he'd been known as Mike.

At this stage in our quest, as Sasha and Russia loomed on the horizon, we had begun to meet other gay and lesbian couples who had managed to have or adopt children, which made the whole reality of it more tangible as well as more uncomfortable.

A quote from my diary:

It is so awkward to talk about our adoption, which is so detailed, and yet so unsure. Despite everything we have on paper and know, it could all evaporate, thus making it hard to discuss beyond our own self-controlled screening process. Imagine a pregnant woman having to do this in her eighth month; never being quite able to just say "yes, we're going to have a child soon." Any wonder we're numb?

To our amazement, Gary's parents, Gladys and Pete, had begun to gently nudge, seeing our friends' children (one of whom was in fact their biological grandchild, a fact they would never know) and telling us that they'd love for us to have our own. Having your Jewish mother-in-law-but-not-legally tell you she wants you to give her grandchildren is kind of a fantastic milestone. Too bad it was as painful as it was pleasing.

The adoption plans with officials in Moscow and Petrozavodsk moved forward. I had gotten so gun-shy from the previous misfires that I found myself trying not to think about it—about *him*, that little half-Roma baby in an orphanage on Lake Onega. I refused to look at his pictures in the file sent to us by the agency. I couldn't bring myself to say his name out loud. As it turned out, Gary caved first, as he and our friends Sue and Faith began to talk baby things and plans for a trip Gary would make to Russia. At one point, a week before he left for Europe, Gary came home from a re-sale children's clothing store with a pile of adorable baby things for our little boy. We sat together in the nursery, my former study, cleared of all of my things, furnished with a borrowed crib and a cheery picture on the wall above it spelling out ALEX-ANDER in big cartoonish letters; and sorted through the baby clothes and the various supplies Gary needed to take with him. We had let ourselves believe at last.

The plan was straightforward enough. Gary would fly to Moscow and then take an eight-hour train journey to Petrozavodsk. He would spend time with the baby each day at the orphanage for a week or so, so that they could acclimate to each other. Then he and the baby would take the train back to Moscow and finalize the adoption before flying back to the United States. He would be back—*they* would be back—by Hallowe'en.

As the trip neared, all our discretion evaporated. We talked with everybody about Sasha and our plans, soliciting advice from my brother and his pediatrician wife, pondering daycare solutions that would suit a little tyke who'd been in an orphanage his whole life so far. I talked to Barry, the rector of my church, about possible baptism plans, and to fellow parishioners about the fact that no whisper of my existence could emerge during Gary's visit, since the prejudice against same-sex couples was a deal-breaker everywhere in Europe, and especially in Russia.

Another note from my journal:

Gary took his wedding ring off months ago, to avoid a tan line on his finger. He'll put it on again when he gets home.

We did everything right.

Gary fell in love with Sasha instantly, and would fill me in with daily telephone reports of the goings-on in Petrozavodsk. He was staying in a high-rise tenement in an unattractive district, chauffeured around the gritty city by his handler, a brusque Ukrainian named Natasha, who was soundly disliked by the Russians around her. The directress of the orphanage liked Gary, felt he looked Russian, indeed looked just as she imagined Sasha's father would look. There was a constant refrain of people telling Gary that he needed to get married as soon as he got home with the baby. The absence of a mother was of concern to nearly everyone involved.

It all went like clockwork. Until it didn't. Unexpected postponements in court appointments. Foot-dragging for no reason. Apparently, the Russian modus operandi is to delay and delay and delay rather than to simply tell the truth. The truth was that, somewhere in the maze of Russian bureaucracy, someone with just enough power finally decided that not having a mother was a deal breaker. Gary was sent home, a week later than he was supposed to have been. He left all of the baby clothes and the antibiotics behind. When I picked him up at the airport, and saw him walking down the concourse, looking exhausted, with the empty stroller, I burst into tears.

My journal the day before Gary returned home ended on a very bitter note.

Written on November 7, I thought it would be the last entry:

Part of me fears that this will destroy our relationship, because we've built so much on this dream. I almost dread seeing Gary again, even as much as I miss him.

And in any case this whole journal has turned into nothing more than a ghastly joke. I was so full of hope and optimism on January 3 this year; and now there's nothing left but dust. Someone's played a cruel joke on us, and I haven't the heart to keep recording it.

The Ballantine House will open on time and is more or less finished. I will continue to get notoriety from the Grant's Tomb publicity. None of it matters, really. Maybe this year has taught me what's really important. All I can see now is a wretched holiday season and my own blinking back tears every time I see a family with little kids.

Down in South Carolina this week, a 23-year-old blonde blue-eyed cheerleader mom strapped her two beautiful little boys, 14 months and 4 years, into the family car and pushed it into a lake to drown them. She threw those little boys' lives away, and we can't even get the goddamn Russian government to give us one unwanted orphan. It's too awful.

On December 2 we got formal notice that the adoption application had been denied. It was the day of the press opening for the Ballantine House, renovated and redecorated at a cost of $4.5 million, the crowning achievement of my career. Three thousand visitors came to see the house in the first week. I smiled and was charming, as if nothing at all was amiss.

Another baby Alexander appeared on the horizon. This time he was in Guatemala, a newborn, through a Latina facilitator in Beverly Hills. Did I ever find it odd that we simply transferred the name, and the nursery, to this new baby? I don't think so. We did, however, really stop talking about adoption to everyone. This time we simply shut up, talking only to our closest friends. Not even our parents knew what was going on.

By early 1995 my father's health had deteriorated beyond just the drinking and the now-apparent dementia. Both he and Pete Berger, Gary's father, developed congestive heart failure at about the same time, putting each in the hospital. Dad got over his crisis, with a strict rationing of two drinks a day to be administered by my mother. Pete, on the other hand, had to go into the hospital in New York for a valve replacement. They used a pig's heart valve, and he joked about his non-kosher valve for the rest of his life.

The good news was that the redecoration scheme for my parents' new condo completely tricked my father into believing that they hadn't moved at all. Even as he withdrew little by little from reality, he settled quite happily into the new house. He had a study downstairs, in which he did little but stare out the sliding doors toward the grassy marsh that was a stand-in for the lake view he'd already forgotten. Mom had a small screened porch upstairs converted to her office. She was still driving, but father was not, which was simply another irritant in his increasingly fretful existence.

That year we suddenly became aware of an upswing in adoptions from Asia. A colleague of mine from the museum, having finished the Ballantine House project with me, retired at forty-seven and adopted a gorgeous baby girl from China. The son of our membership director at the museum adopted a baby girl from China within months of that. We already had friends in Maplewood with daughters from India and China. The stars seemed to be aligned for this moment. When our little Julio in Guatemala turned six months, with no forward progress in finalizing the adoption, I began to shut down again. We only referred to him, when we did, by his birth name, not by the name on the wall in the nursery. We tried to pretend he didn't exist unless we were forced to. The pattern of delayed court dates and requests for further psychological tests for Gary (because, yet again, I was a non-entity, the man upstairs, even though the home study agents always included me in their stateside reports) was all too familiar.

We had learned previously, in March, that Sasha had been adopted by another family in New Jersey quite quickly and without incident after Gary's attempt had been preempted.

That June was the first Gay Pride anniversary in New York since 1976 that we didn't march. We went into the city alone and watched from the sidelines.

August 18 marked my parents' fiftieth anniversary, which was duly celebrated at the Onondaga Country Club. The day before the dinner, my mother played golf with two old friends with whom she'd been golfing at this club since 1945. My mother was seventy-nine, my father newly seventy-five. Outwardly, seeing family and friends from all over the country gather for their party, he seemed mostly himself. All of the adults at the dinner were chosen because they'd known my parents for all of those fifty years. Some of our older relatives were too ill to make the trip, and their children stood in for them. My mother's sister Edith had died just a few weeks earlier, on my niece Edith's seventeenth birthday.

By the fall of 1995, I apparently had had my fill of self-deception. I'm putting in a long citation from my journal, because it says it best:

I had a little epiphany today, working out at the YMWCA in Newark. I realized that I can't keep pretending that the little baby in Guatemala isn't, psychologically, our son. We've been trying to keep him at arm's length, keeping the pictures locked away in the file marked "Julio." Today, on the Life Steps at the Y, a little door opened in my heart, and I understood, regardless of whether or not this adoption goes through the way we planned, Julio is already my little Alexander Ulysses, and there's no point claiming otherwise. We can do all we want to try to protect ourselves from the eventuality of disappointment, and another period of grief; but it won't change anything. Sasha was our son; the first child we lost. Just as if there had been a miscarriage or a stillbirth. I guess the pain of that loss has stopped, but I know I will never lose that scar. Sasha was the child that died before I got to meet him. Even knowing that some other family has adopted him, and that he's probably somewhere in New Jersey now, happily settled, doesn't change it. My Sasha died when that adoption failed, and I'll carry that loss forever. So I cannot deny our second child, even at the risk that he, too will be denied us.

Every time a woman who has miscarried gets pregnant, she must go through this. Can you spend nine months pretending you're not pregnant, to lessen the sorrow should you miscarry again? Can you spend any time pretending you don't love your child, hoping that, should you lose him, you won't grieve? So today I admitted to myself that the baby in Guatemala, whom we've watched grow in snapshots over the last nine months, is no longer Julio Antonio, in spite of what his present birth certificate says. For all the frustration and all the waiting, and in spite of the delays of the Guatemalan bureaucracy, he is, already, Alexander Ulysses, and he is our second child. We may still lose him, as we lost Sasha, and that will be another scar on my soul, another pain we'll have to shoulder together. But he's already mine, as much as if I'd held him, and fed him, and put him in his crib. Not looking at the pictures won't make the reality go away. So I've got the pictures in front of me, and I'm having a good long look at my second son. I've just got to keep praying that we get to keep this one.

I can't talk to Gary about this, because his scars are too deep and too painful still. Once this is over, then we'll talk.

Well.

I'll always be grateful to our loyal and meddlesome friends Sue and Faith for suggesting, as Christmas approached, that we should start a second adoption program, this time looking to China for a little girl. "What's the worst that could happen?" they said. We might end up with two children rather than none potentially. We went for it. Without their nudging, we never would have done it, but by the time we drove to Baltimore for Christmas, with our poodle in the back of the Mercury minivan I'd leased, Gary's application was already in Nanchang, Jiangxi Province. We had told nobody about this second project and were jittery to the point that we announced that we were returning to New Jersey on Christmas Day, leaving my brother and his family mystified after all the presents were opened and the turkey had been devoured. To lessen their puzzlement, we confided to them our second adoption plan. We claimed we had paperwork we needed to do. The truth was that we simply needed to be alone with our fear.

For Christmas that year I gave Gary a small, crib-sized quilt, hand-made by a Chinese American woman who, coincidentally, lived just a few blocks from Gary's parents in Springfield, New Jersey. Debbie Lee Chiu, born in Canton in 1955, had emigrated with her family to the United States during the Cultural Revolution in 1963. She had entered two of her quilts into my fall project, the New Jersey Arts Annual Crafts exhibition. I bought the larger of her entries, a splendid quilt called *Phantoms in a Chinese Restaurant* for the museum's collection. The smaller one, made for a competition sponsored by Campbell's Soup in Camden, New Jersey, was a brilliantly rendered Campbell's Chicken Noodle Soup can in the form of a traditional log cabin quilt. The quilting pattern, something of which Mrs. Chiu was especially proud, was a portrait of her own daughter eating soup. I had figured that it would be appropriate, one way or another, as a combined Christmas and anniversary gift.

For our twentieth anniversary we ran away to New York. We treated ourselves to a room at the Carlyle Hotel on Madison Avenue, and a New Year's Eve dinner at the Townhouse, a famous old-style gay bar and restaurant on the Upper East Side. We had made it through two decades together, and at forty and forty-two, allowed ourselves to revel in a love that had sustained us, for better and for worse, all those years.

After a wretched two years of failure and delay, it all began to happen in early 1996. At the beginning of February the final paperwork went through in Guatemala, and late in the month Gary flew to Guatemala City for a three-day pick-up and finalization process. On February 26, I got a phone call from our Chinese adoption agency to report that a little girl in Jiangxi Province had been assigned to us, and to ask if I was willing to accept her. She was, they told me, four months old and weighed twelve pounds. There was no paperwork, no photograph. I had to say yes before I got those. So with Gary in Central America with our first child, I accepted our second child without consulting him. It only occurred to me later that day, after I'd broken the news somewhat awkwardly to my frazzled partner over the phone, that I might have handled it better.

Alex and Gary arrived home from Guatemala at Newark Airport on February 27. Gary looked tired but radiant. Our little boy, fifteen months old, was plump and brown and smiled shyly at me before reaching out to let me take him into my arms. That first night he slept better than we did, and I remember, at dawn the next morning, turning to Gary in our big Victorian bed and whispering: "There's a *baby* down the hall."

A month later Gary left for China with Faith to get Grace. I love the sound of that, and all those years ago it seemed weighted with destiny. Gary chose our close friend Faith because I couldn't travel with him, and he needed someone experienced with babies. We chose to name our daughter Grace after my great-aunt Grace Root, wife of Edward Root, my grandmother's brother. I had always liked Aunt Grace, and thought it was a name that had been ignored for too long in our family. We rushed to get new wills in place before Gary left, and Alex decided to start walking while everybody sat around signing documents in our dining room.

Gary and Faith left for Beijing and Nanchang, where, in the White Swan Hotel, ten families were joined with ten babies, of whom ours, named Guo Fan, was the smallest.

Meanwhile, I invited my family for Easter church at St. George's, where Alexander Ulysses Antonio Berger was baptized at the Great Vigil. My altar guild team and I had filled the church with flowers for the holiday, and the Rev. Barry Stopfel performed the baptism. I didn't invite, or even notify, Gary's family, since I didn't want to seem to rub their faces in the fact that I (with Gary's blessing, so to speak) had chosen to make our children into Christians. Baptism is not a neutral kind of service and I felt that it would possibly be hurtful for Gladys and Pete to witness what could easily be seen as a rejection of our kids' Jewish heritage. Gary is not religious, and we had agreed that we would try to incorporate both of our religious traditions into our children's lives. My brother and his wife had never baptized their children, despite being married by an Episcopal Bishop; but that didn't prevent them from showing up, with their kids, for a full-blown Eucharist and baptism at St. George's. My younger nephew, Elihu, then eleven, held Alex's baptism candle. Alex, dressed in a little plaid outfit of shorts with suspenders and a white shirt—much like outfits I wore at his age—followed the priest's actions with wide-eyed fascination. Only toward the end of the very long service did I have to take him to the back of the church to play. Since so few (i.e. none) of our friends or colleagues were remotely interested in church, we asked the entire congregation to stand up as godparents to both of our children.

The Good Friday that year, the day before Alex was baptized, the FBI caught the Unabomber, a loner in a cabin in Montana who had been killing random people with mail-bombs over the course of seventeen years. On Easter Day, as Alex slept off the excitement of the night before, we all read a big article in the *New York Times Magazine* about the heresy trial of Bishop Walter Righter, who had ordained Barry as an openly gay man with a same-sex partner. I crowed in my journal at our son's being baptized by a rogue priest, and in my heart I reveled in the fact that somehow, the town we had chosen and the church to which I had returned seemed so perfectly suited to the family we had become.

Two days after Easter, on April 9, I drove to Kennedy Airport in a snowstorm to greet Gary and Faith's Asiana Airlines flight from Seoul. I had elected to leave Alex behind at home with our newly hired nanny, Alma, a warm midwestern grandmother who was a youthful sixty-one. Gary, Faith, and Grace arrived on time despite the weather. Before stuffing my expanded family into the green Mercury Voyager for the return trek to New Jersey, I was briefly introduced to the other nine families who had also adopted babies alongside Gary. There were, in all, thirty families with newly adopted babies on that return flight to the United States. Out of the ten couples in Gary's group, three were same-gender (two male, one female). It was a moment in American family history that would not be repeated. From start to finish Grace's adoption had taken all of four months. That period ended almost immediately, and all international adoptions became much slower, with multiple visits required and even more red tape.

Grace Fan Berger was duly baptized on Pentecost, wearing a Baby Dior outfit given to her by Bishop Spong and his wife Christine. Along with her that morning was another baby, William, whose mother and grandfather, both Episcopal priests, co-celebrated with Barry Stopfel. During the sacrament itself, Gary held Alex and I held our daughter. Legally, I still had no tie to these little ones who had already transformed our lives. After twenty years, the only things that still tied me legally to Gary were our wills and our refinanced fifteen-year mortgage on the Woodhill Drive house.

Because Gary had adopted our kids in two different foreign countries as a single father, this story has a couple more chapters. First, Gary had to re-adopt the children in the United States, although neither of us ever quite understood how legal adoptions in Guatemala and China didn't cut it in the American legal system. Once that was done, requiring another home study and court appearances, it was my turn.

Second-parent adoption was a new and controversial thing on the American family horizon. Right-wing religionists were fighting it on several fronts. Fortunately, those laws had been tested and adjudicated in New Jersey by the time it was my turn, and to our utter astonishment (and after a final home study, in which I was no longer the "man upstairs" but the star witness) my adoption of both Alex and Grace went through quickly. All I needed to do was sign some papers. It was strangely anticlimactic.

In the end, we received American birth certificates for both Alex and Grace, and on the line for parents, Gary and I were both listed. After twenty-two years, Gary and I were legally bound together for life—by our children.

I abandoned my journal at the end of 1996, with this closing commentary:

Perhaps I don't need a diary anymore. The kids are the most fright-ening, beautiful, and blessed thing I've ever experienced. I thank God every day for them, and never stop for a moment worrying about them somehow. I guess that's the way it was meant to be. The jewelry show looms ahead in '97. The kids will change and grow, as will we. I never suspected, when I began this diary back in January 1994, that it would turn out this way.

As I write this, Gary and I are empty nesters again. Alex is in California and Grace is in New York. Raising these children has been every bit the adventure I anticipated in 1997, but not at all what I expected in its details. Of course, like every parent of our generation, we did not make the mistakes our parents made with us. Gary and I found new and creative ways to fuck up our children in spite of our best intentions. This, I have realized, is the way of the world. I think my beloved husband and I have been the best parents we could possibly be, given the twists and turns of fate, biology, and history. Our children say they love us. What more can we ask?

I remember reading a rhetorical headline that humor columnist Dave Barry once used: *Children, bad idea or big mistake?* I laughed at the time, because I understood the fear that underlay it. Gary and I were no strangers to that fear, as we saw our lives change irrevocably with the birth of our family. To this day we see our life together as BK and AK—before and after kids. As parents, we had bad ideas and we made big mistakes, for sure, but I have no regrets, Maybe I'd do it better if I had a chance, but I'd do it again without a doubt.

Pentecost 1996. Gary holds Alex, as I present Grace for baptism by the Reverend Barry Stopfel at St. George's in Maplewood.

CHAPTER TWENTY-EIGHT

HETERONORMATIVITY

I really hate the term heteronormative, which started cropping up in the last decade or so, as identity politics moved to the fore in the face of the increasingly aggressive Right, aided and abetted by the very people whose job we thought it was to protect the civil rights of all Americans. When Gary and I first dated, and even when we first moved to the suburbs and got involved in local gay politics, the word heteronormative did not exist, or at least was not in common use. I know I did not hear the word, or have it used in reference to my life, until the twenty-first century.

As we grew together, Gary and I witnessed the emergence of the LGBTQ+ acronym, a far cry from the early days when "gay" meant everybody (more or less as queer does now, I suppose). Everyone in our circle in the 1970s knew that drag queens and trans folk had been there at the Stonewall Rebellion. I met my first transgender woman when I was twenty, the year I moved into the Winchester Avenue house with Gary in New Haven. Within our earliest gay community in New Haven were men and women who were bisexual, gender-fluid, out and closeted, political and apolitical. Yeah, we were oblivious to a lot, and didn't tend to label things, but it was a new world for us.

The core truth of gay liberation as I understood it and lived it in the 1970s was the freedom to be whom I wanted to be, to express my true self. The judgment of the straight world was our shared obstacle (I won't say enemy,

294 · ULYSSES GRANT DIETZ

because the straight world was changing, too, as proven by our families). The theory was that, within our community, the gay community, there would be no judgment of others.

When I went on my first date with Gary, I had one thing in mind. It was not a long-term relationship or a house in the suburbs of New Jersey, or children. When I met Gary Berger, I was twenty years old and had quite literally never been kissed. There was one goal in my head. Everything after that was improvisation.

In the mid-1970s among gay men in their twenties (especially recently-out gay men), there was a general assumption that we would be promiscuous. After all, sexual liberation implied the freedom to have as much sex with as many people as you wanted. If nothing else, the sexual revolution of the 1960s had left that legacy for everybody, gay and straight.

Promiscuity was easy (in case you didn't know that), especially in the urban gay world that was never far away from me and Gary. I don't need to offer a catalogue of gay hook-up possibilities from my younger years, but will simply note that Tinder, and its gay sibling Grindr, have merely made everything much quicker (if not actually any easier). Plus, there were the baths, which had evolved into the perfect source in urban America for the gay version of what Erica Jong referred in her 1973 novel *Fear of Flying* as the zipless fuck.

Fact is, while I understood the vast options open to me once I came out, and although I sort of felt that I was *supposed to* jump into this new era of sexual liberation headfirst, I pretty quickly realized that this wasn't really who I was. To begin with, I had absolutely no game. I was hopeless at flirting, and almost an imbecile when it came to noticing when someone was hitting on me. Second, by my twenties I had come to understand that I was a romantic. Sure, I was as horny as most twenty-year-olds whose sexual development had been retarded by fear; but I very quickly came to realize that any physical connection I would have with another man would have to be accompanied by an emotional connection. Sex with strangers was not going to do it for me. Interestingly, this idea is hard for some gay folks to accept, because it is so deeply engrained in the mythos of urban gay culture.

In the end, when Gary told me he loved me on that odd New Year's Eve on a stranger's guest mattress in Concord, Massachusetts, I understood who I was and what I wanted. Sex mattered, but love mattered more. Ironically, by ultimately choosing monogamy and embracing the cultural norms of (supposedly) straight suburbia, Gary and I became rebels of a different kind. We chose to confront the enemy where he lived, so to speak, to lay claim to a life that we had been led to believe was our right as Americans. Oh yes, we were white men who had graduated from Yale, so you can assume all sorts of entitlement and privilege and not be wrong. The fact remains that we wanted what we had grown up with (or, at least, I wanted it and Gary didn't object). Our vision of gay liberation was to live the life we wanted, in the place we wanted, in the house we wanted. As was true with the time and place I came out, we were fortunate in our choice (quite by accident). We had no clue that suburban Essex County New Jersey would become, by the time of the Trump/Clinton election debacle of 2016, one of the most liberal demographic areas in the nation. Eighty-six percent of our town voted Democrat in 2016; ninety-two percent in 2020. It would have been the opposite when we moved there in 1980.

AIDS changed everything. A new kind of judgment became the mantra of the right, even as a different kind of unity, forged in sorrow and suffering, emerged from what we all thought of as a gay holocaust. Once the dynamics of the plague became understood, those of us who had chosen to build our lives in suburbia realized that our safety was as much an illusion as that of the revelers in Edgar Allan Poe's horror story, *The Masque of the Red Death*. We were not on the front lines, most of us, but we never doubted for a moment that the battle was ours, too.

We have friends who, quite literally, attended a hundred funerals over the course of the 1980s and 1990s. We were certainly no stranger to funerals as, one by one, handsome, smart, successful young men we knew were brought down by the virus and its opportunistic complications. As for me, I lost my best friend from Exeter, Rick, as well as my closest colleague at the Newark Museum, Gary Reynolds. Both were in long-term relationships and both were blindsided by the disease that eventually took their lives and those of their partners as well. One of my cousins lost two long-term partners to AIDS, nursing both of them to the end, somehow surviving himself. The youngest person whose funeral we attended, with our friends Bill and Michael, was all of twenty-two. During the long Roman Catholic mass, no mention of what killed this boy was made. His family circled their wagons, layering their grief with shame and denial over what had taken that young man's life.

Monogamy was no guarantee of survival, as we learned all too often. I am sure, however, that the nature of my relationship with Gary ultimately increased our odds of avoiding HIV and AIDS. Whatever choices we made were lucky ones. It has been a constant refrain within the gay male world that monogamy is unnatural, and that sexual exclusivity somehow undermines the authenticity of gay male experience. There is no question that, in the days before safe-sex practices, there was a link between promiscuity and HIV. Larry Kramer paid the socio-political price for speaking that truth early in the AIDS epidemic. On the other hand, plenty of promiscuous gay men from that time are still alive today, for a variety of reasons.

The legacy of sexual liberation that we inherited from the 1960s as young men in the 1970s and 80s was full of anti-establishment rhetoric that mocked the very things that Gary and I were looking for in our lives. This had originally been aimed at the mainstream straight world in the 1960s, but became part of the dogma of the left wing of the lesbian and gay world when we were still new to it. Forming couples and moving to the suburbs was seen as imitating our parents (the oppressors, after all). For the first fifteen years of our relationship, the very idea of having children and getting married was largely unimagined because it seemed both impossible and a was portrayed as a kind of betrayal of the freedom for which we had struggled. Of course, Gary and I were far from alone, it turned out, and a phenomenon that really picked up momentum in the 1990s was the movement of lesbian and gay couples to the suburbs in numbers great enough to draw the attention of realtors. When Gary and I moved to Maplewood in 1980, we were still something of a novelty (although we were, I repeat, not alone). By the end of the twentieth century, Gary and I—and our two small children—were featured in a *New York Times* piece about the movement of lesbian and gay families to suburbia. Unwittingly, we, along with our friends Sue and Faith and Bill and Michael, had been at the leading edge of a trend that would transform our *Leave it to Beaver* world into something the Cleavers never anticipated.

Thus, as the new millennium began, and we survived the Y2K bug with our family, friends, and our suburban "lifestyle," the only frontier left was marriage. We didn't know it in 1999, but the single most heteronormative thing we could do would become one of the fastest and most profound cultural changes in our country's history. We didn't see it coming.

My father did not make it to the millennium, but died two days after my forty-fourth birthday in 1999, just a few weeks shy of his own eightieth birthday. Sandy's final decline began dramatically enough. One day, two years after their move, on his way down the stairs to his study in the Fayetteville condo, his body simply forgot how to walk. He collapsed on the stairs, and my mother had to call an ambulance. At eighty-one, my mother Julia was still sturdy, but not strong enough to heft my father. He was taken to the nursing facility at the Nottingham, a high-end assisted living complex a few miles away in Jamesville, New York. My parents knew lots of people at the Nottingham, although Julia vowed never to go there except as a visitor. My father, on the other hand, checked into the Nottingham and never returned home.

Others have written heartbreaking books about losing loved ones to various forms of dementia, and I can attest to its demoralizing, relentless onslaught on the human personality. I saw it happen at a distance, but my mother, who had loved my father for over fifty years, had to watch him disappear day by day. While Sandy was in the nursing home, Julia stopped traveling, not even willing to come for Christmas in Baltimore. She knew, as we knew, that Sandy wouldn't remember whether or not she was there every day; but she couldn't bring herself to leave him alone, not even for a day.

At least in the Nottingham there was no question of liquor, so that problem of Dad's was moot. In the end, Julia was the only person that Sandy recognized. The last time I visited, he was cheerful, but he had no idea who I was. As is not uncommon, Dad's distant memories were intact, so that he and Mom could talk when he was relaxed enough to hold a conversation. At one point, toward the end of his life, a very old friend from New Haven visited— Bob Arnstein, one of his roommates at Deerfield Academy in the 1930s. Mom reported that the two of them chatted away for an hour, my father sounding as lucid as if nothing was wrong. He remembered his friend as a teenager, a rich Jewish boy from New York City who learned about life on my grandparents' farm in Albuquerque one summer in the 1930s. An hour after Dr. Arnstein left, Dad had no memory of the visit at all.

In the end, as is too often the case, it was pneumonia that got him. Physical therapy had no effect on my father's failing body, already besieged with congestive heart failure from years of smoking cigars, drinking too much, and eating without thought to his health. His mind simply couldn't fight, couldn't help his body struggle against the illness.

I was speaking at a jewelry conference in Providence, Rhode Island when my father died. My brother called to give me the news, and to assure me that there was no rush, that the funeral would be the next week. So I carried on with my conference, excusing myself when it was appropriate and heading back to New Jersey to prepare my family for the trip to Syracuse.

Don't, however, imagine me as some wounded hero, nobly keeping a stiff upper lip to hide my grief. Daddy's death was not entirely unanticipated. Of course I was sad; sad to lose a father who had been loving and supportive and generous, no matter what demons he fought. He had voiced his happiness at our successful adoptions, even as his dementia was reaching a tipping point. He was at their baptisms. He understood that we had succeeded.

John Sanderson Dietz's funeral was held at the charming, shingled St. Peter's Episcopal Church in Cazenovia, New York, filled with friends and family who had arrived from across the country to celebrate his life. My brother and I spoke as our children sat in the front pew with our families. I talked about cocktail hour at my grandparents' in Syracuse in the 1960s, and imagined my father with his parents, Aunt Ethel, and my siblings, Ned and Edie, drinking and gossiping "up there" as they looked down on us, just as we had all watched the world from the bay window at 301 Sedgwick Drive. I was aware of the negative role alcohol had played in the long arc of my family's history, but it didn't matter. Cocktail hour will forever remain a sacred space in my memory.

***

Shortly after my father's death, another new adventure began. The year previously, two other women friends, Sandi and Monica, asked us if we would help them have a baby. This time, the honor fell to me, and there was no notion that the child would be an alternative to parenthood, given that Gary and I already had two preschoolers turning our lives upside down. Now, it was about helping our community, helping our friends become parents. In the fall of 1999, another gay family was created, with my assistance. I had to go to court to sign away my legal rights to that child, but to this day I am called "Papa Uly." We choose our families; we can make our families, too.

I managed to go to Paris twice in the summer of 2001. The first time was with Gary, and our children, Alex and Grace, then aged five and six. With us were our friends Sandi and Monica, and their eighteen-month-old Sophia (the one I helped with). The reason we all thought this was a good idea escapes me, but it turned out to be a surprisingly fun vacation. Taking small children around Paris (without a stroller) was challenging at moments. There are long tunnels in Paris' underground subway system, as well as stairs. Lots of stairs. We did a lot of carrying, and little kids are heavier than you'd think. I remember one moment in the Metro, when Gary turned in panic to me, almost yelling: "where is Alex?" only to have Alex himself, snuggly held in Gary's arms, pat him on the cheek and look at me with bemusement.

During that trip to Paris my French cousins, Josie and Antoine Sartoris, brought their young adult children down from Rouen to have dinner with us all in a restaurant they knew near the great Garnier opera house. Antoine, a fellow great-great grandchild of Ulysse S. Grant, is a descendant of the Grants' only daughter, Nellie. Their children are, like Gary's and my children, third-great grandchildren of the president and his lady. After some further conversation that afternoon, we realized that baby Sophia, mine biologically if not legally, was also a third-great grandchild of U.S. Grant—so Sandi and Monica took a fascinated Josie off to our hotel to see this miraculous infant.

The second trip to Paris that summer was with my mother, on a Newark Museum riverboat trip from Paris up the Seine to the Normandy beaches. At eighty-five, Julia was still spry and strong, and wanted to see Paris again. To my horror, Mom confessed that she had not been to the Louvre since 1936, when she had gone to Europe with a college friend and her own mother. So we saw the Louvre together. We also went to the Musée d'Orsay, which hadn't existed when Mom was last in Paris. Once the trip upriver started, we lazed on the top deck of the riverboat, reading as France unrolled alongside us. We visited the Sartoris family again when we got to the beautiful city of Rouen, bringing together three generations of U.S. Grant descendants at a lovely dinner party in our cousins' charming suburban house.

At the end of the boat trip, Mother and I saw the military graveyards in Normandy, the Bayeux Tapestry, and climbed Mont Saint Michel together. We walked on the beaches that saw the fierce fighting on D-Day in 1944, the same beaches my father crossed with the financial corps a week after the fighting was over. Mom and I, at eighty-five and forty-five respectively, were the oldest and youngest people on the riverboat. It would be Julia's last trip abroad.

A month after the second trip to France, we sent our daughter off to kindergarten after Labor Day in September 2001. Alex was in first grade, and he and Grace were in a small modern school building in South Orange, built in the 1960s to hold the overflow from the Baby Boom.

Gary headed up the Garden State Parkway as usual that morning, while I drove to park at St. George's and walk to the train station to catch the train into Newark. It happened to be Gary's forty-eighth birthday. Any celebration had been put off until later in the week, because my cousin Claire and I had made plans to meet at the World Trade Center's main concourse after work that evening, and from there to go to dinner to talk about Grant Monument Association matters. As I listened to our public radio station, WNYC, during the short drive to Maplewood Village, the announcer reported something about a fire in one of the World Trade Center towers. As I grumbled to myself that I hoped this wouldn't screw up PATH train service into the city, the radio went to static.

Walking into the Maplewood train station to buy my morning coffee a few minutes later, I looked up at the television mounted on the wall in time to see the second tower hit by what was clearly a large commercial jet. That was the moment I realized that something really bad was happening. Stupidly, I, and all the other commuters, got on the train that went from Maplewood to Hoboken. We were all on our cell phones trying to check in with family. Gary was already at work. All our cell phones were jammed, by other callers, or simply the loss of the signal. When I got off the train at Newark's Broad Street Station, I could see the mortally wounded towers billowing smoke just ten miles away. I kept my eyes on them as I walked the three blocks to the museum.

As I sat at my desk, pretending to work, my brother called. He was stuck in Elizabeth, New Jersey, on a train headed into Manhattan. It was Jed who told me that there had been four planes with four targets, and that the Pentagon had also been hit. He said he was planning to get off the train at Penn Station Newark and find his way to me at the museum. Mid-morning, the director called all the staff into the museum's central sky-lit court. There were staff people at the museum, she told us, who had lost family members in the towers. As she talked to us about the price of a free society, how our freedoms would always make us vulnerable to attacks like this, she was told—and passed on to all of us—that both of the towers had fallen. After that, she sent us home. I'm embarrassed to say that I completely forgot my brother and his plans. When Jed finally found his way to the museum, he found it closed and locked. Bless his heart, he shrugged it off, and made his way, eventually, back to Baltimore in a rented car.

Strangely enough, the suburban trains were still running—away from New York at least—and I got home and to my car in time to drive to Alex and Grace's school to collect them. I was barely holding myself together as I gathered them, puzzled at my unexpected appearance, into my arms. As we would later learn, two of their classmates' parents had died in the towers, a man and a woman, both executives just beginning a normal workday on a bright, cloudless Tuesday in September.

I took the children home and settled them in, and when Gary got home, drove to St. George's, where I checked in with Karen, the parish administrator, to see what she had heard. Lots of people at St. George's worked on Wall Street, and I was terrified at the thought. I remember hugging Karen and crying, completely undone by my fear. Amazingly, St. George's lost nobody directly. Hoboken and Middletown were the two New Jersey zip codes with the highest number of deaths. That our two towns lost so few seemed bizarrely random.

It felt at the time that the world had tumbled down around us, and that we would never feel safe again. That evening, after we put the kids to bed, with songs and stories as we always did, Gary sat at his computer trying to find out more. I was curled up on the sofa in our library, listening to something gentle by Mozart, and reciting a kind of mantra-like prayer to regain some control over my spinning, freaked-out brain. Not since my little brother's death in 1969 had I felt so disoriented, so yanked off my axis. It felt, quite simply, as if the life we had created together had ended.

Sometime before New Year's Eve 2000, Gary and I had given each other new rings to mark our twenty-fifth anniversary. The first rings that we had exchanged in 1985, purchased from the jewelry store on Christopher Street in Greenwich Village, had to be cut off our fatter, middle-aged fingers. This was done quite publicly and with some hilarity, at a jewelry store in Millburn, New Jersey, after we had picked out replacements. Wide gold bands inset with a recessed band of platinum, they were comfortable, easy to remove, and subtle. After twenty-five years, two houses and two children, we still had no thought of marriage. Marriage was for straight people and not an option for us. Oh, there had been rumblings about same-sex unions, but it all felt so impossible and distant that we thought nothing of it. We had begun our relationship alone in a stranger's house in 1975, our silent vows shared with nobody but each other. We had made our own life together, and our rings were symbols of our mutual defiance of the larger world.

We, the now-middle-aged children of Stonewall, survivors of a plague, parents of two non-white children, increasingly less-rare denizens of deepest suburbia, had no thoughts of marriage. That could never be.

Imagine our surprise.

Why did Gary and I even *want* to get married? What purpose would it serve? We were bonded, not just by a mortgage, but by the lives of two other humans who were ours as much as if we'd given birth to them. We knew the feminist rejection of marriage as the continuation of a patriarchal passing of women around as chattel. We had no argument with that. If my years listening to the Episcopal Lectionary in church every Sunday had taught me anything, it was the truth about what marriage really was, historically. We also understood the gay liberation take on marriage as something that was unnatural and an impediment to the kind of freedom gay men had been fighting for over the past two generations. To seek marriage was to embrace an outdated institution, a double sanction by state and religion as a means to control the generational movement of wealth and the sexual behavior of the population. Anyway, half of all marriages failed, didn't they? Yeah, we got it.

What all these arguments missed, however, was a basic truth: lots of gay men and women simply wanted to have what their happily married parents had. Gary's parents, my parents, and three sets of our grandparents were all married for more than fifty years. We wanted the sort of civic status that would make us equal to our straight neighbors. My brother had resisted marrying his girlfriend for years, somewhat to the despair of my parents and me. We had adored Julia from the moment we met her in 1967. She had lived through our family's darkest hours and stuck by Jed and by us. My joy at the announcement of their engagement was huge. Their wedding in Chapel Hill in 1974 was one of the great moments of my then young life. Why wouldn't I want that, too?

We kept close track (even before the Internet) of what was going on in the world. We could easily see the hatred focused on gay people, and the appalled reaction to the idea of same-sex marriage, as it bubbled up here and there across the country. I don't need to enumerate all the events that we read about from Hawaii to Vermont in the 1990s, the final insult being Bill Clinton's signing of the Defense of Marriage Act in 1997, a year after we became fathers. Oh, we might be white men of privilege, but here was a man of our generation, supposedly one of us, denying us the right to something he took for granted (and abused).

There were two sides to our wanting legal union: practical and political. We wanted the simplicity of spousal inheritance; but we also wanted marriage simply as a way to say 'fuck you' to all the haters in the world. Every volley in the political game of same-sex marriage became either an attack against us personally, or a point won for our team.

We were thinking back to the 1986 Bowers vs. Hardwick decision by the Supreme Court, which basically affirmed that sexual relations and personal privacy were not protected for gay people in the United States, as they were for straight people. We learned of the Hardwick decision on the way to meet our friends Allen and Paul at a concert at Carnegie Hall. I had all but snatched a newspaper out of someone's hands on Seventh Avenue when I saw the headline. The next day I wrote my parents an angry letter, with a copy to my brother, telling them that the Supreme Court's action made us feel "like Jews in Munich in 1933."

This wasn't about mimicking archaic heterosexual rituals. This was about claiming ownership of our lives. Unlike some of our friends, who went to states that had allowed same-sex unions earlier, we were determined to stick it out in New Jersey. Our first step was to get domestic partnership, made law in 2004 by our not-yet-known-to-be-gay governor Jim McGreevy. We went to town hall in Maplewood, filed our application with the town clerk, who had been there for decades, and got our certificate. That date was July 10, a date I only remember because it is my sister-in-law Julia's birthday.

After New Jersey's Supreme Court upheld a ban on same-sex marriage in 2005 (claiming that the state constitution did not guarantee marriage as a civil right for same-sex couples) the fight began to heat up. When that same court decided in 2006 that same-sex couples were guaranteed, if not marriage, all the rights of straight couples, that opened the door for civil unions. This felt bigger for us. My mother (by this time, aged ninety, our only surviving parent) had been following the news and asked me pointedly if we were going to run off and get married without her being there. We took advantage of her coming to New York for a party honoring her cousin John Root, and incidentally accompanying me to the annual commemoration of Ulysses S. Grant's birthday at Grant's Tomb. A dear friend's husband, a state judge, insisted on performing the ceremony, which took place in the living room at 11 Woodhill Drive, with our family and friends (and one random neighborhood child who, although uninvited, enjoyed himself and appears in all the pictures). This date was April 28, the day after President U.S. Grant's birthday.

You realize, don't you, that civil union was nothing more than a straight/gay version of "separate but equal?" It didn't work, particularly for crucial financial things such as insurance and pensions. In terms of healthcare, Gary could not be put on my museum health plan, although our children already were on my plan. Fortunately, Gary's job offered excellent health benefits, so for us at least it was not a financial issue so much as one of principle.

Meanwhile in 2010, I turned fifty-five and started a quiet internal melt-down. Having kids at forty had spared me the usual mid-life crisis. Two children kept me young and wore me out during my forties. By fifty-five, however, Alex was fourteen and Grace was thirteen. There is no greater assault on a middle-aged psyche than teenagers. Soon after my birthday, I looked in the mirror one morning and saw my father looking back at me. As much as I loved my father, this was a shock. I realized two things that morning: my thirty years going to the YMCA in Newark had not kept me young; and I would never again be sexually attractive to anyone. I had become invisible, especially to the gay world. It is stupid to confess, but for some reason this was a crushing blow.

I have a strangely bittersweet memory of that summer, walking to the train from the museum with a close colleague who lived in my town. Several years older than I, she was as svelte and elegant as she must have been thirty years earlier. She also had a very handsome husband. We chatted about the horrors of aging as we walked, and she suddenly blurted out to me, completely out of character: "we should have had so much more sex when we were in our twenties!" We laughed together in agreement at the time, but I didn't tell her one thing. Every time I tried to fantasize about being sluttier back in my youth, I couldn't suppress a shudder at the idea that the result, for me, might well have been an early death.

In October 2013, I accompanied a group of contemporary art curators on a ten-day visit to Israel. My only decorative arts peer was a curator from the Musée des Beaux Arts in Montreal, Diane Charbonneau. Our trips were funded by a group called AIDA (Association of Israel's Decorative Arts). Not only were we old enough to be the parents of most of the other travelers in our group, we were also the only participants in this adventure who cared about contemporary craft. She was a great traveling companion and we made the most of our mutual professional interests, visiting artists the others didn't see, getting private tours of exhibitions of contemporary Israeli glass and ceramics and jewelry, as well as photographing each other knee-deep in the Mediterranean on the beach in Tel Aviv.

To prove that this is not a random insertion into my story, the day before we returned to the United States, I got a call from Gary. The ongoing tussle between the New Jersey legislature and the Governor, which was ultimately resolved by the State Supreme Court, resulted in the legalizing of same-sex marriage—full-on marriage—as of October 21, 2013. This was the day after I got back from Israel. Gary had arranged our paperwork, and we would be married on the first day it was legal in New Jersey. This was the most romantic thing my beloved partner, never prone to romantic gestures, had ever done.

And so it happened, with our teenaged children at our side. Mayor Vic DeLuca, who had known us for years, officiated in the mural-lined town council assembly room in Maplewood's Colonial Revival town hall. I had posted a quick notice about this on my Facebook page, and was touched and surprised that some fellow parishioners from St. George's showed up to witness, as well as some of the museum's marketing team. Of course, our closest friends from town were there. We were the first male couple to be married in Maplewood.

We held hands. We kissed in public. Pictures were taken. At sixty and fifty-eight, after thirty-eight years together, Gary and I became a legally married couple. As one of the kids said, somewhat sheepishly, it felt like we had become, at last, a real family.

In 2015 the United States Supreme Court decided a case that made same-sex marriage legal in all fifty states. Even as I write this, an unconstitutional plot hatched by the religious and political right in this country is still engaged in trying to undo it. How much do you have to hate someone to want to take away their civil rights?

CHAPTER TWENTY-NINE

FAREWELL TO UPSTATE

By the time Julia Grant Dietz died on March 20, 2014, at the age of ninety-eight, my ties to upstate New York had already grown thin. Since 1976, Gary and I had been driving to central New York State at least once, sometimes twice a year to visit Sandy and Julia, either in Syracuse or later at the lake house in Cazenovia. Once Jed and Julia had decamped with their family for Baltimore when Julia started her long career at Johns Hopkins Medical Center, Christmas had shifted there, thus dividing our annual pilgrimages between southern and northern destinations. This carried on after my father's death, with visits to Mom's condo in Fayetteville.

Back in 1978 my mother and her sisters had decided to sell Ulysses and Edith Grant's house at 101 College Hill Road in Clinton, New York. Edward and Grace Root's house next door, the Homestead, had long since become the Root Art Center, and would later be transformed into an alumni center. Grace Root had lived out her life in her husband's converted painting studio behind the Homestead, at the top of the Root Glen, a woodland garden she bequeathed to Hamilton College, and in which the ashes of members of my family had been scattered since my brother Ned's death in 1969. At Grace's death, the studio and her gardens became another part of the Hamilton campus.

Up the hill, Elihu Root Junior's house stayed in the family until 2004, when it went to Hamilton College and was made, appropriately, into the art history department. The Root tenant farmhouse and land had been acquired by Hamilton long since, and was the site of Kirkland College, intended as an all-female counterpart to the all-male student population of Hamilton. That experiment failed when Hamilton went coeducational and Kirkland merged with Hamilton.

With the death of my cousin John Root in 2010, the last of my mother's generation of Roots was buried in the Hamilton College cemetery. The luncheon after John's funeral was held at the house where my godparents, Ann and Philip Rogers, had lived during my younger years. A grand colonial revival country house built for Philip Rogers's father, a Utica banker, it had been sold to the college and converted to a dormitory. Every building associated with my family and Clinton now belonged to Hamilton College.

When my mother's died in 2014, the last of my family's ashes were scattered in the Root Glen. Who knows where my brother and I will end up; but we have our own families to consider.

Back in Syracuse, the R.E. Dietz Company, founded by my great-great-grandfather in 1840 in Brooklyn, had been sold to a national conglomerate called Federal Mogul in 1990. The sale of the company after 150 years put a strain on the family. Two of the four Dietz siblings who owned the company, my father and his eldest brother, Robert E. Dietz III, were anxious to sell, while Gerry Dietz and their sister Olga Turner were resistant. The family worked it out, and the sale went through. The buyer's purpose, it turned out, was to dismantle the century-old factory and eliminate a big-name competitor from the marketplace. The family sold the Hong Kong plant separately to a Chinese buyer, and it still manufactures kerosene lanterns with the Dietz logo for sale all over Asia and Africa. The Syracuse factory sat empty for years, as the Syracuse of my childhood withered and struggled, along with every other city between Albany and Buffalo. Virtually every commercial entity in my hometown had disappeared; all the department stores, all of the manufacturing companies, including my own family's. All the names that had mattered in small-city life in the 1950s faded from public memory, their archives either tossed or packed up and deposited in the vaults of the Onondaga Historical Association. That's where the Dietz Company archives went.

Few of my childhood friends remained in Syracuse by the time of Mom's death. Larry, who had been part of my triad with our mutual friend David, was now the senior partner in a leading Syracuse law firm—in fact he was my mother's estate lawyer. David had died of cancer in his fifties a few years before. Larry and his marvelous wife lived in our old neighborhood of Sedgwick Farm, and next door to them was Tony, one of our middle school friends, who had been with my brother Ned the night he was killed.

Mother's funeral took place at St. Paul's Episcopal Cathedral in downtown Syracuse, where I had attended Sunday school and been confirmed, up the street from the YMCA where I took swimming lessons. Lofty and somber, its mahogany pews and fantastic stained glass intact, St Paul's looked almost exactly as I remembered it from college years. The parish building was also nearly the same, only somewhat shabbier and somehow smaller than my memories painted it.

My brother and I organized the funeral, contacting the rector of St. Peter's in Cazenovia to do the service, and working with the cathedral staff and altar guild to arrange for flowers, catering, and an organist. We had no idea who would show up, in spite of the obituary I wrote and placed in the surviving Syracuse newspaper. Most of mother's friends had died. Her best friend, my aunt Cynthia, was one of the last. It occurred to me that Mom, passing her ninety-eighth birthday, might have decided the time had come, unable to face losing Cynthia as she had lost all her other close friends of the past seventy-four years. Aunt Cynnie was surely brokenhearted at her sister-in-law's death; but she was strong and philosophical about it, as my mother knew she would be.

A weirdly slapstick moment occurred just before the funeral started, as Jed and I were conferring with the priest celebrant. Mom had been cremated, and it hadn't dawned on Jed that we would (or, at least, I would) want the ashes, properly veiled, in the church in place of a casket. The priest asked Jed where our mother was, and my brother's nonplussed response was "in the trunk." The absurdity of the situation made me laugh out loud. We got Mom out of the trunk and she was there, among her family and friends, one last time.

Episcopalians don't go in for lavish floral displays or extended eulogizing. It is hard to grieve deeply for someone who has lived so long and so well. On the other hand, if you manage to be nice right to the end of your life, people will cry for you no matter how old you were. The wonderful crew of women who had been my mother's caretakers and constant companions for her last three years were all there, weeping visibly. Over a hundred folks showed up in the vast old church, each of them with some memory of life in Syracuse when we were young and *Leave it to Beaver* had been on the air.

As we had done at Dad's funeral, Jed and I spoke. I focused my remarks on three moments in my life that, for all their smallness, exemplified my feelings about my mother. One, in Bermuda just after we learned of our grandfather's death in 1968, was when Ned and I were sassing our sister and generally being irritants. Mom, lying on the little jetty by the water, yelled at us, "Do as you're told." I could see from her face that she had been crying and was overwhelmed with shame that my own behavior had forced my grieving mother to raise her voice – something she almost never did.

Second, I remembered a quiet night at Cazenovia in 1977, when my mother chided me for nagging my boyfriend Gary, urging me to communicate with him more effectively. In her typical low-key way, she let me know that she took my relationship with this man seriously. It was a validation of who I was that meant more to me than she could possibly have known.

Third, on our 2001 river trip in France, I teased Mom about wearing a baseball cap with floral embroidery, which struck me as not quite the right tone for a lady like her.

Her response to me was, with a sly smile, "I'm an old woman, I can do what I like."

Without the slightest note of criticism, she punctured my balloon of pretension and reminded me of her own hard-won self-assurance. Even at forty-five, I needed to remember to get over myself.

It is a stereotype that gay men are close to their mothers, but Mom and I were close in a way I will never forget. We were never "friends," but we always enjoyed each other's company. She was not a romantic, but she understood her emotional, high-strung little boy, and never failed to see who I was and what I needed from her.

Julia Dietz, at ninety-eight, was the last living great-grandchild of President Ulysses S. Grant and his First Lady Julia. With her death, a witness to everything from the invention of the radio to the invention of the Internet slipped away.

We didn't have to put Mom's condo on the market quickly, so Jed and I took our time to deal with her estate, going through the contents of the townhouse, dividing up what we wanted and figuring out how to dispose of the rest. The whole process became an extended conversation with each other about our lives, each object evoking memories that covered not just our lifespans but three generations of our family history. It was cathartic and exhausting, giving my brother and me more time alone together than we had enjoyed in years.

We had only a single moment of, not disagreement, but disconnection perhaps. A carved rock-crystal jar from China, something that had come from my great-aunt Ethel's house, was a thing I had pegged for myself because of my Chinese daughter. To my surprise, Jed wanted it too. We ended up negotiating a deal whereby I sacrificed a much-coveted U.S. Grant relic (a gold match safe from the 1860s with his initials on it) in order to claim the rock-crystal jar. My daughter's response when I told her this story: "Why the hell would you think I'd want that?"

Sigh. Curators are idiots, apparently. I still love that Chinese jar.

We moved U-Haul trailers full of stuff to Maplewood and Baltimore, contracted with a mover to bring the big things a week or so later; and consigned a bunch of things to a regional auction house. This included a large assortment of the 1868 monogrammed Chinese export porcelain commissioned by Ulysses and Julia Grant during the general's first election campaign. The design is a lavish frenzy of pink and green enamel, highlighted in gold, featuring flowers and Chinese figures. I had one piece from that so-called Rose Medallion service in Maplewood and had gotten my parents to give seven dinner plates to the Newark Museum early in my career. The Rose Medallion china had loomed large in our childhoods, and the thought of being burdened with the rest of it was too much for Jed or me. It garnered a lot of interest and sold very well. I heard from several of the buyers who were interested to know the details of its provenance and descent.

Whatever else remained in the house was left in place for an estate sale, including my mother's 1960s mink coat and various pieces of furniture that I had known my entire life. Even my insatiable acquisitiveness was defeated by the contents of my parents' last home. I realized that Gary and I had built our own memories and our own life. We had a house full of children and stuff. It made it easier to let go.

I went back up to Syracuse in the spring of 2019 to celebrate Aunt Cynthia's one-hundredth birthday at the Century Club, where we had shared family meals with my grandparents in the 1960s. It was a joyful mob scene, bringing cousins and friends from all over the country to celebrate this gentle, smart and resilient old lady. I drove up there again a few months later to have a quiet dinner with her at the Nottingham, the senior complex where my father died and into which my mother refused to go. My aunt's body was bent over with arthritis, but her mind and her humor were all there. She told me that she still missed her friend and sister-in-law, Julia.

Along with Aunt Cynnie, her son Michael and his husband Fouad, who live in Cynthia's parents' house on Skaneateles Lake, are my last Dietz family upstate.

CHAPTER THIRTY

OTHER PEOPLE'S MONEY

I n November 2017, I was called to a meeting by the co-chairs of the Newark Museum's board of trustees, in an office in Springfield, New Jersey,
not far from where Gary had grown up. I assumed it was to discuss the
terms of my pending retirement, less than two months away.

Well, no. I was asked to step in temporarily as interim co-director of
the museum, owing to the current director's decision to step down. I didn't
exactly bang my head on the conference table, but I did say to Christine and
Cliff, the board co-chairs, "This is way worse than I expected." They laughed.
I did, too. Their laughter was tinged with relief; mine with resignation. It was
the second time I'd been asked to step in as interim co-director of the museum.
The museum had been my life since I was twenty-four; how could I refuse?

I retired, officially, from the Newark Museum on December 31st,
2017, having been the decorative arts curator there for thirty-seven years, the
chief curator in addition to that since 2012, and interim co-director for a month
and a half. Morrie (Morrison) Heckscher, who ended his long career at the
Metropolitan Museum as the head of the American Wing (I don't even know
the correct title), always referred to people like us as "lifers." There are quite
a few lifers in the curatorial world of my generation, but we represent a trend
that is fading, perhaps for the best. I, at sixty-two, was looking forward to

retirement. I had writing to do, places to go, a retired husband to irritate constantly.

Instead, after I retired as curator, what I got was nearly a year under contract as a part-time museum administrator, charged with oversight of the curatorial and exhibition side of operations, while my colleague and co-director Deborah took on the really hard work of carrying out the business and marketing side of the museum (on top of her two other jobs). My five years as a chief curator had given me good insight into the administrative side of museum work, as had my previous reluctant stint as interim co-director back in 2013. This time around, at least, I was no longer a curator, and thus could do my best at just one job. For eleven months I sat in the director's office, at a crumbling reproduction Louis XV *bureau plat*, and dealt with my friends and colleagues as their boss for the first time. I realized that, as a notoriously anxious-to-please type of guy, I had virtually no power to effect change, or even to get art installed in my office. I loved my colleagues at the museum, and they knew it. They knew they could largely ignore me and not get yelled at or fired. They knew I knew how overworked and stressed out everybody was—had always been.

I never wanted to be anything other than a decorative arts curator. Absurdly, Newark had hired me with no real experience right out of graduate school and made me, by default, a department head. Technically, I could have happily stayed my entire career at the Newark Museum without a promotion. Circumstances, and the fact that people seemed to like and trust me, pushed me upwards as the years piled up behind me. I am glad that I was not a chief curator for a larger part of my career, and grateful that I was better for the experience. In the end, the co-director position made the transition from working to not working less jarring. I never felt that I was a particularly effective chief curator, or a particularly effective co-director. I was, more or less, a good mediator. I worked well with people and made them feel appreciated.

My temporary job, fortunately, was to keep the museum moving forward and to prepare the exhibition and curatorial staff with the necessary groundwork for the next CEO. I also served on the search committee for the museum's new director, a rewarding experience. I have no regrets and am happy simply to think that nobody cheered when I finally left for good on November 1, 2018. The volunteer organization put my name on one of the seats in the auditorium.

All my life I have been object-oriented, a term I didn't learn until I was in graduate school at the Winterthur Museum in 1978. As a child I collected Corgi, Dinky, Matchbox, and other miniature automobiles. Family memories are rife with embarrassing stories of me, on Christmas morning, carefully unwrapping each box, removing the little metal car, and then taking it up to my room to play with it for a few minutes before putting it carefully in my cedar toy chest. Not only did I get to milk the joy of Christmas Day; but I got to feel the pleasure of holding each little car in my hand before moving onto the next. I loved the feel of these cars, the cool smoothness of the paint, the spring of the tiny rubber tires. I loved the colors, the design, and especially the stories I could weave from them. These cars were characters in my childhood fantasies, something that lasted until I went to boarding school at fifteen.

As a teenager, I tried to get my parents to become collectors, having discovered through them the auctions at Palmiter's in Waterville, New York. I managed to get them to buy two things: a late eighteenth-century silver tea caddy by London silversmiths Peter and Ann Bateman, and a jazzy Boston federal chest of drawers with lushly veneered drawer fronts and carved corner columns. The chest sat in Julia and Sandy's dining room for decades, in two different houses. The tea caddy was always somewhere visible. In 2000, my mother gave the tea caddy to Gary and me for our twenty-fifth anniversary, having filled it with twenty-five silver dollars from the 1970s in a flannel pouch. I kvelled over it immediately, touched by the fact that it was the same tea caddy I had convinced her and Dad to buy all those years ago. Julia had no memory of what I was talking about, no idea that this piece wasn't just another family thing they had picked up along the way.

Oddly, I never collected much of anything personally other than those little cars, not until years into my career and my life in New Jersey. Oh, Gary and I bought things as we settled into the long-term nesting process together, including antiques. It was never, however, collecting. The closest thing to collecting I've ever done was made possible by the emergence of online shopping, especially Ebay. That phenomenon has made possible collecting a group of Newark-made gold cufflinks, a direct result of my big 1997 book and exhibition project on Newark's jewelry industry, *The Glitter & The Gold: Fashioning America's Jewelry*. Then, after collaborating with Charles Venable at the Dallas Museum in 1999 to premiere his brilliant exhibition on tableware, *China and Glass in America, 1880-1980: From Table Top to TV Tray*, I began to buy random dinner plates and sterling forks and spoons for myself, captivated by the idea that all I had to do was go online and look, finding what I wanted quickly and just clicking on a button to buy it.

I arrived at the Newark Museum knowing a tremendous amount about early American decorative arts and related European and Asian objects. I as yet did not fully appreciate how much I did *not* know, a lesson that would be taught to me gradually—relentlessly—over the next three decades. As for the administrative part of being a curator, that I picked up as I went along. Administration is the ugly secret about which they never warn us object-oriented people in graduate school.

A curator is a caretaker. The British still use the term keeper, which is both archaic and accurate. Our role is to care for a collection, but usually not in the literal, physical sense of the word. Museums have collections care people, called registrars and art handlers, collection managers and conservators, who are charged with the physical conditions under which the collections are shown and stored. A curator cares for the intellectual and historical information that surrounds every object, great and small, under their purview. A curator should be able to tell you everything you need to know about an object. A registrar can tell you where that object is in the building, and what sort of work has been done on it or needs to be done on it.

Another thing a curator does is to think up exhibition ideas, organize and coordinate those ideas into finished projects, working with the whole range of staff at their museum. Newark is a huge collection in a mid-sized building with an undersized staff. As a curator there I worked with everybody, face-to-face, from the maintenance crew who built the exhibit cases and platforms, to the director who had final approval on all label and text copy. I also wrote press releases for the PR department, prepared lectures for the education department, gave tours, and wrote books and articles when I got the offers and had the time. I quickly discovered that I loved to give lectures every bit as much as I loved giving guided tours in the museum. My love of writing—the actual physical part of putting pen to paper—made it a pleasure for me to knock out articles and create texts for books and exhibitions. Getting my own office computer in 1992 was a game-changer for me, allowing me to write even faster. Having always figured that I had no real creative talent, I realized that my love of words was my gift. I wouldn't dare say that I got it from Ulysses S. Grant, but I have been known to wonder.

By the end of my career at Newark I had given 565 lectures outside the museum, and a further 806 lectures and tours inside the museum. We were asked to keep track of our audience numbers for our monthly and annual reports, so I know that I spoke to approximately 60,000 people face to face, in groups large and small, over thirty-seven years. I can remember feeding slides by hand into a broken projector for a dozen rapt listeners in the basement of a church, and also having three large screens behind me in a ballroom filled with a thousand people. It was all joy for me, and I got paid to do it. How lucky was that?

Every museum collection is a cultural narrative, and every object in a collection is a word or phrase or sentence that expands that narrative and provides a chance to enrich the experience of a museum visitor. It is totally understandable, especially for young curators, to want to dump everything they know into every label they write. In the first two decades of my career, people were beginning to understand that long labels packed with information were often not read—and thus did not do their intended job. A new school of thought, spearheaded by museum education departments, insisted that shorter labels, as free of jargon as possible, would go farther in encouraging the public to read, enjoy, and learn. This was all being formulated as my career evolved, and the truth is that it was a rare curator who actually thought about the people that might be looking at their lovingly crafted labels and wall panels. The idea that writing concise, understandable labels was "dumbing down" museum content echoes the intellectual snobbery that began to shape American art history studies in the nineteenth century, and simultaneously shaped the museums created by the academic and cultural elite during the Gilded Age from the Civil War to World War I. Despite my own personal and professional fascination with the Gilded Age, I long ago embraced the notion that a museum that receives public funding needs to keep its audience in mind.

Even at the Newark Museum, which was consciously founded to be unlike other major urban museums in the country, it was easy to fall into the unreadable label trap. I was taught, eventually, that we curators were not supposed to write labels to impress our friends and colleagues; we had to think about the people who came to the museum, understanding that they more than likely walked in knowing either nothing, or a fraction of what we knew. Objects, even familiar objects, do not tell their stories without help. The very idea that art and objects "speak" to people is only partly true and only for a small part of the general population.

Art museums in the United States were conceived of, from 1870 on (whether they admit it or not), as cultural clubs for the best and the brightest. Museums today must be, impossibly, all things to all people. Very rich museums with huge staffs have an easier time of it, but they are not always the best at it, because their very wealth can make them careless or indifferent. My challenge as a curator was to take folks who didn't care, or even disliked my objects, and convert them into people who loved the stuff I loved as much as I loved it. This may not sound very highbrow, but to me it's the most important thing I ever did in my career: open a door for someone who didn't even know there was a door and lead them into a new world.

As much as I loved the rest of being a curator, I confess that collecting for the museum was probably my chief pleasure and my most lasting legacy. As with everything else at that job, I started out with no guidance, just knowledge. I was expected to figure it out on my own, and I had a lot of fun doing just that. The collections falling under the Decorative Arts Department at Newark today numbers tens of thousands of objects, one quarter of which are textiles and fashion. The date range of my department's holdings runs from the Renaissance to the present day, with large clusters in the nineteenth and twentieth centuries. My first task after I was hired was to explore the store-rooms and the ground floor period rooms of the 1885 Ballantine House, just to see what was there. I had to ponder what I might do with all that stuff, and wonder what we might need to fill gaps.

I had no idea what I was doing. The blessing is that I didn't know that, either. I was a natural with objects and big old houses, and I was curious about everything. The collection ran from the sublime to the ridiculous, and all of those things had value in the overall narrative of the museum's mission. We were not a historical society, but we did actively pursue things that reflected Newark and New Jersey history, either by ownership or by manufacture. Although my training at Winterthur and Yale had been primarily in American material culture from the colonial, federal and nineteenth-century periods, I had been taught how to look at objects from any period, and to evaluate them contextually based on material, design, function, and cultural meaning. What it boils down to is that I had no set boundaries except for the collection itself, which was huge and messy and full of holes.

The first object I purchased for the museum, in 1980, was an art-deco vase made by the Fulper Pottery Company of Flemington, New Jersey. It was offered to me by a local dealer, priced at ninety dollars. I knew that the museum had acquired a lot of Fulper Pottery, New Jersey's most famous art pottery of the early twentieth century, in 1914 and 1915. I also knew that the museum had nothing like this, showing the new modernism of the late 1920s and early 1930s, just before the firm left the Fulper family. It wasn't, and isn't, the most important thing produced by Fulper, known for their great glazes. On the other hand, it still tells exactly the story I wanted it to tell when I bought it, and thus is an acquisition of which I am still proud.

A less successful, but no less thoughtful, purchase came the next year, when I was visiting a dealer in Passaic, New Jersey. I was captivated by a piece of Rookwood Pottery from 1923. It was small, a classic squat Chinese vase form, covered in a limpid orchid-hued glaze created by putting a transparent sky-blue glaze over a pink matte ground glaze. It was delicately painted with a frieze of cherry blossoms by Kataro Shirayamadani. Japanese-born, he was the most famous decorator at Rookwood, and worked for the company, with a gap, from the nineteenth century until his death in 1948. We had nothing by this artist in the collection, and I simply loved the color and its resonance with the modernist aesthetic of the 1920s. At $760, it seemed expensive to me, but I forged ahead and got permission to add it to the collection.

Looking back, while I still love the piece, I realize it is something that I'd like to own personally, but that it doesn't really hold up to the best Rookwood acquired by the museum in 1914. It is not an impressive piece, nor is it a striking art-deco design by one of the firm's major 1920s decorators. It is lovely, but it is not "important." I can justify it still in terms of the museum's collecting history—we purchased plenty of more modest modern objects in order to demonstrate the notion that "museum quality" is a meaningless term unless you understand the museum's mission. Not everything in Newark needs to be a masterpiece, and by that token, this little orchid-colored vase is still useful and something that can open the minds of our visitors. It is not, however, a purchase that makes me proud.

So, it seems, my collecting needed to mature, and I needed to sort out the difference between what the museum had collected in the past and what I, as a curator, needed to purchase to enrich the collection's narrative and to raise its overall significance. I had to learn to think nationally as well as locally, and to know my subject in order to justify anything I proposed that the museum pay for. I had to think: *what would the Met buy? Chicago? Houston? Los Angeles?* I had friends in all those museums. What would my friends acquire for their institutions and why? Sometimes I was forced to compromise because of Newark's limited acquisitions budget—made up then largely of a series of paltry endowments and supplemented heavily with membership dues. Buying the best thing I could afford with the money I had available was not always completely successful, but it forced me to strategize and to think through each acquisition.

Oh, just to make one point clear: during my long career, no matter how well-known I became in the field and among collectors, only a few people ever gave my department truly important gifts. A lot of useful and interesting things came our way from generous donors, but rarely did they approach the realm of what I thought of as "transformative." I realized early on (and noted it faithfully every year in my annual reports) that if I was going to raise the profile of my departmental collection, the Museum was going to have to pay for it. The board and the boss would need to let me shop.

Now, I'm going to contradict myself. To this day, I am very suspicious of notions of "museum quality," because I think many—in fact most – "masterpiece" museums do a very poor job of representing the real diversity of world culture. If you only collect the most valuable and rarest of material culture, then you're not telling the story of most of the people on earth. All of this, for me, goes back to a series of exhibitions that the Newark Museum's founder, John Cotton Dana, mounted the year he died. Carried out by his brave and patient Associate Director, Beatrice Winser, the shows' collective premise was: *Beauty has no relation to price, rarity, or age.* I have been known to joke that the subtitle should have been: *You get what you pay for;* but at heart I agree. If everyday people are going to feel that art is something they can embrace, then they need to have the opportunity to see art that is accessible to them in some way, and that includes objects that are both beautiful and affordable. Most major museum curators and collectors would likely disagree with me, if not to my face then behind my back. No matter.

In some ways, I suspect all curators collect the same way. Some of it is, inevitably, an acknowledgement of institutional needs. What gaps are there in any given type of collection? How can I build a better, more coherent, collection that tells the story I want to tell in the best possible way? This was certainly my initial approach as a new curator. I started looking for holes in the decorative arts narrative for each main medium: ceramics, furniture, glass, silver, textiles, and, eventually, jewelry.

I was also, from the very start, attuned to the New Jersey angle. A great object with a history in a New Jersey family was better than a similar object with no history at all. Something made in New Jersey, even if it was a modest object, could be important, or even rare, and could tell a story that would be important for *my* museum's unique mission. I can think of at least three pieces of New Jersey furniture I purchased, none of them headline-makers in terms of design or craftsmanship; but each one remains the sole example of an otherwise unknown cabinetmaker or a unique document that expands our understanding of a known maker's output.

One of these, a plain little two-drawer mahogany stand, I purchased from another institution in 1981. It was made by Albert E. Noe of Rahway, New Jersey in 1845. It is not only stenciled with the maker's name, but he happens to have written out the making costs, the price, and the date on the bottom of one of the drawers. Most museums wouldn't have taken it as a gift—well, one museum had—and then sold it to us many years later. What is irrelevant for one place becomes a fascinating document for another. It is a plain, straightforward, well-made object, and it demonstrates someone's small-town idea of elegance in the 1840s. It tells as much about material aspiration in American life as a rich man's masterpiece could.

Being faithful to this institutionally specific kind of collecting path is a double-edged sword, because it can lead to parochialism. Newark's collections are global in scope, even though they are slanted in a domestic, contextual way that allows for embracing objects that are not as fancy as the sort of things big, rich museums tend to favor. So, while the New Jersey narrative influenced a great many purchases and gifts for me over the years, I developed a parallel agenda. It was less noble, maybe, but it also led to acquisitions that, I think, made my department's holdings better, and added stature to my institution in the national arena.

Of course, that's what I told myself. Buying important objects also made me look good in my professional colleagues' eyes. "Whoa, look at what Ulysses bought for Newark. Impressive." That, of course, made me feel good about myself. Don't for a minute doubt that every curator's ego is deeply invested in the collecting they do for their institution.

It is also true, however, that I have always collected to protect things. An object in a museum storeroom is safe from the vicissitudes of time. It is cared for and cared about, even if it's not displayed for decades. Even if something is not on display, it is *there,* available to scholars and collectors. I've been told by people who ought to know better that there's no point in acquiring something if it goes into storage. Not true. The point of collecting something is to keep it away from the world, because the world tends to be destructive and uncaring.

Oddly enough, my first large purchase for Newark was somewhat unsatisfying because it was in response to a crisis. In the summer of 1980, three weeks after I started my career, someone broke into the Ballantine house, scooped up all the flatware off the dining table, and exited through another window. This required the thief to remove two window air conditioners (yes, that was our climate control) while setting off all the alarms. The report was that our night security officer was so terrified at the idea of a burglar in the house that he hid until the police came. This was at the height of the Hunt Brothers' attempt to corner the silver market, and silver had skyrocketed to fifty dollars an ounce. The saddest part of this is that the silver was part of a unique art nouveau service, made in Newark as a wedding gift in 1908. The lucky bride happened to be the daughter of the silver manufacturer. Without doubt it was all thrown into a portable crucible and melted instantly for its scrap value. Fortunately, half the service survived in storage, but now I was not willing to leave it exposed on the dining table in the Ballantine House. I took our insurance money and went to auction, buying a service for twelve by Tiffany & Co. in the *Renaissance* pattern designed by Paulding Farnham. Made in Tiffany's Newark factory, this set had the local origin and the requisite grandeur for the Ballantine dining room, but no personal history to give me emotional anxiety. It is there to this day.

With silver as one of my great passions and realizing that I needed to think about contemporary decorative arts, I got it into my head to commission a major silver service—in other words, a Victorian form in modern style—for the museum's seventy-fifth anniversary in 1984. My friend Jeanne, a Winterthur classmate who had started working at Christie's, took me to visit Ubaldo Vitali in his New Jersey studio, bringing with her a Paul Revere teapot that needed a hinge repaired. Ubaldo is a Roman-born silversmith, from a dynasty of Roman silversmiths. He happened to fall in love with a beautiful Newark girl in Rome in the 1960s. He was and is one of the dearest, gentlest men I've ever known, and the Museum gave me a green light to commission this fantasy tea and coffee service from him. Titled *The Anniversary Service,* it was delivered in 1984, and gave me my first taste of what fun spending other people's money could be.

This was also the era of post-modernism, and the rise of architect-designers like Princeton's Michael Graves. A New York gallery offered a group of highly publicized architect-designed silver tea and coffee services produced by Alessi in Italy. Among them was a now iconic service by Michael Graves, whom I knew because his firm had become the museum's architect for a massive renovation that took up most of the 1980s. With secret permission from my board chair, I approached Mr. Graves to design a centerpiece bowl to commemorate my director Samuel C. Miller's twentieth anniversary at the museum. The piece I had in mind would represent Grave's style but would also be functional and appropriate for a modern home. Then, with Grave's blessing,

I approached Tiffany & Co. through my friend Janet Zapata, who had become their archivist in 1982. Working through the acquisitions committee of the board, behind my boss's back, I pushed the project along, in time to unveil the *Samuel C. Miller Cup* at a museum opening during his anniversary year, 1987. A shimmering, elegantly classical centerpiece bowl, with two ribbon-like handles, the Miller Cup was designed in New Jersey, and made in New Jersey. Aside from having great local significance, the cup was also something of national importance in modern design. It was the perfect object. I was all of thirty-two and felt like I was flying high.

The year before, my first really "transformative" purchase at auction in New York, had been an outlandish three-piece coffee service designed by Paulding Farnham and made by Tiffany & Co. in their Newark factory for the 1901 Pan-American Exhibition in Buffalo, New York. An insane confection of Nordic interlacing, studded with American gemstones and enameled in lavender, chartreuse, and dark green, it was known as *The Viking Service*. It reflected an international interest in Viking-style objects that were appearing at international expositions at the turn of the twentieth century. I spent quite a lot of other people's money on this juicy little masterpiece in 1986. It fulfilled my desire to honor New Jersey's legacy as a making state, but also my inner wish to bring glory to my museum by making its collection better and better.

Tiffany's factory in Newark, which I toured in operation in 1983, would close in 1985, its once-huge staff having dwindled to only 100 people. For the next two decades, Tiffany's New Jersey headquarters, largely a secret to the outside world (as the factory had been before it), would serve as their silver shop and the home of their astonishing archives. My friend Janet managed to arrange for the two surviving drawings for the Viking Service to be donated to the museum by Tiffany & Co., the rationale being that, since the object itself was unique, and it was in a public collection, the drawings should stay with it.

In the mid-1980s, as the museum itself was being transformed physically by Michael Graves, I pushed myself into the world of contemporary craft.

Since the museum had been acquiring modern decorative arts literally since the year it was founded in 1909, I felt I had to school myself and become a collector in that realm as well. At my director Sam Miller's suggestion, I wandered into Garth Clark's gallery in Manhattan on West 57th Street one morning in 1985 (going to museums and visiting galleries is part of a curator's job description—perhaps the greatest single perk of such a career). I was there ostensibly to see an exhibition on George Ohr, an eccentric early-twentieth-century Mississippi potter about whom Garth Clark was passionate. I ended up meeting the collectors who owned that Ohr pottery, but more importantly I purchased two pieces of contemporary studio ceramics for the museum. One of these was by a New Jersey maker; the glorious Anne Kraus, prickly and profound, whose decorated whiteware gave me my first important window into contemporary ceramics. Thus began a long relationship and friendship with Garth, his partner Mark, and that gallery. I not only would buy lots of ceramics from them over the rest of my career, but as friends they would give the museum some important pieces, and steer still more gifts from other collectors. They were mentors and helped me find my footing in a new sphere of collecting. They helped me step outside my parochial bubble, and to think nationally and internationally (within my budget) about contemporary craft and design as it related to my institution's founding mission.

Asking a curator to name his favorite object is like asking parents to name their favorite children. The question "what would you grab first if there was a fire" has circulated in my field for decades. Although I was always proud of my New Jersey acquisitions, I never was entirely sure if anyone cared about this other than me. New Jersey is not a state with a great sense of self-pride. Trapped between New York and Philadelphia for three centuries, it has always been the butt of jokes, and seen as the slightly embarrassing relative to the great cultural centers at either end. It only shames me a little to admit that it was the "great" acquisitions, the expensive purchases that got me and my museum a little notoriety, that were especially gratifying. As a curator who loved his collection for many years, I care about all my inanimate children. Between you, me, and the door, however, there are favorites.

To normal people these things won't necessarily mean much, but to decorative arts curators, they will, as the current expression goes, spark joy. The Alexander Roux sideboard from the 1850s, the mate to which the Metropolitan Museum purchased a few years later; the "Arabic" style armchair designed by Louis Comfort Tiffany for his first great interior design scheme in 1879; the opulent Anglo-Japanese lady's secretary custom-made for the long-lost Mark Hopkins mansion on Nob Hill in San Francisco; the "Henri II" silver charger made by Tiffany & Co. for the 1876 National Centennial Exhibition in Philadelphia; the "Dancers" tray, bejeweled and gilt silver, set with enamel plaques, made by Gorham for the 1893 World's Columbian Exposition in Chicago. These are objects that, to this day, make my heart beat a little faster, and knowing that I acquired them for the museum, makes my ego swell with pride. Though John Cotton Dana would have disapproved of spending so much of other people's money on things like this, I think I honored the Newark Museum's founding mission and also pushed it farther.

I want to end this palaver with a note on jewelry. I always loved jewelry but had never much thought about it as an art form. When I was seventeen, I dragged my father into the jewelry store at the Royal Hawaiian Hotel in Honolulu and encouraged him to buy jewelry for my mother. Even as a teenager I knew about and coveted a few family jewels left to my mother by her ancestors: a diamond necklace that had been Julia Grant's, and a Tiffany & Co. diamond spray that Elihu Root had purchased for his wife Clara in the early 1900s. At the time my brother married in 1974, my mother let me have a pearl and diamond choker of my grandmother Grant's from her safe deposit box. Because Mom and Dad had given Jed four diamonds to make into earrings for his bride Julia, they let me have the pearl choker. What my parents (or I) thought I would ever do with such a thing, I have no idea.

In the early 1980s the museum received three pieces of opulent jewelry from a grand old lady named Mary Shanley Dempsey. Her family had been the most important Irish Catholic family in Newark in the heyday of the city's wealth and power. They were responsible for the building of the first Catholic cathedral in New Jersey, and the founding of Seton Hall University. Her nephew Kevin was the chairman of the museum's board, as his father had been before him. So when Mrs. Dempsey sent her nephew to me with some gifts, I accepted them. They were fabulous. There was a large diamond brooch in the shape of a dagger wrapped in a bowknot, made by Theodore B. Starr in New York, one of the great Gilded Age jewelers. There was an eighteen-karat gold mesh evening purse purchased at Cartier in Paris in the 1910s, its frame set with cabochon emeralds and diamonds. Local history aside, these jewels dazzled me and planted a seed that would flower twenty years later.

There was also something more intimate and modest in Mrs. Dempsey's gift: a fourteen-karat gold spectacle case, its original pince-nez still inside, the front cover elaborately engraved with art-nouveau scrollwork. Given to Mrs. Dempsey's father by his wife for their tenth anniversary in 1908, it was an object redolent of marital love and Gilded Age luxury. As it happens, it was also made in Newark, and by a jewelry company owned and operated by the very man who had received it as a gift.

Newark, it seems, had once had a great jewelry industry. I had no idea.

That discovery was the result of a small exhibition on jewelry I did in the Music Room Gallery in the Ballantine House, a show I lamely called *Human Plumage*. This turned into the most important exhibition and book project I ever undertook: *The Glitter & The Gold: Fashioning America's Jewelry*. With a team of authors and the full support of the museum, my friend Janet Zapata and I embarked on a five-year project to research Newark's once-vast gold jewelry industry, produce an exhibition, and publish the first major book ever written on the topic.

If the 1994 reinterpretation of the Ballantine House was the most important thing I ever did as a historic house curator, *The Glitter & The Gold* was my most important accomplishment as a decorative arts curator. The Newark jewelry project also whetted my appetite for jewelry. Quite logically, despite the huge success of the exhibition, I figured that only so many people would make their way to Newark just to see pretty, middle-class jewelry. Given that I had some real doozies in the collection already—including the Dempsey jewelry—I had an excuse to start pushing forward with other jewelry, "important" jewelry, that told a larger, international story.

The last decade of my career was heavily focused on building the large, messy, uneven jewelry collection, and turning it from a slightly incoherent assemblage of random things into a broader, calculated narrative that included major names and critical design moments in the history of jewelry. I also purchased a good many great works by contemporary studio jewelers. Obviously, I didn't finish the job, but I had the fun of being a major player in the very small world of American museum curators collecting jewelry (including colleagues in Boston, Toledo, and in New York at the Cooper-Hewitt, and, eventually, the Metropolitan Museum).

As I prided myself on saying to audiences during my travels across the country speaking about jewelry, I spent more money on jewelry than any other curator in North America. The flip side of this, which I also confessed as a kind of punch line, was that this was true because other museums were given great pieces of jewelry, while Newark had to purchase almost every major acquisition. Mrs. Dempsey's jewels were the most important jewelry we ever received as a gift, until 2014, when Gary and I gave, in memory of my mother, my grandmother Grant's pearl-and-diamond choker, the one my parents let me have when I was a teenager.

The greatest coup in my jewelry collecting years was the purchase, in 2013, of what I named the *Rehan Jewel.* Made around 1900 by Marcus & Co. of New York, it had been commissioned by Catharine Lasell Whitin, wife of a textile millionaire from Massachusetts, for the celebrated Shakespearean character actress Ada Rehan. The jewel, a confection of fragile transparent openwork enamel known as *plique-à-jour*, is in the form of a triangular cluster of three morning-glory blossoms, each of which is articulated to move when worn. Symbolically the jewel referred to the hope of resurrection, unrequited love, and the biblical notion of Hope, Faith and Love. Not only did it survive in its original case, complete with an enameled gold necklace to which it could be attached once the pin was detached, but it seemed to represent a Gilded-Age celebrity crush that lasted until Ada Rehan's death in 1916. Mrs. Whitin commissioned John Singer Sargent to do a full-length portrait of Ada Rehan in 1894 and left that portrait to the Metropolitan Museum at her own death.

Ada Rehan left the jewel to Mrs. Whitin, in whose family it remained until it hit the market in the early 2010s. At auction, two major jewelry-collecting museums (with rich patrons waiting to pay) bid on it; but it went to a New York dealer for five times the high auction estimate. That's whom I bought it from, after paying a fair but substantial markup. It was the most expensive thing ever purchased for Newark's decorative arts department, and justifying it to the board meant that I had to present it as a full-on work of art. They bought my rationale, and the museum bought the jewel.

In the end, did it matter? Yeah, I think so, but only if you think museums and their collections matter.

By the end of my curatorial career in 2017, I had brought in nearly 5500 objects as gifts to the decorative arts department at Newark, and purchased nearly 1100 objects, spending something over $5.3 million. The larger purchases that my directors and board allowed me to pursue by the end of my career had been made feasible by a carefully thought-out program of deaccessioning—a word which is still widely misunderstood and often used as ammunition against museum practices. In Newark's case, we had accumulated a badly curated and mediocre collection of European fine art, even though it had never been our mission to collect in this area. Over the century-plus of the museum's history, people had unloaded their "old master" reproductions, "school-of" paintings with genuine age, and, in the 1950s, a number of good works by important artists. In the 1980s and 90s, we had deaccessioned a few of these works in order to pay for otherwise unaffordable masterworks by American artists—a Toulouse Lautrec grisaille traded for a great Thomas Cole landscape; a James Tissot, a Bouguereau, and a Byrne-Jones sold to pay for a fantastic John Singer Sargent portrait. It dawned on us that this piecemeal dismantling of an unused collection wasn't the best long-term financial strategy, and the board followed up with a regulated program to deaccession the entire European fine art collection to create an acquisition endowment shared by all curatorial departments. In my last years as chief curator, I oversaw the completion of this project. It was that endowment that allowed me, and all the curators, to collect world-class objects for Newark in the absence of major donors. The Newark Museum's collections represent the people of the world, and also the diaspora of immigrants to the United States. Collecting allows the museum to continue to enrich the stories our objects tell.

When I arrived at Newark it was still very much a mom-and-pop museum. By the time I retired, after serving under three directors, it had become the complex institution it is today. The museum was, for thirty-eight years, quite literally my life. I love it with all my heart, and I still feel that it is one of the most underrated and underappreciated art museums in North America. If I have any sense of failure as a curator, it is that I did not, somehow, manage to bring in any transformative gift of money or objects to my department. Oh, we got some nice gifts, and lots of useful gifts; but I have friends in lots of museums, and I have seen them bring in millions of dollars and amazing gifts of important objects to improve their departments and enrich their galleries and reputations. I'll always wonder why I couldn't do the same.

I have, in retrospect, managed to attain a certain celebrity in an arcane subdivision of an esoteric profession. I am astonished that this was my fate. I've made friends far and wide and have always treasured those relationships. I've had the opportunity to lecture in scores of museums all around the country. I have taken enormous pleasure in guiding hundreds of wide-eyed fancy folks through my museum, enjoying their surprise at the quality, breadth, and depth of Newark's holdings.

On the other hand, none of those tours ever translated into something really big for the museum I love. After the first twenty years, even the highest praise began to feel hollow to me, because I knew it would lead nowhere, do us no good. Even my ego isn't quite big enough to take joy in accolades for myself without support for my institution. Maybe this was part of the deal for me: personal satisfaction but no ultimate triumph. New Jersey has kept me humble. Or, at least, humbler than I might have been if I'd ended up somewhere else.

CHAPTER THIRTY-ONE

Speculation #8
SPIRIT OF CHRISTMAS
YET TO COME

With a start, I found myself in an opulent Victorian parlor, and no idea how I'd come to be there. As I raised my head and did a quick survey of the room, it seemed oddly familiar, but for reasons I couldn't quite grasp. The walls and ceiling were painted in soft, saturated colors of rusty red, ochre yellow and olive green, their simplicity in contrast with the elaborately milled and carved rosewood of the door casings and mantelpiece. The mantel shelf was cluttered with silver and porcelain vases, and in front of the hearth were two small carved Chinese tables, each holding a massive, enameled porcelain urn. In each of the corners flanking the doorway into what I could see was a library, were tall Chinese teakwood cabinets with still more vases and bric-a-brac.

As my eyes scanned to the left, I noted the substantial painting on the wall to the right of the fireplace. It was *Sheridan's Ride* by Thomas Buchanan Read. I knew this picture. I had seen it before. I tried to focus my thoughts, dropping my eyes as my mind whirled through its internal hard drive. Then I noticed the two black-lacquered parlor chairs on either side of the library doorway. On the crest of each was inlaid a circular cipher in gilt metal of the initials USG. The penny dropped.

I was inside 3 East 66th Street in New York, a house I had only seen in photographs, published in a book called *Artistic Houses* in 1883. This was Ulysses and Julia Grant's house. Instinctively, I looked down at myself, and noted with some surprise that I was wearing what appeared to be a long black velvet dressing gown tied with a black silk cord. The full sleeves fell almost to the tips of my fingers. Weirdly enough, I was barefoot. The elaborate carpet felt lovely and soft under my feet.

As I pondered the strangeness of the situation, I heard a faint sound, a voice, as if from far away. I turned, pushed past the velvet portieres into the entrance hall and paused, listening. Again, I heard the voice. It was slightly louder, but still muffled.

"Hello?" I called out, not too loudly.

This time I could make out the answer, barely. "Who is it?"

I had no idea how to answer him—for I knew who was addressing me and why his voice was so muted. All I could think to do was go to the elaborate mahogany staircase and climb to the second floor, lifting the skirts of my robe so I wouldn't trip myself. I knew where I was going and what I would find. The fact that the house seemed utterly deserted no longer felt strange. I understood that I was there for a reason.

As I came to the top step, I turned to my left and moved down the carpeted hall to the front of the house, where I could see, through windows facing what I knew to be East 66th Street, that it was snowing gently. There was no sound from outside. Stepping into the room, I saw that I was in a study, piles of books stacked on every surface. From what I could make out of the room's décor, it had clearly been a woman's room before its current occupant took over. Seated at a desk against one wall was an old man—looking older physically than he was in years, I knew. His body had been stout but showed the signs of significant weight loss in the hollowing of his cheeks. His hair and beard were heavily silvered, and he wore a knitted scarf knotted closely around his throat.

The old man looked up at me, and I saw both fear and curiosity in his blue eyes.

"What is your name?" His voice was hoarse and quiet, and I thought of the pain his words caused him.

"My name is Dietz, sir."

This seemed to surprise him. "You mean like the fellow who's buying up all those lots downtown to build his new lantern factory?"

It was my turn to be surprised. "Um, well, yes, sir. I am of that family."

The old man dropped his eyes, as if thinking, motioning me absently to a nearby chair. I sat, arranging the folds of black velvet around me and pulling the long sleeves up and away from my hands. Then he looked up at me, and I could see the strength in his gaze, despite the pain in his face.

"Why have you come?" He asked.

I had no idea what to say, how to answer him. I stammered a bit, until he interrupted me.

"I was told you would come." His expression was no longer afraid. Curiosity had taken over, and he watched me with keen interest.

"By whom, may I ask?"

"My mother," he answered.

"Hannah?" I blurted out, startled.

This provoked a small smile, followed by a wince.

"Yes. She came to me in a dream last night. She said you would visit me."

I'm sorry to say I actually chuckled when he said this, and without thinking replied, "How very Charles Dickens."

He took no offense, but smiled his small, pained smile again. "You know *A Christmas Carol*, Mr. Dietz?"

"Very well. I've read it many times. It's a favorite of mine."

"Mine as well," he said, but this time his voice was so faint I barely heard it. His face settled into a calm study of me. Abashed, I dropped my gaze to my lap, and noticed again the intense blackness of the strange velvet robe I was wearing. Suddenly it hit me.

"May I ask, sir, what time of year is it? I see that it's snowing."

Another tired attempt at a smile. "December. A fortnight before Christmas." He was silent a moment, and then added. "The last Christmas I shall see on this earth." Pain shimmered in his eyes, but an emotional pain this time.

I now understood what I had to do. I steeled myself and clasped my hands in my lap.

"Apparently, General, I am the spirit of Christmas yet-to-come." I tried to smile, but I failed. Perhaps making Dickens jokes wasn't quite the right tone at a time like this.

Rather than offending him, my words seemed to set him back. His whole body stilled as he gazed at me.

"Then what have you come to tell me?" He looked resigned, but no longer afraid.

I wracked my brain for a way to proceed, having decided to go down this road, and finally grasped the direction I needed to take.

"Fear not," I said softly, trying to put some urgency in my tone.

He raised his eyebrows.

I raised a hand and gestured to the manuscript pages on the desk and to the piles of books around him. The deep sleeves of my robe made it seem very theatrical.

"You will complete your great work, General. Not only will you complete it, but it will save your family and find an honored place in history."

A sigh escaped him, as if a weight had been lifted off his shoulders.

"My Julia will be all right?"

"More than all right," I said, trying what I hoped was a comforting smile.

Then the general sat quietly, his eyes on me, but unfocused, as if thinking. When they came back into focus, he continued.

"Will people read the book?"

I almost laughed. Even in such pain and worry, his author's ego was still very much alive. I hesitated over how to respond. How much could I properly say? In the end, I made a choice.

"A million people will read your book, general. Thanks to Mr. Clemens."

This brought another smile to his weary face.

He whispered, "Ah yes, Sam, my new best friend. My savior, I might believe."

"The book will have a long and celebrated life. It will stand as a beacon for your memory more than a hundred thirty years from now."

I stopped with a gasp. I had gone too far. I was certain I wasn't supposed to say this kind of thing to him. His only response was to look at me more closely and with ever-stronger curiosity.

"Who *are* you, kind sir? You look to be my age, but in good health."

I was flummoxed by the question. What could I say now? What was I allowed to say in a situation like this?

We simply stared at each other for a long moment. My hands fidgeted in my lap, while his lay still as he waited.

I cleared my throat. "Your little grandson Ulysses, sir? Fred and Ida's child?"

He nodded slightly, his eyes going wider.

"He will grow up and marry. He will have a daughter named Julia."

Another smile, a real smile regardless of any pain. "Go on."

"That little girl will grow up and get married as well. She will have four children, of whom I will be her third."

The old man said nothing, just stared at me with what looked like hope.

"My given name is Ulysses, grandfather. I was named for your grandson. And there are other Ulysses, two generations beyond me."

I could see tears well up in his eyes, but none escaped. The gray tone of his skin seemed to grow pink, and he blinked several times. Suddenly he leaned forward slightly and reached out a hand toward me.

"It is worth it, then?"

I dropped forward on one knee so I could take his proffered hand in mine. Without thinking, I kissed the back of his hand and looked up into his blue eyes.

"Yes, it is worth everything."

The next thing I knew I was lying in my bed, the tall Victorian headboard looming over me. My face was wet with tears, and my heart was racing. To my right, my husband was asleep, his back to me, snoring softly. Our black poodle, Pete, was stretched out along the footboard at our feet, also sleeping soundly.

CHAPTER THIRTY-TWO

BREAKFAST EVERY FIFTEEN MINUTES

A ll through my life I have been prone to the Imposter Syndrome. From childhood on, my anxiety to please was always driven by a nagging worry that I wasn't quite up to snuff; that somehow, I was faking my way through my life and succeeding without quite deserving it. I'm sure that my emerging awareness of being gay played a role in this, but it persisted long after I came out. This feeling of being a faker followed me through Yale, where I carefully chose courses at which I knew I could do well, and on into graduate school where the same notion continued. Even as a curator, I looked around me at my new friends and colleagues in all sorts of museums and somehow felt that they were really doing it right, while I was still, one way or another, a bit of a fraud.

Rationally, I know it's not true, but I confess that, when I finally retired, there was a huge sense of relief that I had gotten through it all without getting caught.

I do hope I'm wrong.

Kitty Carlisle, onetime actress, longtime television personality and widow of Broadway impresario Moss Hart, commented in her autobiography that when you pass the age of fifty it begins to feel that you're having breakfast every fifteen minutes.

That's exactly what it feels like.

I hate aging but have learned to give thanks for every new day granted me. I think of my brother and sister, neither of whom made it past their teens. I think of Ulysses S. Grant and his son, my great-grandfather Fred. They were both dead by the time they were my age. I am the most blessed and most privileged of all people, and there is not a minute of any day in which I am not aware of that fact.

As a voracious reader of romance literature over the last decade (specifically gay romance literature, because I found that I am hungry to see myself, somehow, in the books I read), I have begun to realize that the Happy Ending is a drug for me. I need what the romance writing world refers to as the HEA, the Happy Ever After. As a gay man who lost two siblings in his adolescence; as a gay man who survived the AIDS epidemic; as a gay man who chose monogamy, the suburbs, and raising children; I have always felt that the Devil is waiting in the wings, ready to step out and snatch away my happiness. For all my privilege and good fortune, my life has not been without bumps in the road. I am only in my mid-sixties; there is still (I hope) a long story to be told.

In the end, we're all alone. There is no happy ending in any human life, no matter what the church has tried to tell us. All the people who came before me, famous and forgotten, each of whom contributed to the person I am, faced this truth whether they wanted to or not. One of us, either Gary or I, will die first, and the other will be left to cope. We can't control what happens, and we can't predict how the world will turn. All we can do is hold onto whatever happy memories we have managed to create and imagine them to be the happy ending we desire.

I guess I'm good with that.

ABOUT THE AUTHOR

The author with his grandfather, Ulysses S. Grant III, in 1956

Ulysses Grant Dietz grew up in Syracuse, New York, where his *Leave it to Beaver* life was enlivened by his fascination with vampires, from Bela Lugosi to Barnabas Collins. He studied French at Yale (BA, 1977), and was trained to be a museum curator in the University of Delaware's Winterthur Program in American Material Culture (MA, 1980). A decorative arts curator at the Newark Museum for thirty-seven years before he retired, Ulysses has never stopped writing for the sheer pleasure of it. Aside from books on Victorian furniture, art pottery, studio ceramics, jewelry, and the White House, Ulysses created the character of Desmond Beckwith in 1988 as his personal response to Anne Rice's landmark novels. Alyson Books released his first novel, *Desmond*, in 1998. *Vampire in Suburbia*, the sequel, appeared in 2012. His most recent novel, *Cliffhanger,* was released by JMS Books in December 2020.

Ulysses lives in suburban New Jersey with his husband of 46 years. They have two grown children, adopted in 1996.

Ulysses is a great-great grandson of Ulysses S. Grant. His late mother, Julia, was the President's last living great-grandchild; youngest daughter of Ulysses S. Grant III, and granddaughter of the president's eldest son, Frederick. Every year on April 27 he gives a speech at Grant's Tomb in New York City. He is also on the board of the U.S. Grant Presidential Library and Museum at Mississippi State University.

CPSIA information can be obtained
at www.ICGtesting.com
Printed in the USA
BVHW071935130122
626175BV00005B/155